MAMMALIAN FERTILIZATION

An Atlas of Ultrastructure

Seeing once is better than hearing hundred times
CHINESE PROVERB

MAMMALIAN FERTILIZATION

An Atlas of Ultrastructure

ROBERT HADEK

DEPARTMENT OF ANATOMY
STRITCH SCHOOL OF MEDICINE
LOYOLA UNIVERSITY OF CHICAGO
HINES, ILLINOIS

1969

 ACADEMIC PRESS New York and London

ACADEMIC PRESS, INC.
111 Fifth Avenue, New York, New York 10003

United Kingdom Edition published by
ACADEMIC PRESS, INC. (LONDON) LTD.
Berkeley Square House, London W.1

LIBRARY OF CONGRESS CATALOG CARD NUMBER: 69-13482

PRINTED IN THE UNITED STATES OF AMERICA

PREFACE

The morphology of fertilization and gamete cytology is an intriguing topic. The application of the electron microscope has made the study of the gametes particularly rewarding. Heretofore unthought of structural details and, in their wake, an understanding of function came to light.

Before this book received its title it was called "Ultrastructural Aspects of Mammalian Fertilization." Its present title notwithstanding, it only deals with certain aspects of the topic.

The principal effort of this work is to depict in sequence the ultrastructural appearance of the mammalian gametes before, during, and after fertilization. It is hoped that by looking at the submicroscopic components of the gametes their structural significance will come to be understood more fully. Electron micrographs have been arranged in sequences which appear most logical. I hope I have succeeded in my effort. Comments from readers will be appreciated.

To enable the reader to understand the electron micrographs, each picture is matched by a line drawing. These depict the approximate part of the gamete from which the section was taken and do not represent the exact conditions. I hope that they will serve their purpose. Comments from readers will be appreciated.

The study, however, was not prepared single-handed. I am greatly indebted to many who, directly or indirectly, contributed to this effort. Professor Joseph Thomas Velardo, Ph.D., Head of the Anatomy Department in this Medical School, and his Research Associate, Miss Barbara Kasprow, M.S., generously gave of their time to read the manuscript; Frederick Selfridge, M.D., Assistant Dean, kindly allocated his secretary for manuscript reading and typing; Mr. Louis S. Pedigo printed the micrographs; Miss Jane Hurd, M.A., drew most of the illustrations; Miss Helen Huelsman, B.A., M.A.L.S., kindly checked the references; Messrs. T. M. Beringer, L. P. McCallister, J. C. McMahon, M.S., and H. D. McReynolds, M.S., all graduate students in the Anatomy Department in this school, verified technical details. Of the typists, Miss Erminia Maddalena and Miss Shirley Saldanha, M.S., should be mentioned. That this work was completed in great measure is due to the devoted and painstaking efforts of Mrs. Doris E. Shaw, my secretary. I am greatly indebted to her and to all the aforementioned co-workers and helpers. Ultimately, it is a pleasure to acknowledge the cooperation of the publisher.

I gratefully acknowledge the help received from the United States Public Health Service through National Institutes of Health Grant No. RO1 HD00552.

Robert Hadek

Chicago, Illinois
January, 1969

CONTENTS

LIST OF ILLUSTRATIONS

INTRODUCTION

Research Procedure

The work reported herein has been performed on laboratory animals; namely, the rabbit, golden hamster, and ferret. Some specimens, however, were obtained from the mouse and gerbil.

Since the original work by Hammond (1925), the rabbit has been one of the most frequently used experimental animals due to the amount of information available on its anatomy and physiology. Namely, in the rabbit, ovulation follows copulation within 10 to 12 hours and the egg is fertilizable within 8 hours after ovulation. The cleavage divisions occur within the first 12 hours after fertilization and at an ever-accelerating pace thereafter (Hammond, 1934). It is also comparatively simple to cause superovulation in the rabbit with the use of follicle-stimulating hormone, or to induce ovulation without mating by the injection of progesterone (Parkes, 1943). Although the ovulatory pattern in the rabbit is not quite matched by the pattern of the golden hamster and the ferret, they are for the most part dependable experimental animals, as previous investigators have shown (Hammond and Walton, 1934; Ward, 1946).

In the hamster, the sexual cycle is of 4 days' duration, and ovulation takes place 7 to 8 hours after the onset of heat. Our hamsters were kept in a closely watched colony, and the presence of spermatozoa in the vaginal smear in the morning was accepted as an indicator that ovulation occurred between 2 and 3 A.M.

The ferret is on estrus twice a year, and ovulation follows coitus.

TECHNIQUES

Female Gametes

Eggs were recovered either from the ovary or by flushing from the oviduct with physiological saline or Ringer's solution. After isolating them, they were fixed for 20–60 minutes in various fixatives at a hydrogen ion concentration (pH) between 7.2 and 7.4.

Fixatives used included: (1) veronal acetate-buffered 1% OsO_4 (Palade, 1952); (2) phosphate-buffered 1% OsO_4 (Millonig, 1962); (3) 2% K_2MnO_4 (Luft, 1956); (4) 2–4% phosphate-buffered glutaraldehyde (Sabatini et al., 1963; Tormey, 1964).

Brief washing in chilled distilled water was followed by dehydration in a graded series of ethyl alcohol baths. As a rule, before dehydration the specimens were embedded in an agar sandwich (Samuel, 1944). After clearing in propylene oxide, specimens were embedded either in Epon 812 or 815 (Luft, 1961), or alternately in Durcupan (Stäubli, 1963), or Maraglas 65.5 (Freeman and Spurlock, 1962). Sections were cut on a Porter-Blum (MT-1) ultrathin sectioning microtome and contrast was enhanced by "staining" with uranyl acetate (Swift and Rasch, 1958), or with one of the lead stains (Glauert, 1965).

For studying the presence of the enzyme acid phosphatase Gomori's acid phosphatase reaction was performed as described by Barka and Anderson (1963).

Male Gametes

For studying the male gamete, spermatozoa were either obtained from the male genital tract, from ejaculatum, from the female genital tract, or observed in the perivitelline area of the egg.

The ejaculated spermatozoa were washed and centrifuged to eliminate the secretion of the accessory genital glands (Hadek, 1958), subsequently fixed, dehydrated, and embedded in one of the previously mentioned polymers. For the rest of the investigation the specimens were handled identically with the female gamete.

FIGURE A

THE ROLE OF THE CELL ORGANELLES IN THE FORMATION
OF THE MAMMALIAN SPERMATOZOON (drawing)

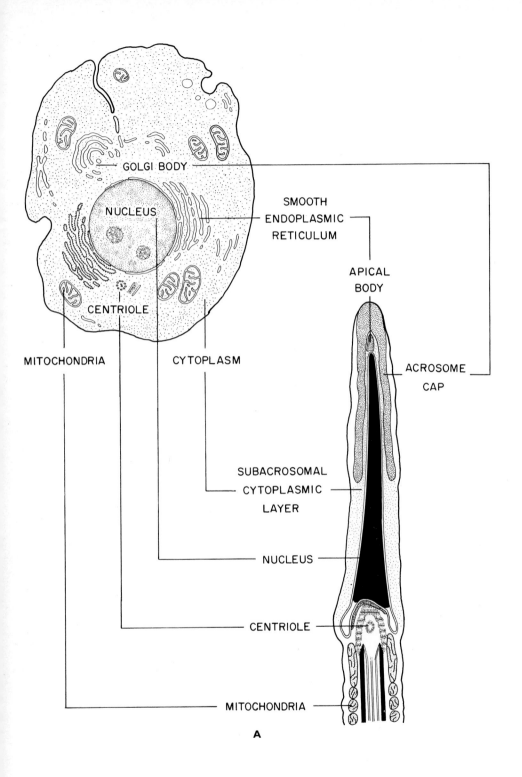

GOLGI BODY

SMOOTH
ENDOPLASMIC
RETICULUM

NUCLEUS

APICAL
BODY

CENTRIOLE

ACROSOME
CAP

MITOCHONDRIA

CYTOPLASM

SUBACROSOMAL
CYTOPLASMIC
LAYER

NUCLEUS

CENTRIOLE

MITOCHONDRIA

A

FIGURE B

HAMSTER SPERMATOZOON, LATERAL VIEW
(phase contrast, × 1200)

FIGURE C

MAMMALIAN SPERMATOZOON—FRONTAL VIEW (drawing)

   This work is devoted entirely to the ultrastructural morphology of the gametes. Therefore, unless otherwise indicated, it should be understood that the features described refer to the fine structural organization of the gamete as it is observed under the electron microscope.

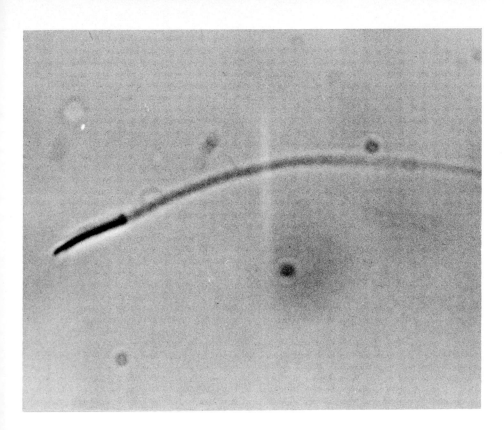

B

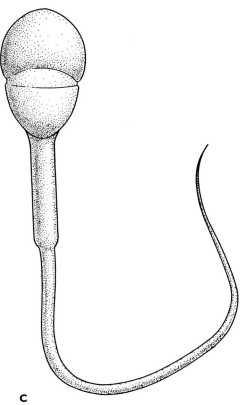

C

I

THE MAMMALIAN
SPERMATOZOON

The Ejaculated Sperm

INTRODUCTION

The mammalian spermatozoon, as a rule, measures around 60 μ and is composed essentially of two parts: the head and the tail. The proportions between them can vary from 1:5 to 1:12.

The components of the head are: the nucleus, the acrosomal cap, and the subacrosomal (or cytoplasmic) layer which includes the apical body. On its posterior surface, the nucleus forms an implantation fossa in which one observes the basal plate.

The tail is divided into: neck, middle piece, principal (or main) piece, and end (or terminal) piece. The core of the tail is formed by the axial filament complex: a combination of two central filaments (tubules) with a double set of nine peripheral fibrils (doublets). These in turn are surrounded by nine coarse outer fibers. The variation of the enclosing structures delineates the different segments.

The neck contains the connecting piece which terminates in the capitellum that is attached to the implantation fossa of the head of the spermatozoon. The connecting piece is formed by the fusion of nine horizontally segmented columns into a ribbed body. This continues caudally into the nine dense peripheral fibers that surround the axial filament complex. The peripheral fibers in the middle piece are surrounded by a mitochondrial sheath. The end of the middle piece and the beginning of the main piece are marked by a dense ring, the annulus. The fibers in the main piece are surrounded by a fibrous sheath. At the terminal end, only the cell membrane surrounds the gradually disappearing components of the axial filament complex.

THE HEAD

In most mammalian spermatozoa, to paraphrase Fawcett (1965), the form of the head is determined by the shape of the nucleus. Some notable exceptions, however, exist. In the guinea pig the covering layers are responsible for the shape of the head. In the two species on which most of this study was conducted, the rabbit and the golden hamster, the sperm head has an elongated, circular shape, being wider in its anterior third than toward the posterior end. Examination of a sagittal section shows an elongated, elliptical profile.

Starting from the center of the head, one observes the nucleus. The rabbit sperm nucleus is composed of electron-dense material in which irregular cavities, or nuclear vacuoles, or "defects in the chromatin" (Fawcett, 1958) are occasionally present. On its anterior two-thirds, the nucleus is covered by a cup-shaped structure. The term "acrosomal cap" has been used of late (Fawcett, 1965) to describe this single-membrane limited, rather electron-dense, homogeneous layer situated immediately beneath the cell membrane.

The cone-shaped area between the acrosomal cap and the nucleus has been assumed to be empty. It has been designated as "subacrosomal space" because, in osmium-fixed epididymal semen, this layer usually shows very little contrast and thus appears empty. Alternately, it was assumed to be formed by the separation of the two layers of the nuclear envelope and, at best, to contain some cytoplasmic remnants left behind in the spermatid. There is, however, an indication now that this is not an empty space. Rather, it appears to be a layer or a sheath formed by a cytoplasmic matrix, which in its anterior part is located between the nucleus and the acrosome, and in its posterior aspect, between the nucleus and the cell membrane. In the ejaculated rabbit sperm, the cranial part of this layer (which is also a morphological entity) is composed of structureless cytoplasmic material, while its posterior segment is formed by irregular cytoplasmic tubules and channels. Admittedly, such a sheath is mostly unobservable in the epididymal sperm of the common laboratory animals, although a similar layer has been detected in the spermatozoon of the bat (Fawcett and Ito, 1965).

In the mature, ejaculated spermatozoon of the rabbit, a cytoplasmic sheath is in evidence which enwraps the nucleus except for its posterior aspect. The presence of a similar "opaque layer" between the nucleus and acrosome cap has been observed in the sperm of the boar (Nicander and Bane, 1962a,b), and around the caudal aspect of the sperm of the bull (Saacke and Almquist, 1964).

The nature of this subacrosomal layer, or cytoplasmic layer has been the subject of controversies (Bishop and Walton, 1960; Rahlmann, 1961; Nicander and Bane, 1962a,b; Saacke and Almquist, 1964). In the bat sperm it was observed to show a periodicity (Fawcett and Ito, 1965). The caudal segment of the cytoplasmic layer (or sheath) has been termed the "postnuclear cap" by earlier cytologists, since it is strongly argyrophilic with histological stains. In the sperm of rabbits, after penetrating through the zona pellucida and in the spermatozoon of hamsters after sojourn in the female genital tract, this layer is particularly prominent and at certain locations shows a ringlike thickening.

In ejaculated spermatozoa of laboratory animals, one can observe in the apical portion of the cytoplasmic layer (which fills the area between the acrosome cap and the nucleus) a cone or semicircular blade-shaped structure which, as a rule, shows a greater electron density than the rest of the material around it. This discrete body has been designated as "perforatorium" (Moricard, 1960) or "apical body" (Hadek, 1963c; Bedford, 1964; Wimsatt *et al.*, 1966).

In all the spermatozoa studied in this laboratory (mouse, hamster, rabbit, ferret), the apical body was constantly present. In the mouse spermatid it appears to originate from membranous material, and in the rabbit from an amorphous, cytoplasmic droplet. Of course, it is also possible that it evolves from the same source in both, and the variation observed only represents different phases of development. Species variation in the shape of the apical body also was observed. In sagittal section its outline is cone-shaped in the rabbit, irregularly pointed in the golden hamster, and disc or crescent-shaped in the bat. In the latter animal, Wimsatt *et al.* (1966), suggested the term "apical lamina."

THE TAIL

The core of the sperm tail is composed of the longitudinally running, axial filament complex. This includes the two centrally placed thin tubules (one above the other in a dorsoventral axis), which are surrounded by a double set of nine fibrils (18 tubules in all), one set empty, the other solid (Telkka *et al.*, 1961; Nicander and Bane, 1962a). [This composition is similar to that of cilia and flagella (Gibbons, 1961; Gibbons and Grimstone, 1960).] These fibrils in turn are enclosed by nine rough fibers, of which numbers one, five, and six are thicker than the others.

The delineation of the different segments of the tail is due either to the morphological modification in this central core, e.g., neck and filamentous end, or alternately, by it becoming surrounded by additional structures, e.g., mitochondria in the midpiece and a fibrous sheath in the main piece. The whole spermatozoon is enclosed by the cell membrane.

Within the frame of this inquiry, no special study was conducted on the sperm tail; consequently, only a general description will be supplied insofar as it is related to the general purpose of the narrative.

The Neck

The neck, the shortest part of the tail, is situated between the head and the first mitochondrial spiral of the middle piece. In its cranial aspect, the neck is limited by a modified section of the nuclear membrane, the basal plate, on which it abuts with its own cranial plate, the capitellum. It is composed of nine cross-striated columns, which form a ribbed connecting piece. Two pairs of these join one another, thus their number is reduced to seven (Fawcett, 1965; Blom and Birch-Andersen, 1960). Although this connecting piece has been assumed to be a direct continuation of the coarse outer fibers, contemporary research workers contradict this view (Fawcett, 1965; Wimsatt et al., 1966). Within this ribbed body is a centriole in an oblique, angular position with reference to the longitudinal axis of the tail. Two nonspiral, longitudinally placed mitochondria can be also observed in the region of the neck.

At the anterior aspect of the neck, laterally from the ribbed connecting piece, a collar of membranous outpocketing can be observed. This structure, quite prominent in the evolving spermatozoon, contains a number of membrane scrolls or loops. These folds are either in loosely arranged rolls as in the hamster sperm, or form tightly packed scrolls, as in the aging rabbit sperm. The loops represent the excessive length of the nuclear envelope which remains empty when the spermatid transforms into the spermatozoon. They gradually disappear from the mature sperm. For example, only a dense lamella showing irregular periodicity can be seen in the ejaculated spermatozoon of the rabbit, and no membrane at all can be observed in the penetrating sperm of rabbit and hamster. Neither were membrane scrolls observed in the sperm of the bat, *Myotis lucifugus*, which has been recovered from the uterus of the female (Wimsatt et al., 1966), suggesting that the disappearance of the surplus nuclear membrane and the aging of the spermatozoon are related.

Middle Piece

The middle piece is characterized by the mitochondrial layer. A single sheath of mitochondrial spiral, composed of approximately 43 gyri, in the rabbit, is found outside the nine rough fibers. The spiral starts beneath the two vertically placed mitochondria of the neck and terminates above the fibrous annulus. The mitochondria are arranged circumferentially end-to-end in a continuous spiral, in such manner that the terminations of two mitochondria in one winding of the coil are bordered by the middle of a mitochondrion in the turning above and below.

Changes in mitochondrial morphology are characteristic of mammalian gamete development in the male (Andre, 1961a; Fawcett, 1959) as well as in the female (Hadek and Swift, 1961a; Adams and Hertig, 1964). All the mitochondria in the sperm tail show an almost identical morphology that is related to the species and to the age of the spermatozoon. For example, epididymal spermatozoa from the rabbit contains mitochondria with irregularly filled lumina.

Principal Piece

The principal piece is the longest part of the tail of the spermatozoon. It is surrounded by a stout, fibrous cover that replaces the mitochondrial layer. This fibrous sheath is composed of two parallel-running longitudinal columns on opposite sides of the tail, which are joined to one another by circumferentially running ribs. Admittedly, in most instances the columns appear to be composed of smaller units, but fortuitous fixation will reveal them to be of one continuous piece. The encircling ribs are connected with barblike filaments contributing to the continuity of the sheath.

The End Piece

In the end piece of the sperm tail, there is a gradual disappearance of the structures which form the principal piece. First among these are the rough fibers, most of which disappear excepting numbers one, five, and six. There is also a decrease in the thickness of the fibrous sheath. At the termination of the principal piece, the structure of the sperm tail is similar to a flagellum: composed of the two central and the nine peripheral double fibers. At its very end, only the cell membrane surrounds the remaining filaments.

FIGURE 1.1

IDEALIZED REPRESENTATION OF MAMMALIAN SPERM

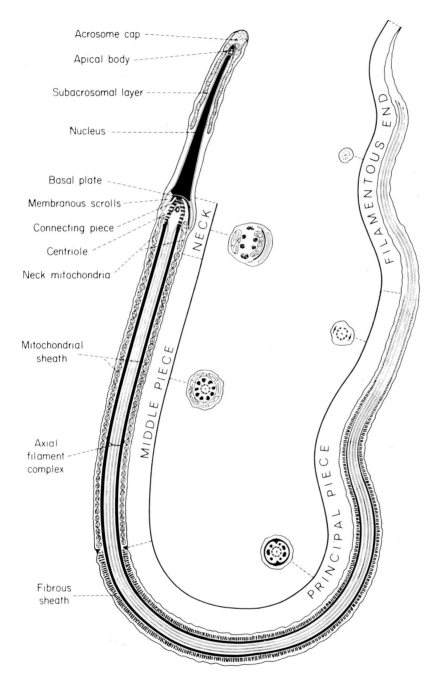

Acrosome cap

Apical body

Subacrosomal layer

Nucleus

Basal plate

Membranous scrolls

Connecting piece

Centriole

Neck mitochondria

Mitochondrial sheath

Axial filament complex

Fibrous sheath

NECK

MIDDLE PIECE

PRINCIPAL PIECE

FILAMENTOUS END

I.1

FIGURE 1.2

HEAD OF EJACULATED RABBIT SPERMATOZOON

The accompanying micrograph shows the sperm head and cross sections of the spermatozoon's tail at different levels. In this sagittal section, the central part of the sperm head is occupied by the elongated oval nucleus which shows greater electron density than the other structures of the head. In some areas the nucleus appears vacuolated. These nuclear vacuoles, or nuclear defects, apparently do not interfere with spermatozoon function. Since they are visible in osmium-fixed specimens and are mostly absent from aldehyde-fixed material, one wonders whether they could be artifacts. The nucleus is surrounded by the double-layered nuclear envelope which can be distinguished as a thin, dark line.

The subacrosomal layer surrounding the nucleus has been the subject of controversies. Some authors assume that this layer, which shows lower electron density than either the nucleus or the acrosome cap (outside of it), is an accumulation of residual cytoplasmic material located between the two membranes of the nuclear envelope. Since it is formed by cytoplasmic material, it could be referred to as a "cytoplasmic" layer. Abutting on the apical portion of the head, one can observe a separate body within this cytoplasmic layer. In rabbit sperm this is a well-delineated structure often appearing triangular in sagittal and parasagittal sections and fitting snugly in the area between the nucleus and the acrosome cap (the next layer outside).

Outside the subacrosomal layer is the acrosome cap. Forming a thickened, cupolalike structure at its rostral extremity, not unlike a thimble, it encloses the anterior two-thirds of the nucleus, the apical body, and the subacrosomal (cytoplasmic) layer. Its caudal extremity is rounded, and it abuts on the wider section of the cytoplasmic layer.

The cell membrane loosely fits around the sperm head except at the tip of the acrosome cap to which it is firmly attached.

SPECIMEN

1.2. Rabbit ejaculatum. Veronal acetate-buffered 1% OsO_4; Epon 812; uranyl acetate ($\times$ 30,000). The bar on this and all following photographs represents 1 μ unless otherwise noted.

A, acrosome cap; AB, apical body; C, cell membrane; N, nucleus; S, subacrosomal layer; V, nuclear vacuole.

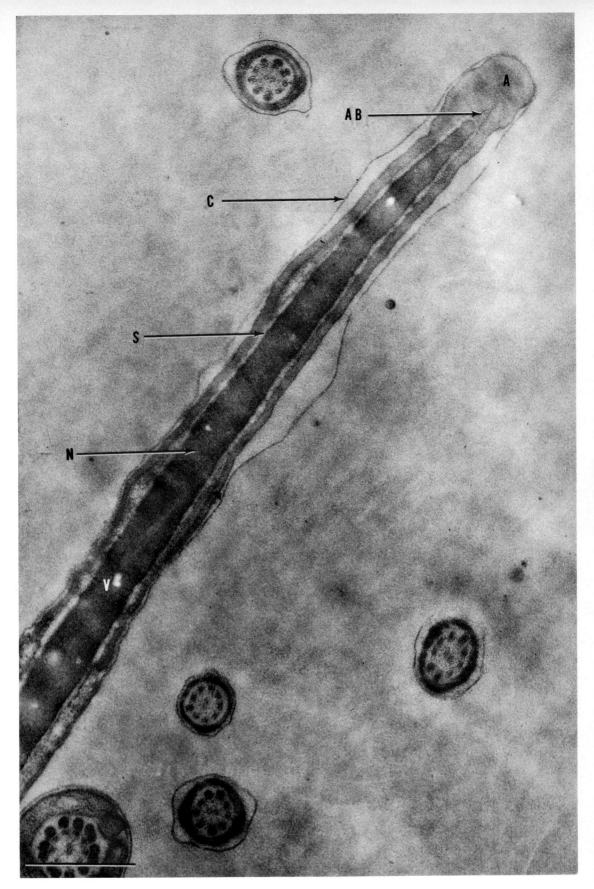

I.2

FIGURE 1.3

RABBIT SPERM HEAD—APICAL BODY; SAGITTAL SECTION

This electron micrograph shows at higher magnification the head of the ejaculated sperm of rabbit. The apical body is particularly well delineated. It appears that the apical body, acrosome cap, and subacrosomal (cytoplasmic) layers each, are enclosed by single membranes.

SPECIMEN

1.3. Freshly ejaculated rabbit sperm head. Sagittal section. Veronal acetate-buffered 1% OsO_4; Epon 812; uranyl acetate ($\times$ 65,000). A, acrosome cap; AB, apical body; C, cell membrane; N, nucleus; S, subacrosomal layer; V, nuclear vacuole.

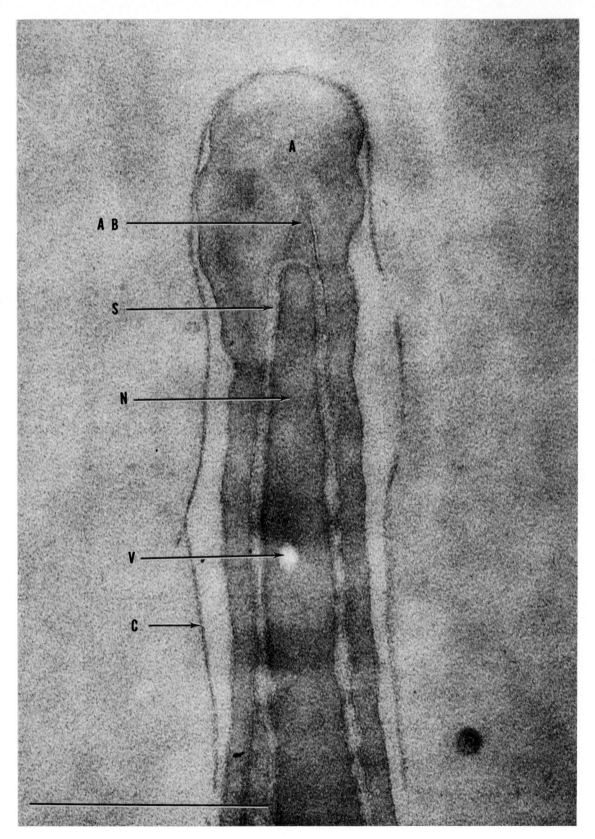

A

A B →

S →

N →

V →

C →

I.3

FIGURE I.4

CAUDAL THIRD OF EJACULATED RABBIT SPERM HEAD; PARASAGITTAL SECTION

In this spermatozoon the subacrosomal (cytoplasmic) layer, which lies partly medial and partly caudal to the acrosome cap, reveals a structure of its own which is not visible in epididymal or testicular sperm. The filling apparently is composed of moderately dense, granular material in which single membrane-bound profiles and channels are visible. In publications which appeared prior to the era of ultrastructure research, the posterior aspect of the sperm head often was referred to as being enclosed by a "postnuclear cap." This is understandable since this is the only area in which this layer is thick enough to be perceived with the light microscope.

This subacrosomal (cytoplasmic) layer appears at places to be delineated by a single membrane.

The salient points about the subacrosomal, or cytoplasmic, layer are that: (1) it surrounds the sperm nucleus, excepting its caudal end; (2) it contains or encloses the apical body of the sperm; (3) it shows a ringlike thickening. This ring or beltlike thickening can be in any position along the nucleus except at the level of the apical body. In the spermatozoon that penetrates the egg, the subacrosomal layer disintegrates in the form of circular to irregularly shaped profiles. It is possible that this layer is partially responsible for the dissolution of the vitelline membrane around the egg.

SPECIMEN

I.4. Rabbit ejaculatum. Veronal acetate-buffered 1% OsO_4; Epon 815; uranyl acetate ($\times$ 50,000).

A, acrosome cap; N, nucleus; R, ringlike thickening of subacrosomal layer (around sperm head); S, subacrosomal layer; V, nuclear vacuole.

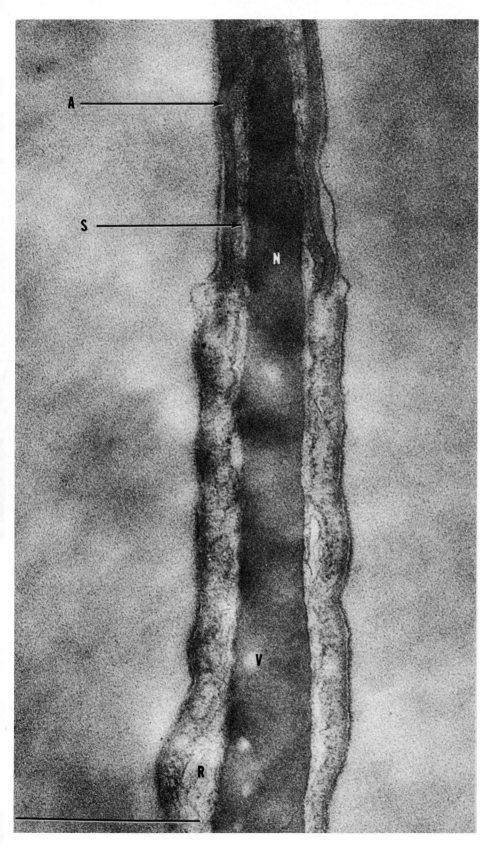

1.4

FIGURE I.5

FORMATION OF SUBACROSOMAL (CYTOPLASMIC) LAYER

The evolution of the spermatid into the spermatozoon involves a gradual "thinning," or loss, of excess cytoplasm. Through this process, the spermatid becomes the fishlike organism, the spermatozoon, as it appears in the ejaculatum. The first structure which becomes free of cytoplasm (but nevertheless remains surrounded by a Sertoli cell) is the sperm head. The disappearance of cytoplasm starts at the rostral extremity of the head. Consequently, one may observe developmental stages in which the apical part of the head already has been freed from the cytoplasm, while its caudal portion is still surrounded by it. In many of these specimens, the cytoplasm often contains parallel-running, small tubules around the caudal portion of the nucleus.

On this oblique section of developing hamster spermatid [head-sleeve stage (Clermont-Leblond, 1955)], one can observe the well-developed acrosomal cap abutting caudally on the cytoplasm of the cell. A thin cytoplasmic subacrosomal layer composed entirely of ground substance is between the acrosome cap and nucleus (arrow). That part of the cytoplasm which is situated around the caudal part of the nucleus below the termination of the acrosome contains a number of microtubules. A membrane around this layer which later will separate it from the rest of the cytoplasm is not visible yet. The nucleus is composed of a centrally placed, dense, granular part and a lighter peripheral part.

SPECIMEN

I.5. Hamster testis. Phosphate-buffered 1% OsO_4; Epon 815; uranyl acetate ($\times$ 40,000). A, acrosome cap; CY, cytoplasm (or vitellus in egg); N, nucleus; arrow, subacrosomal layer between nucleus and acrosomal cap.

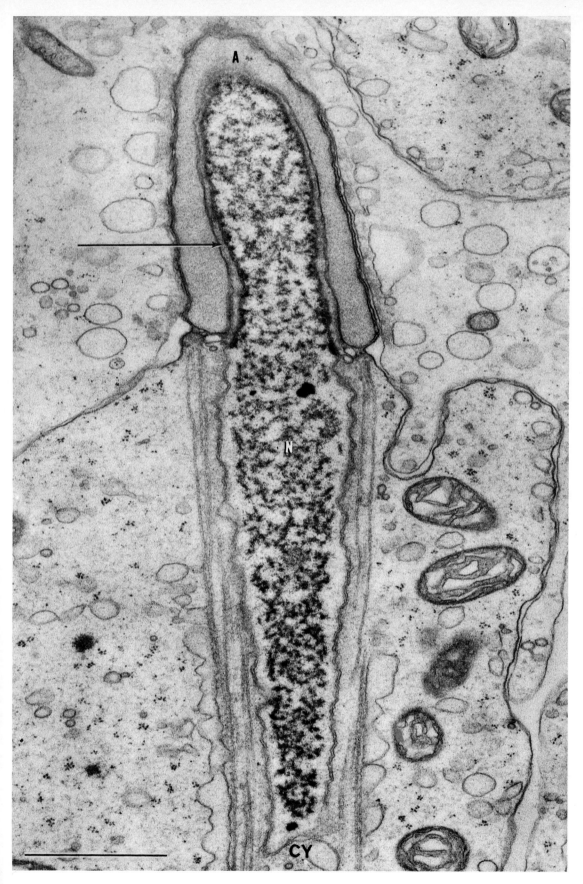

1.5

FIGURE 1.6

DEVELOPING APICAL BODIES IN HAMSTER SPERMATID; SAGITTAL AND FRONTAL SECTIONS

Apical bodies are best observed in the ejaculated spermatozoa or in those which have been recovered from the female genital tract (Hadek, 1963a; Piko and Tyler, 1964; Wimsatt *et al.*, 1966). The cell organelle from which the apical bodies are derived has not yet been determined, although one possible source of their origin could be the concentric (whorllike) agglomeration of smooth membranes (smooth endoplasmic reticulum). These whorls are visible in the developing hamster spermatid between the nucleus and the acrosomal cap (arrow). A possible support for this hypothesis is that the smooth membrane whorls in the developing spermatid and the apical body in the fully developed spermatozoon are in identical location. Further, no membranous whorls were observed in any of the fully developed spermatozoa examined.

The transverse section of hamster spermatid head opposite shows the presence of circular strands formed by a concentration of smooth membranes. These membrane whorls are located at the apex of the spermatozoon between the nucleus and the acrosome cap within the cytoplasmic layer.

The shape of the apical body has been a subject of some controversy (Wimsatt *et al.*, 1966). On the strength of observations of the ejaculated sperm of rabbits, it was assumed that the apical body has a conical shape (Hadek, 1963c; Bedford, 1964). However, studies on spermatozoa of the hamster and the bat (Wimsatt *et al.*, 1966), have shown that in the three mammals studied the apical bodies may differ in shape. While it still is regarded as conical in the spermatozoon of the rabbit, it apparently is irregularly conical in the sperm of the hamster, and has a circular, blade shape in the spermatozoon of the bat.

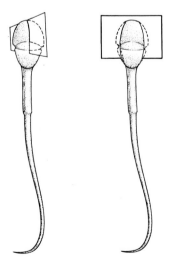

SPECIMEN

1.6. Hamster testis. Phosphatase-buffered 1% OsO_4; Epon 815; uranyl acetate ($\times$ 28,000). A, acrosome cap; arrow, membrane whorls in developing subacrosomal layer (assumed origin of apical body).

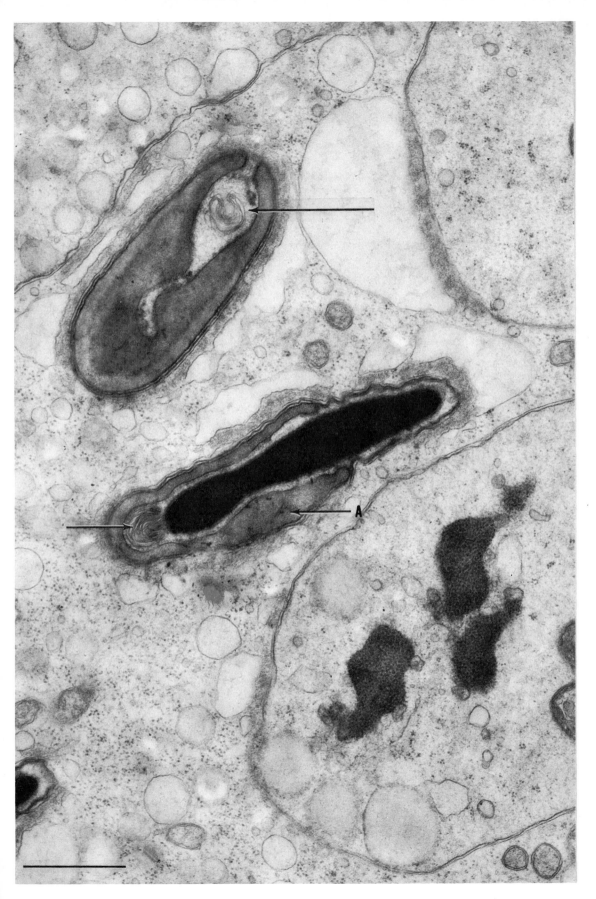

1.6

FIGURES I.7, AND I.8

APICAL BODIES IN SPERMATOZOA OF RABBIT AND HAMSTER

Sagittal sections of epididymal and ejaculated spermatozoa of rabbit (epididymal) and golden hamster (ejaculated) are shown.

In the fully developed spermatozoon, the apical body as a rule assumes a greater electron density than the cytoplasmic layer immediately around it.

In these pictures the subacrosomal cytoplasmic layer lacks any fillings in the spermatozoon of the hamster, while it forms a ringlike protuberance in the sperm of the rabbit. Outside this is the acrosomal cap. In both sperms between the acrosome cap and the apex of the nucleus, a small, dense apical body is visible. This can be observed as a separate body in the sperm of the rabbit, but cannot be discerned as a separate structure in the sperm of the hamster.

SPECIMENS

I.7. Epididymis, rabbit. Veronal acetate-buffered 1% OsO₄; Epon 815; uranyl acetate (× 28,000).

I.8. Hamster vaginal plug. Veronal acetate-buffered 1% OsO₄; Epon 815; uranyl acetate (× 28,000).

A, acrosome cap; AB, apical body; N, nucleus; S, subacrosomal layer.

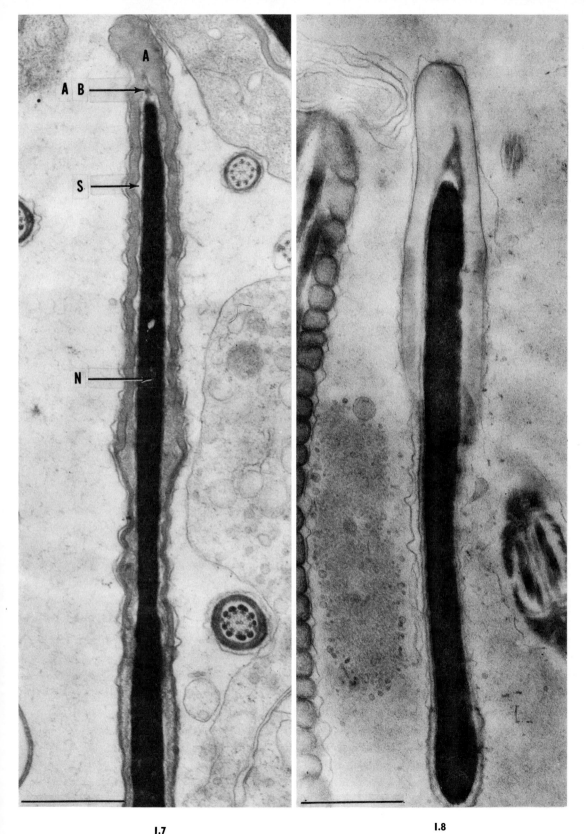

1.7   **1.8**

FIGURE I.9

SPERMATOZOON NECK (The Proximal Part of the Tail)

This is a frontal section through the lower part of the head and neck in a developing hamster spermatid. The center of the neck is occupied by a slanting centriole located within and surrounded by the elements of the ribbed connecting piece. This body appears to be the apical continuation of the dense peripheral fibers of the spermatozoon's tail, though the two do not show similar densities (Fawcett, 1965).

SPECIMEN

I.9. Testis, hamster. Phosphate-buffered 2% glutaraldehyde; Epon 815; uranyl acetate (× 50,000).

CE, centriole; CP, connecting piece (in sperm neck); CY, cytoplasm (or vitellus in egg); M, mitochondria; N, nucleus; PF, peripheral rough fibers (in spermatozoon's tail).

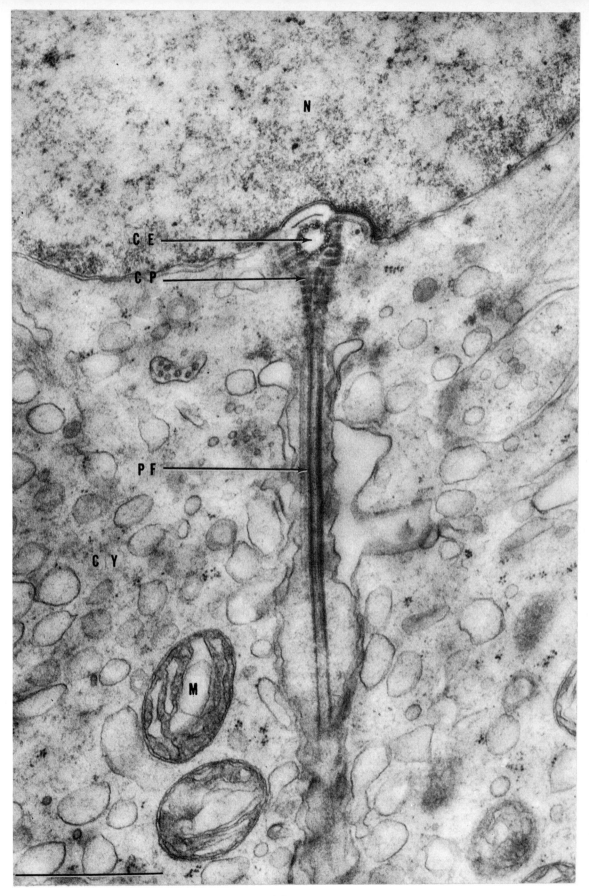

1.9

SPERMATOZOON NECK IN DIFFERENT ANGLES
These four pictures illustrate the spermatozoon neck in different phases of its evolution and from various aspects.

FIGURE I.10
FRONTAL SECTION THROUGH THE NECK OF EVOLVING HAMSTER SPERMATID
Observe the apparent continuity of the rough filaments into the ribbed (possibly helicine) connecting piece. A folded membranous scroll, enclosed within the nuclear membrane outpocketings, is cut transversely on both sides of the neck. The basal plate is in the process of evolution, while the capitellum is still absent from this picture. Mitochondria are beginning to align along longitudinal axis of spermatozoon. Left drawing.

FIGURE I.11
PARASAGITTAL SECTION THROUGH SPERMATOZOON NECK
This picture shows some of the components of the spermatozoon neck. At the base of the nucleus, the dense structure is the basal plate (only partially visible). Actually, it is a thickened segment of the nuclear membrane. Opposite to it is the capitellum, the most apical portion of the neck (tail), which is the termination of the ribbed connecting piece that is continuous with the rough fibers of the central core in the sperm tail. The nuclear membrane fold, visible on each side, is flatter than on the previous picture. Right drawing.

FIGURE I.12
OBLIQUE SECTION THROUGH SPERM NECK
In addition to the basal plate, part of the capitellum is visible; also the termination of some rough fibers. In the center of the capitellum, the outline of the centriole is barely perceived, surrounded by the termination of the ribbed body elements. In addition to one of the neck mitochondria, some elements of the mitochondrial spiral are partially visible. Membranous folds on both sides of the neck are in evidence. Center drawing.

FIGURE I.13
A SOMEWHAT OBLIQUE SECTION THROUGH BENT SPERM HEAD AND NECK
Of the components which form the neck, the basal plate and part of the capitellum are visible. Condensation of the membranous folds into dense, whorllike structures is in evidence. The continuous spermatozoon evolution apparently causes a shortening of the nuclear membrane. This is assumed to be responsible for the ultimate separation of the nuclear membrane from the protruding fold formed during spermatozoon development. Thereafter, the separated fold disappears at a fast pace. Right drawing.

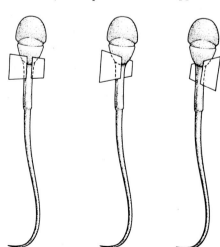

SPECIMENS

I.10. Hamster testis. Phosphate-buffered 2% glutaraldehyde, postosmicated; Epon 815; uranyl acetate ($\times$ 45,000).

I.11. Epididymal spermatozoon, hamster. Phosphate-buffered 2% glutaraldehyde, postosmicated; Epon 815; uranyl acetate ($\times$ 50,000).

I.12. Epididymal spermatozoon, hamster. Phosphate-buffered 2% glutaraldehyde, postosmicated; Epon 815; uranyl acetate ($\times$ 50,000).

I.13. Ejaculated rabbit spermatozoon. Veronal acetate-buffered 1% OsO_4; Epon 815; uranyl acetate ($\times$ 50,000).

B, basal plate (of sperm head); CA, capitellum (of sperm neck); CE, centriole; CP, connecting piece (in sperm neck); M, mitochondria; N, nucleus; O, outpocketings of nuclear membrane.

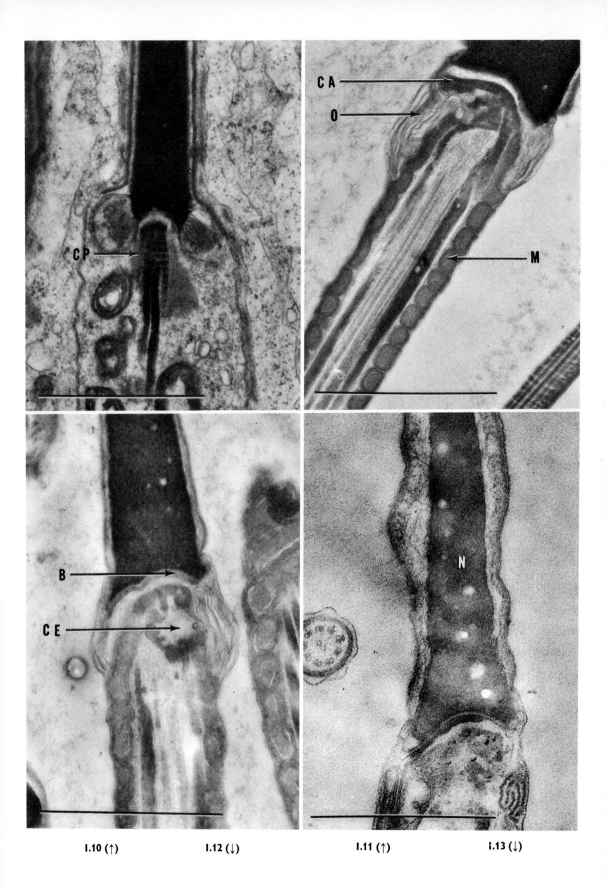

I.10 (↑)   I.12 (↓)   I.11 (↑)   I.13 (↓)

FIGURE I.14

PARASAGITTAL SECTION OF THE NECK OF EJACULATED SPERMATOZOON OF HAMSTER

Due to transecting the outpocketings of the nuclear membrane, membrane whorls appear on each side of the neck. The central part of the ribbed connecting piece is visible as the direct continuation of two peripheral rough fibers. Also visible is the proximal part of the mitochondrial spiral and its rostral termination with the wedge-shaped, vertically oriented mitochondria at the apical part of the neck, advancing almost to the basal plate.

SPECIMEN

I.14. Ejaculated hamster spermatozoon. Veronal acetate-buffered 1% OsO_4; Maraglas; uranyl acetate ($\times$ 20,000).

CP, connecting piece (in sperm neck); MS, mitochondrial spiral (around midpiece of sperm tail); NM, neck mitochondria (of spermatozoon); O, outpocketings of nuclear membrane (around sperm neck); PF, peripheral rough fibers (in spermatozoon's tail).

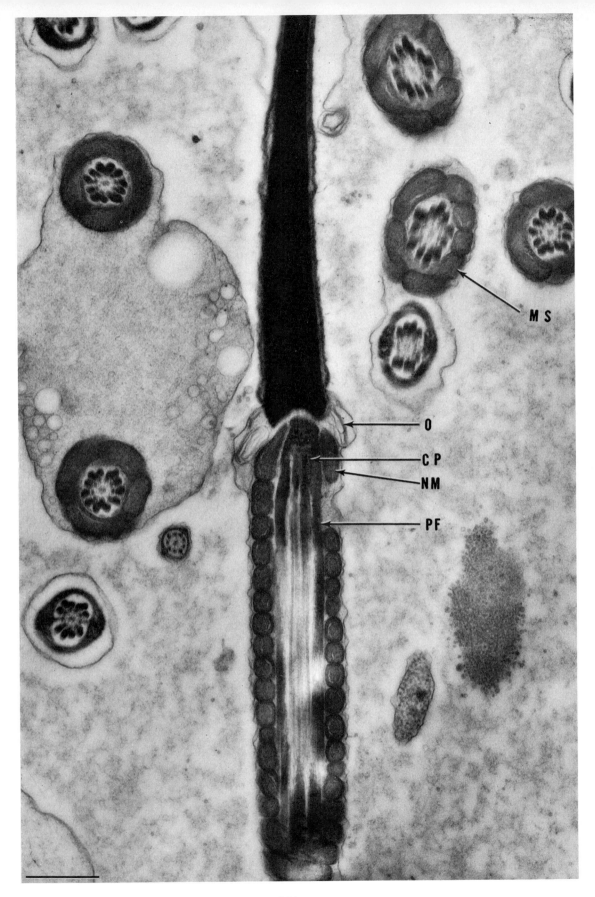

I.14

FIGURE I.15

MIDPIECE SPERM TAIL OF RABBIT

Change in mitochondrial morphology is characteristic of gametogenesis in general, and of spermiogenesis in particular. It is interesting to point out that in the *female* gamete a rounding of the mitochondria, decrease in the number of cristae, and a change in their morphology, have been observed (Adams and Hertig, 1964; Hadek, 1965). In the *male* the cristae elongate and subsequently assume their characteristic shape and location in the mitochondria. All the mitochondria in the sperm tail show an almost identical morphology characteristic of the species and of the stage of spermiogenesis (Fawcett, 1959). They form a continuous spiral around the peripheral rough fibers starting immediately caudal from the two longitudinally oriented neck mitochondria, and are lying end-to-end in such manner that the ends of two apparently correspond to the middle of the one below and the one above (at lower part of picture). This spermatozoon shown in the electron micrograph has a cytoplasmic bead attached, evident in the lower half of the picture.

SPECIMEN

I.15. Ejaculated spermatozoon of rabbit. Veronal acetate-buffered 1% OsO_4; Epon 815; uranyl acetate ($\times$ 30,000).
C, cell membrane; CD, cytoplasmic droplet (attached to spermatozoon); MS, mitochondrial spiral (around midpiece of sperm tail); PF, peripheral rough fibers (in spermatozoon's tail).

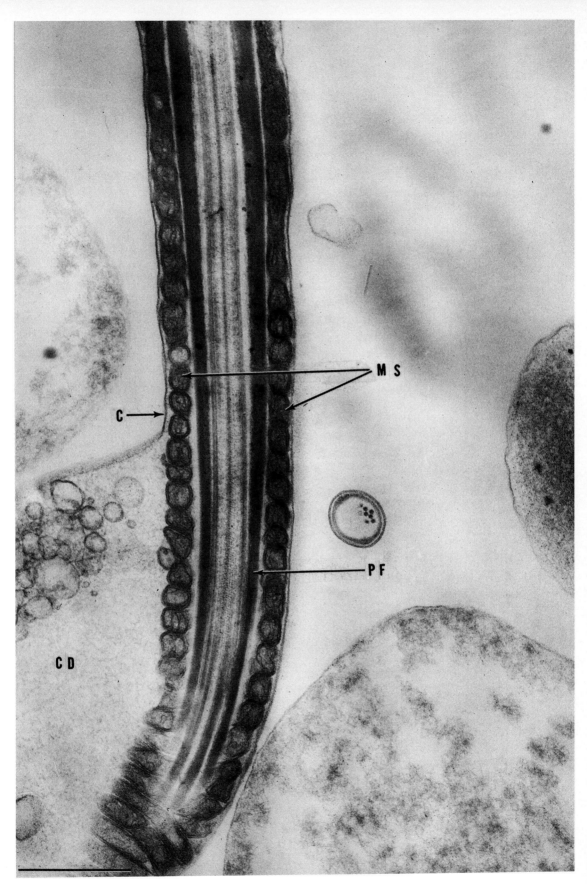

I.15

CROSS SECTIONS OF SPERM TAIL

The purpose of these pictures is to show the polarity and organizational details of the sperm tail.

Running through the center of the tail is the axial filament complex which originates in the neck. The axial filament complex consists of the two central filaments. They are situated one above the other corresponding to a dorsoventral axis, actually two small tubules in transverse section when seen with the electron microscope. These are surrounded by the nine double fibrils (doublets). One of the doublets is an empty tubule, and the other is solid. From the solid filament two armlike projections are directed toward the nearest empty tubule. In addition, spokelike densities emanating from the area of the central tubules toward the peripheral nine fibrils are also observable in these pictures.

Although by no means universally accepted, a number of studies have indicated that minute crossbands, or spokes, are present in the mammalian spermatozoa, e.g., in the human (Anberg, 1957), and in the boar (Nicander and Bane, 1962a), which connect the two central filaments and the double set of nine fibrils. A similar feature has been observed in the sperm tail of the butterfly (Andre, 1961b).

SPECIMENS

I.16–I.18. Sperm from rabbit testis. Veronal acetate-buffered 1% OsO$_4$; Epon 815; uranyl acetate ($\times$ 50,000).

I.19. Sperm from hamster epididymis. Veronal acetate-buffered 1% OsO$_4$; Epon 815; uranyl acetate ($\times$ 50,000).

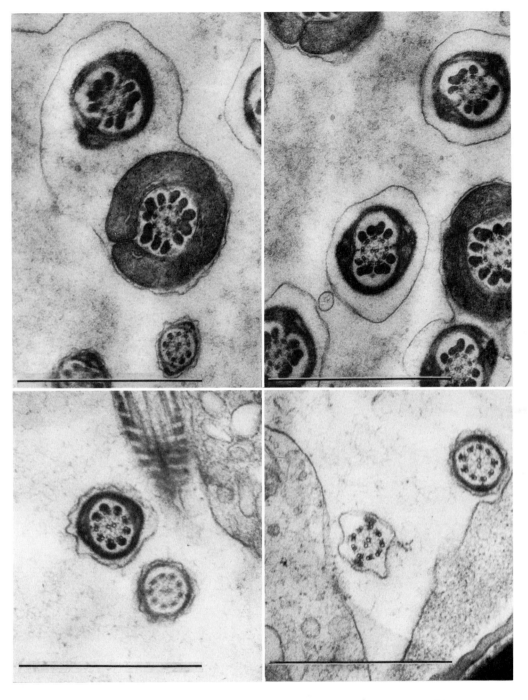

1.16 (↑)   1.18 (↓)   1.17 (↑)   1.19 (↓)

FIGURE I.20

MAIN PIECE SPERMATOZOON TAIL OF RABBIT

Oblique longitudinal section through the sperm tail of rabbit. The two outer columns under the cell membrane appear to be composed of individual units which seem to be continuous with a lateral arm connecting one to another. This led earlier investigators to assume the existence of a spiral-shaped "tail helix." However, in transverse sections, as seen earlier, and in successfully fixed longitudinal sections, these two columns are revealed to be solid bands. These solid bands are joined to one another by transversely running arms which show occasional branching. The other significance of this electron micrograph is the demonstration of very thin connecting bands, or "secondary fibrils," or transverse filaments originating from the double axial filaments and running to the outer set of nine (double) fibrils (seen previously in transverse sections).

SPECIMEN

I.20. Ejaculated spermatozoon of rabbit; transverse section of main piece of sperm tail. Veronal acetate buffered 1% OsO_4; Epon 815; uranyl acetate ($\times$ 50,000).

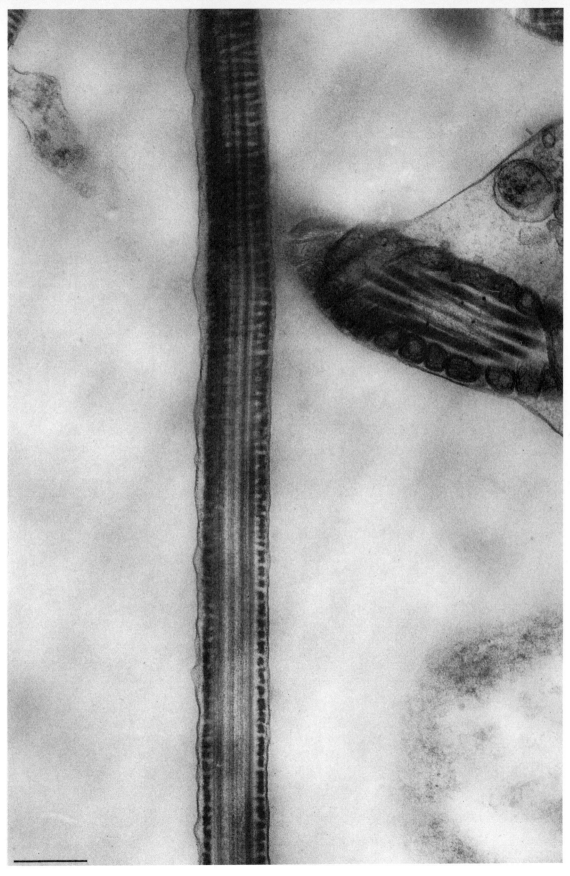

I.20

FIGURE I.21

BEATING SPERM TAIL

Rabbit spermatozoon inside zona pellucida. It is located within the perivitelline area in the vicinity of the vitelline membrane. The appearance of the fibrous sheath in the beating sperm tail is somewhat similar to the organization of a metal coil, thus giving some reason for the earlier assumption that the fibrous sheath is of a spiral nature. There is an apparent segmental organization within this sheath. Particularly prominent are the rough fibers which run in a wavelike manner, at places closer, at others farther from the axis of the tail. Upon consideration, this is feasible only if contraction of these rough fibers is regulated by the transverse filaments (or secondary fibrils). In transverse sections these secondary fibers are seen to run like the spokes of a wheel. Accordingly, this electron micrograph suggests that the flagellar movement of the sperm tail is apparently coordinated with (or possibly caused by) the contracting transverse filaments (or secondary fibrils).

SPECIMEN

I.21. Rabbit egg approximately 18 hours after mating. Veronal-acetate buffered 1% OsO_4; Epon 812; lead acetate ($\times$ 85,000).
PF, peripheral rough fibers (in spermatozoon's tail).

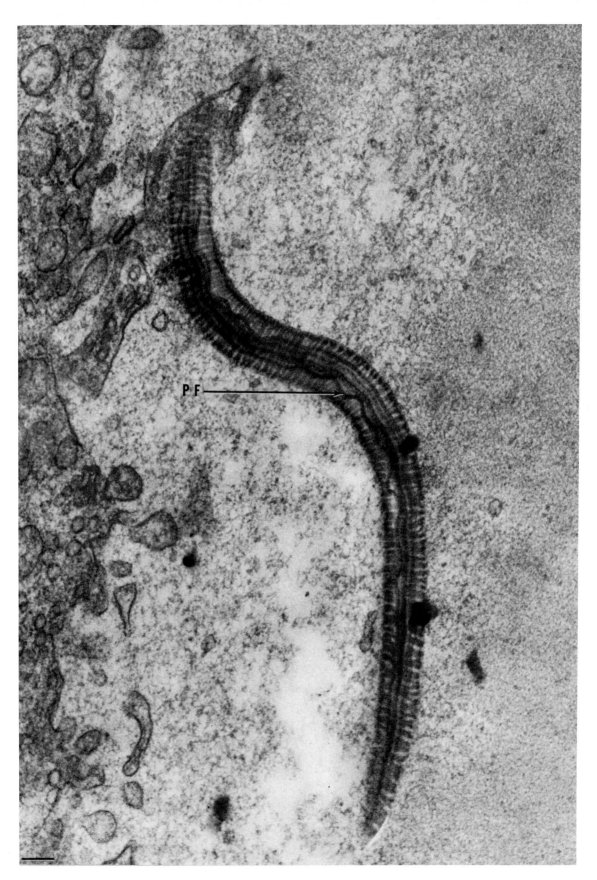

I.21

FIGURE I.22

CYTOPLASMIC DROPLET IN SPERMATOZOON TAIL

Even in the normal ejaculatum an occasional spermatozoon will have an attached cytoplasmic remnant, or "middle piece bead," or "protoplasmic droplet," as it has been variously called. This represents immaturity since cytoplasmic droplets usually are present in the head region of those sperm which have been recovered from the head of the epididymis, and are attached to the tail of those which have been recovered from the tail of the epididymis (Bloom and Nicander, 1961; Nicander and Bane, 1962b; Fawcett and Ito, 1965). Thus a gradual caudal displacement of the droplet occurs in the maturing spermatozoon. When the sperm leave the tail of the epididymis, they become completely detached. This electron micrograph shows the presence of a cytoplasmic droplet at the border of the midpiece and main piece, and at only one side of the tail. It is composed of somewhat electron-dense cytoplasmic fillings, a number of smooth-walled vesicles of various sizes, tubules, and occasional membranes. The picture also shows the terminal mitochondrial spiral (arrow) at the border of the midpiece and main piece, which has a straight circular course instead of being slanted like the others nearer the head (arrow).

SPECIMEN

I.22. Tail, ejaculated rabbit spermatozoon. Veronal acetate buffered 1% OsO_4; Epon 815; uranyl acetate ($\times$ 24,000).
CD, cytoplasmic droplet (attached to spermatozoon), arrow, terminal mitochondrial spiral.

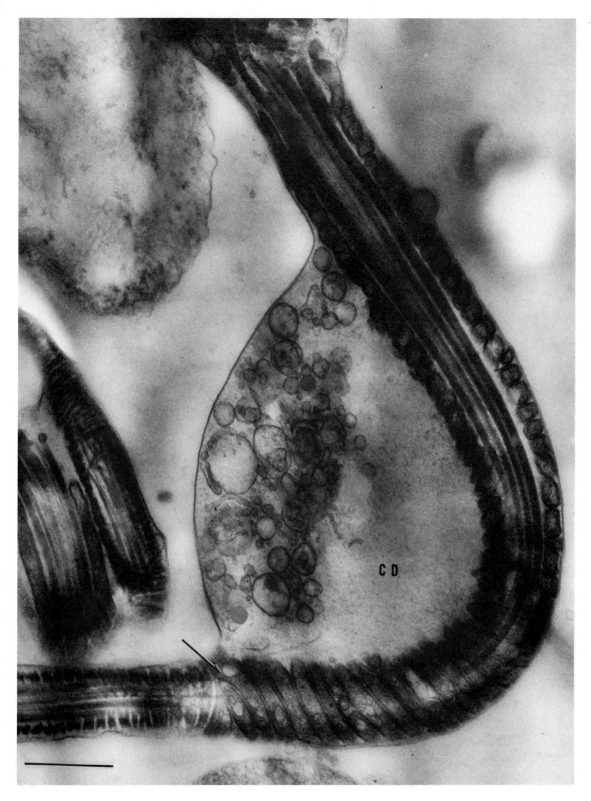

CD

1.22

Changes in the Morphology of the Ejaculated Rabbit Sperm: The Assumed Pattern of Capacitation

Capacitation (Austin, 1951, 1952) is an acquired condition of the sperm that enables it to conjugate with, or penetrate into the egg. The freshly ejaculated mammalian spermatozoon, as a rule, acquires this ability in the female genital tract. For the time being, however, neither its morphological, nor physiological implications are known, with the exception that the acquired "capacity" is manifest only by its effect, which is the fertilization of the egg.

Capacitation can be achieved in a variety of ways, for example, by incubating spermatozoa with female genital tract lavage (Thibault and Dauzier, 1961; Yanagimachi and Chang, 1963), or with peritoneal fluid (McDonald and Sampson, 1957; Hadek, 1958) or by removing the decapacitating effect of the male genital tract (Weinman and Williams, 1964). Since the various layers around the sperm nucleus have been demonstrated (in a variety of genera and species) to participate in fertilization, it has been assumed that the effect of capacitation is on the sperm head or, to be precisely stated, on the layers around the nucleus.

As part of this study a number of experiments have been performed in an effort to study changes in mammalian sperm in situations closely resembling physiological conditions. For example, sperm in rabbit ejaculatum were washed [since the secretion of the accessory male genital glands is known to interfere with fertilization (Chang, 1950)] and subsequently incubated with oviduct lavage from rabbits mated to vasectomized males (Hadek, 1959). Sperm was also obtained from the uterus and oviduct of golden hamsters which had been mated normally. The morphological changes observed in the sperm of these two species could be assumed to be indicative of capacitation. Further morphological changes (when compared to the freshly ejaculated sperm) were observed in the heads of those rabbit spermatozoa that were obtained in the process of penetrating the zona pellucida of the egg, or which were within the perivitelline area (Hadek, 1963a, 1964).

The spermatozoon which is in the process of penetrating into the egg is known to have been capacitated. Consequently, particular attention was paid to the morphology of those spermatozoa which were in the vicinity of the vitelline membrane, assuming that they were "capacitated."

For the purpose of this study mammalian sperm with two different penetration patterns will be put into juxtaposition with one another: (1) the rabbit, an animal in which, as a rule, a number of spermatozoa penetrate through the zona pellucida, and (2) the golden hamster in which the zona acts as a barrier preventing the access of more than one sperm into the perivitelline area. In both species, under physiological conditions, only one sperm has access to the vitellus, thus becoming incorporated into the egg (Austin, 1951). When comparing the gradually changing morphology of golden hamster spermatozoa that have been obtained from the female genital tract with the rabbit sperm penetrating the zona pellucida, a similarity of alterations has been observed. Only the location where these changes are taking place is different in each animal.

Actually, the sperm advancement or ascent pattern itself also differs in the rabbit and the hamster. In the rabbit, sperm ascends into the oviduct within a short period (Adams, 1958), whereas in the hamster the apical part of the uterine horn (Orsini, 1961) appears to be the location where sperm maturation, or "capacitation" takes place. Hamster sperm recovered from the uterus often show a number of morphological changes dependent on the length of time the sperm have spent in the uterus. The sequence of changes is as follows:

1. Enlargement (swelling) of the acrosomal cap, accompanied by the gradual separation of the cell membrane
2. Separation of the acrosomal cap from the subacrosomal "cytoplasmic" layer
3. In the ultimate stage, dissolution of the acrosomal cap, leaving the nucleus with the surrounding cytoplasmic layer

In the rabbit it was shown that the first in a series of morphological changes occurs upon exposing the sperm to oviduct fluid activity. There is enlargement of the head cap which is followed almost simultaneously by a turgescence of the subacrosomal or "cytoplasmic" layer.

The next change in rabbit sperm morphology occurs during sperm penetration through the zona pellucida. Namely, those sperm heads which are observed in zona pellucida channels, i.e., areas wherein zona pellucida has been dissolved, show the acrosomal layer in the process of disintegration. By the time the rabbit spermatozoon has reached the vicinity of the vitelline membrane, the acrosomal cap has disappeared (Hadek, 1963a; Piko and Tyler, 1964). As a result the rabbit sperm nucleus is covered only by the subacrosomal layer.

FIGURES I.23 AND I.24

HAMSTER SPERM HEAD AND ASSUMED CAPACITATION CHANGES

The two electron micrographs assumedly represent the morphological aspects of hamster sperm capacitation. Both spermatozoa were obtained from the uterine content 6 hours after mating. Capacitation in the hamster and the rabbit is assumed to occur in different places and possibly has different morphological concomitants.

In the rabbit, in which multiple spermatozoa can penetrate through the zona pellucida (though only one of them is going to be incorporated into the vitellus), sperm advance rapidly through the female genital tract and spend a longer period of time in the oviduct. Although, in the rabbit capacitation takes place in the oviduct, the sperm are still intact when they start their penetration through the zona pellucida. But, by the time the spermatozoon has reached the perivitelline area, it is devoid of cell membrane and acrosomal cap.

In the hamster, sperm spend a long period in the uterus where capacitation occurs. This involves the disintegration of the cell membrane and the acrosomal cap long before the spermatozoon has reached the zona pellucida. In the hamster only one spermatozoon (which may subsequently fertilize the egg) penetrates through the zona pellucida. The electron micrographs on the opposite page illustrate: (a) the gradual enlargement and (b) subsequent dissolution of the acrosome cap in the hamster sperm. In Figure I.23 the cell membrane is adhering to the apex of the acrosomal cap (most probably due to swellings), while it is loose toward the caudal part. The acrosomal cap shows a denser peripheral fringe and a lighter inner layer, apparently in the process of expansion (swelling), which did not affect the subacrosomal (cytoplasmic) layer. This is clearly visible in this picture.

SPECIMENS

I.23. Parasagittal section through hamster sperm head recovered from uterus 6 hours after matings. Phosphatase-buffered 2% glutaraldehyde; postosmicated; Epon 815; uranyl acetate ($\times$ 35,000).

I.24. Veronal acetate-buffered 1% OsO$_4$; Epon 815; uranyl acetate ($\times$ 35,000).

A, acrosome cap; AB, apical body; N, nucleus; S, subacrosomal layer.

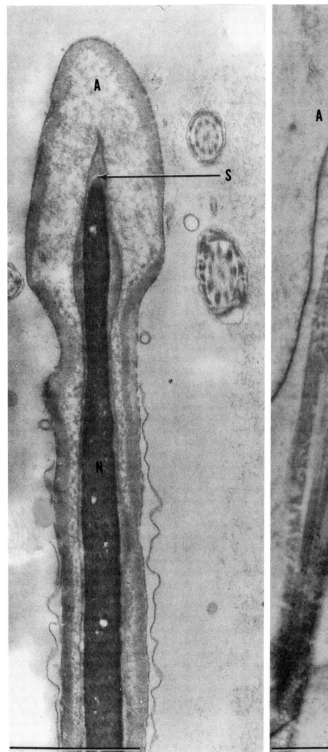

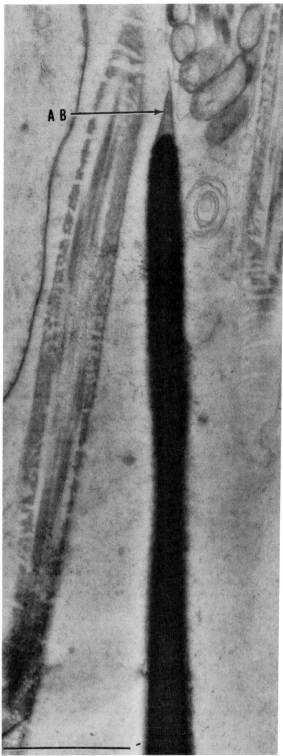

1.23

1.24

FIGURE 1.25

RABBIT SPERM HEAD DEMONSTRATING (ASSUMED) CAPACITATION CHANGE

Washed sperm suspension was incubated in oviduct lavage with freshly shed egg. The changes in the head region associated with the phenomenon of capacitation include an enlargement of the head profile, particularly at the apical extremity of the nucleus accompanied by rounding and caudal displacement of the acrosomal cap. This gives an impression of cranial advancement by the apical body and nucleus. In some instances there is a swelling observable in the cytoplasmic layer and a gradual dissolution of the cell membrane.

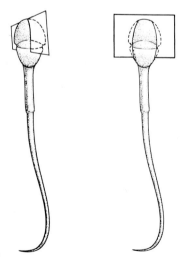

SPECIMEN

1.25. Parasagittal and transverse section through incubated rabbit sperm heads. Veronal acetate-buffered 1% OsO_4; Epon 815; lead citrate ($\times$ 50,000).

A, acrosome cap; AB, apical body.

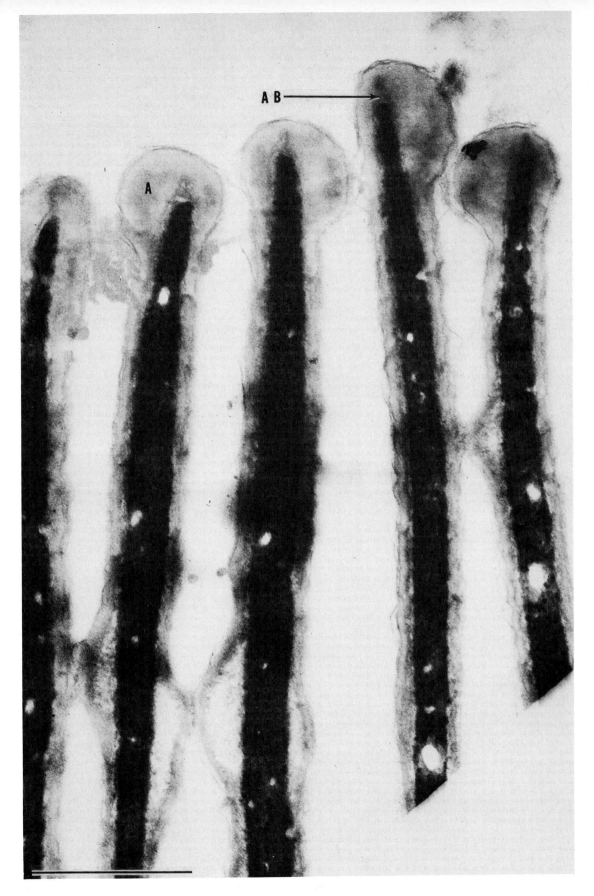

1.25

FIGURES 1.26 AND 1.27

HEAD OF RABBIT SPERMATOZOON SHOWING (ASSUMED) CAPACITATION CHANGES

Transverse and parasagittal sections of rabbit spermatozoa incubated with oviduct lavage and freshly shed rabbit egg.

These spermatozoa are actually attached to the outside of the zona pellucida, contributing to the sunburst effect that one sees when spermatozoa are incubated with mammalian eggs. These transverse and parasagittal sections show: (a) enlargement of the acrosomal cap; (b) changes in its shape from oval to round; and (c) apparent advancement of nucleus and apical body.

SPECIMENS

1.26, 1.27. Parasagittal and transverse section through rabbit sperm head. Veronal acetate-buffered 1% OsO_4; lead acetate ($\times$ 26,000). A, acrosome cap; AB, apical body.

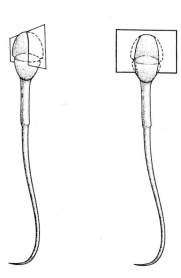

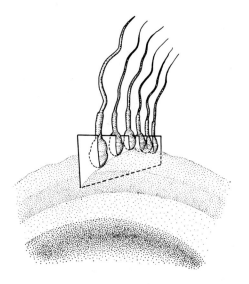

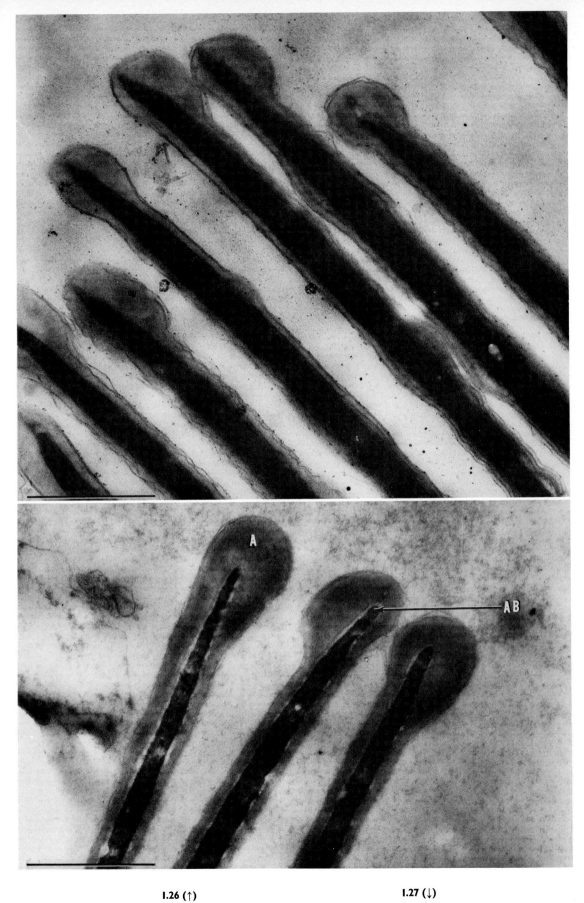

1.26 (↑)   1.27 (↓)

FIGURE 1.28

HEAD OF RABBIT SPERMATOZOON AT THE START OF PENETRATION THROUGH ZONA PELLUCIDA

Rabbit spermatozoon at the outermost part of the zona pellucida. The cell membrane is absent and the acrosomal cap is in the process of apparent dissolution. The sperm head and neck are located in a trough or channel (or funnel) within the zona pellucida. This particular area shows little contrast, indicating the dissolution of the zonal material in the immediate vicinity of the sperm head.

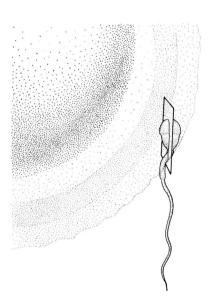

SPECIMEN

1.28. Rabbit sperm head in zona pellucida. Veronal acetate-buffered 1% OsO₄; Epon 812; uranyl acetate ($\times$ 22,000).
A, acrosome cap; Z, zona pellucida.

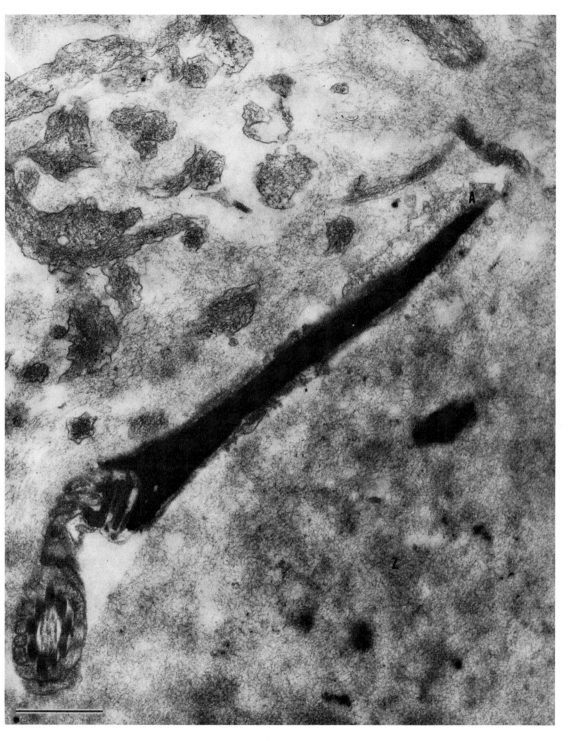

I.28

FIGURE 1.29

THE DISINTEGRATING ACROSOMAL CAP (1)

Parasagittal section through spermatozoon head of rabbit, fixed while penetrating through zona pellucida. Cell membrane is absent, and the acrosomal cap is represented only by the equatorial region on the left side and by a loose profile on the right. The subacrosomal layer and the darker staining apical body are well in evidence. A lighter area is visible within the zona pellucida around the sperm head, which is due to its dissolution by enzymes released from the sperm head.

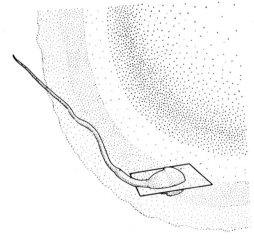

SPECIMEN

1.29. Parasagittal section through rabbit sperm head in zona pellucida of rabbit egg. Veronal acetate-buffered 1% OsO_4; Epon 815; uranyl acetate ($\times$ 33,000).

A, acrosome cap; AB, apical body; S, subacrosomal layer; Z, zona pellucida; ZD, area of dissolved zona pellucida.

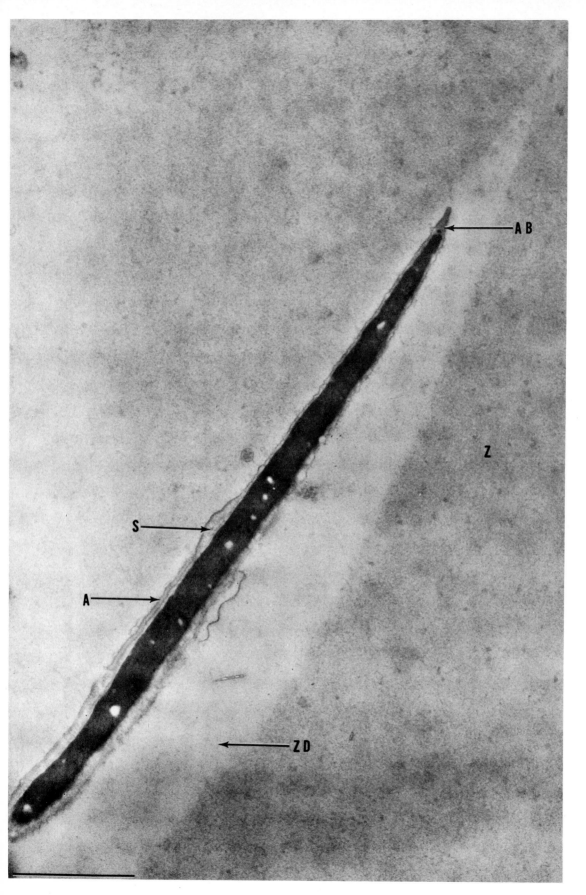

1.29

FIGURES 1.30 AND 1.31

THE DISINTEGRATING ACROSOMAL CAP (2), AND TAIL OF RABBIT SPERM IN ZONA PELLUCIDA

Slightly oblique section through rabbit sperm head while penetrating through the zona pellucida of rabbit egg. Observe the absence of the cell membrane and the narrow profile of the acrosomal cap remnants. The remainder of the caudal segment of the acrosomal cap (equatorial region) is still present. It is abutting on the subacrosomal (cytoplasmic) layer. On the left side bleblike protrusions are apparent, which dissolve the zona pellucida. An apparently empty profile, part of the dissolving acrosomal cap, is visible on the right.

Parasagittal section through rabbit spermatozoon tail, main piece. It is in the passage within the zona pellucida (of rabbit egg), which assumedly was dissolved by the acrosome of the spermatozoon.

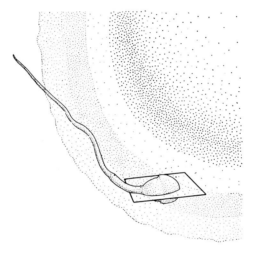

SPECIMENS

1.30. Slightly oblique section through rabbit sperm head while penetrating through zona pellucida of rabbit egg. Veronal acetate-buffered 1% OsO_4; Epon 812; uranyl acetate ($\times$ 50,000).

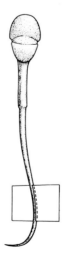

1.31. Parasagittal section through rabbit sperm tail within zona pellucida of rabbit egg. Veronal acetate-buffered 1% OsO_4; Epon 815; uranyl acetate ($\times$ 50,000).

A, acrosome cap; E, equatorial region of sperm head; S, subacrosomal layer; Z, zona pellucida.

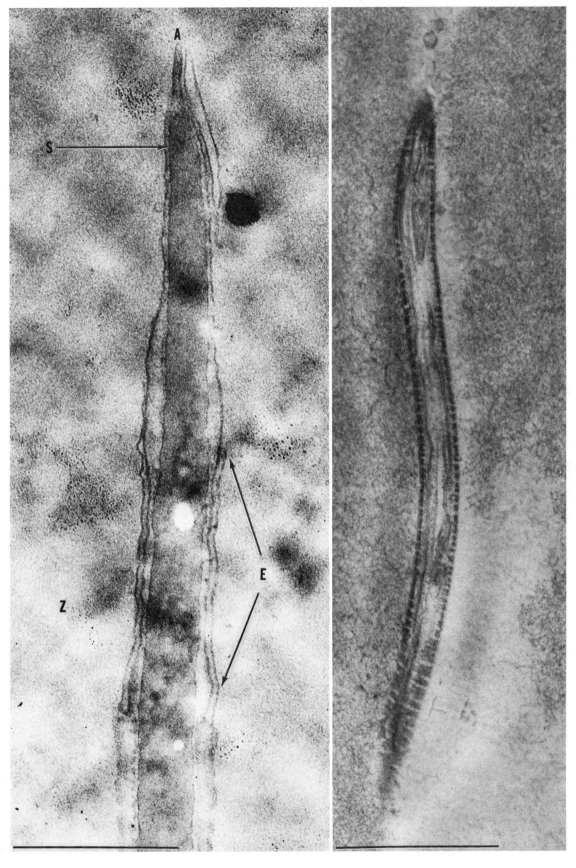

I.30   **I.31**

II

THE
VAGINAL PLUG

Study on the Vaginal Plug

Vaginal plug is the name given to a jellylike substance that has been observed in the vaginal vestibule of certain mammals following copulation.

Although mammalian semen is emitted from the urethra as a fluid, after entrance into the vagina it remains fluid in only a few mammals. The notable exceptions are the Lagomorpha, Canidae, Felidae, Equidae, and Bovidae (Price and Williams-Ashman, 1961). In the majority of mammals the semen forms a plug which, at least temporarily, blocks the uterine orifice. This copulation plug, of course, is to be differentiated from the cellular plug formed by hypertrophied epithelial cells in the vagina of the bat, *Nyctalus noctula* (Grosser, 1903) and the European pipistrelle (Courrier, 1924).

This vaginal plug, or "bouchon vaginal" (assumedly the term originates from Rollinat and Trouessant, 1896), can be of a variety of consistencies. In some species, it is quite soft as, for example, the newly formed vaginal plug in the golden hamster (Orsini, 1961), or it may show a cheesy consistency as in the British horseshoe bat (*Rhinolaphus ferrum equinum*). Ultimately, in some animals a hard, waxy plug may form, as in the wild mountain viscacha (*Lagidium peruaneum* Meyer) (Pearson, 1949). The plug may fill the whole vagina, as in the golden hamster (Orsini, 1961), or merely pockets in the vagina, as may be the case in bats (Courrier, 1927; Matthews, 1937).

The plug may be deposited during copulation as it happens in the chimpanzee (Tinklepaugh, 1930), or may be formed only after copulation as in the guinea pig (Leuckart, 1847).

The length of time the plug is extant may also vary widely. For example, in the golden hamster it disappears about 18 hours after copulation. In other species, however, it may last for days, as in the guinea pig (Stockard and Papanicolaou, 1919). The exception is when it takes a number of months until it disappears, as in the bat, where it persists from fall to spring (Eckstein and Zuckerman, 1956).

It is assumed that in the opossum (Hartman, 1924) and in some bats(Courrier, 1924), the vaginal plug is the female secretion that has been coagulated by the seminal plasma. In other species, however, e.g., the rat and guinea pig, the semen coagulates on its own due to a chemical reaction between the prostatic fluid and the seminal secretion. Specifically, in these animals the anterior prostate gland (Walker, 1910a,b) has been shown to produce the enzyme "vesiculase" (Camus and Gley, 1896, 1899), which is responsible for this reaction (Mann and Lutwak-Mann, 1951). On the other hand, in the horseshoe bat the plug is formed by densely packed sperm and denuded vaginal epithelial cells only (Matthews, 1937).

Opinions about the importance of the copulation plug vary. Species difference, as well as experimental techniques, may play an important role in determining its function. In the rat, the copulation plug is important since, without its cervical stimulation, the corpus luteum does not become functional (Long and Evans, 1922). On the other hand, Blandau (1945) thought that in most animals the main function of the plug is to prevent the outflow of semen. Whichever the case, removal of the accessory sex glands in the male rat leads to infertility (Blandau, 1945; Mann and Lutwak-Mann, 1951). However, there is no similar effect in the mouse (Merton, 1939).

In addition to preventing the outflow of semen (Blandau, 1945), other functions have been ascribed to the vaginal plug, for example, the blockage of a second batch of spermatozoa (Matthews, 1937).

Since it has been known that freshly ejaculated spermatozoa are not capable of wrtilization, the plug has been regarded also as a storage place for sperm in bats Rhich mate in the fall but shed their eggs only in the spring (Nakano, 1928; feedenz, 1926; Hartman, 1933; Wimsatt, 1942, 1944). It has been assumed that the vagina could provide a desirable environment for the sperm to undergo the required maturation prior to ascending in the female tract at the time of ovulation.

Concerning the two species of mammals which we studied most extensively, vaginal plug is never present in the rabbit and does not necessarily form after each copulation in the golden hamster (Orsini, 1961). In those hamsters in which it was present, it was observed to form immediately following mating and, as a rule, persisted up to 16–18 hours after copulation.

The newly formed plug in the golden hamster is an accumulation of viscous material, off-white in color, which subsequently shows time-related changes in its consistency. Three to four hours after its formation (6 hours after mating), the sticky plug changes into a somewhat harder body which has a well-delineated cortical layer separating it from the vagina. This pliable, comparatively tough, material begins to shrink and, by 10 hours after mating, has the shape of an oblong body consisting of a thick skin (or membrane) and practically no fillings. Twelve hours after mating the plug begins to dissolve, though one may be able to recover chunks of vaginal plug material up to 24 hours after mating.

Studies with light microscopy and ultrastructural techniques reveal changing cytological patterns. Four phases have been differentiated in the cycle of the vaginal plug.

1. The mucous plug fills the vagina with a jellylike mass. This stage lasts up to 4 hours. Light microscope studies show it to be strongly PAS-positive, composed of spermatozoa intermixed with mucin and a few cells. Ultrastructure studies show sperm intermixed with mucin, vaginal epithelial cells, polymorphonuclear leukocytes, and macrophages.

2. Four to eight hours after fertilization, in the second phase, the withdrawn vaginal plug shows a gradual increase in density—a jelling process. According to ultrastructure observations, apparently there are two processes evolving gradually side-by-side, most probably one aiding or contributing to the other.

a. First a large number of cytoplasmic droplets appear on the border of the phagocytes, thence detach from the cells, and appear in the intercellular area. They are assumed to be partly lysosomes, partly microbodies—surrounded by single, smooth membranes. Some of these detached profiles appear empty, others contain discrete circular shapes (spherules).

b. The second phenomenon is an apparent process of delineation or "boxing in" of the spermatozoa. Many of them are surrounded by fluid mucus, others by epithelial cells or by macrophages. The amorphous substance appears to jell, i.e., denser areas appear in the diffuse background.

3. The solid plug stage (8–12 hours) is characterized by the presence of a pliable, yet firm material which seemingly fills the whole vagina. Usually it can be extracted in one piece and will keep its shape in air. Its color is predominately yellow, and on occasion it emits an unpleasant odor. Histological studies show it to

be composed mostly of intercellular fibrillar material interspersed with cells and spermatozoa.

Ultrastructural studies reveal the presence of a variety of cells. In addition to vaginal epithelial cells, macrophages also are present. A large number of spermatozoa appear, surrounded either by erythrocytes or by columnar cells, or often within the cytoplasm of macrophages. In the early phase of incorporation, well-known contours (e.g., the sperm head) still can be recognized; but after longer incorporation, the nuclear mass dissolves.

4. The lysed plug. Twelve to 16 hours after mating, the vaginal plug becomes dissolved, although blebs may yet be recoverable from the vagina. Upon light microscopic observation (phase contrast), the plug appears to consist of cell groups (macrophages) surrounded by spermatozoa.

FIGURES II.1 AND II.2

THE APPEARANCE OF THE VAGINAL PLUG

Golden hamster vaginal plug 6–8 hours after coitus is a slightly protruding, whitish-yellow body which can be prolapsed by massaging or prolapsing the vagina.

SPECIMENS

II.1. Golden hamster vaginal plug 6–8 hours after coitus ($\times$ 3).
II.2. The same as II.1, slightly prolapsed ($\times$ 3).
Arrow, the vaginal plug.

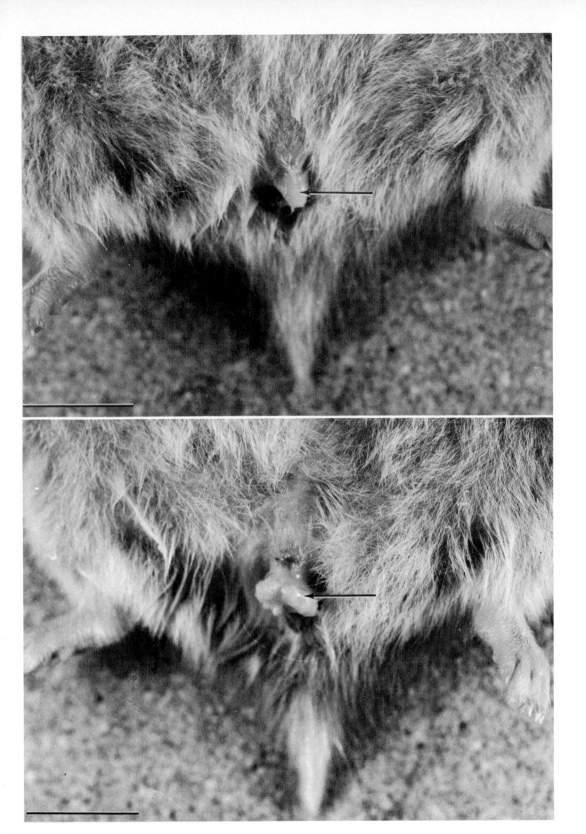

II.1 (↑)   **II.2 (↓)**

FIGURE II.3

HAMSTER VAGINAL PLUG, FIRST PHASE (light microscopical picture)

Detail of small, teased part of hamster vaginal plug, shortly after mating. Low magnification shows profusion of spermatozoa in a watery mucoid milieu. Some cellular debris and macrophages also present.

SPECIMEN

II.3. Hamster vaginal plug 3 hours after mating. Phase contrast ($\times$ 260).

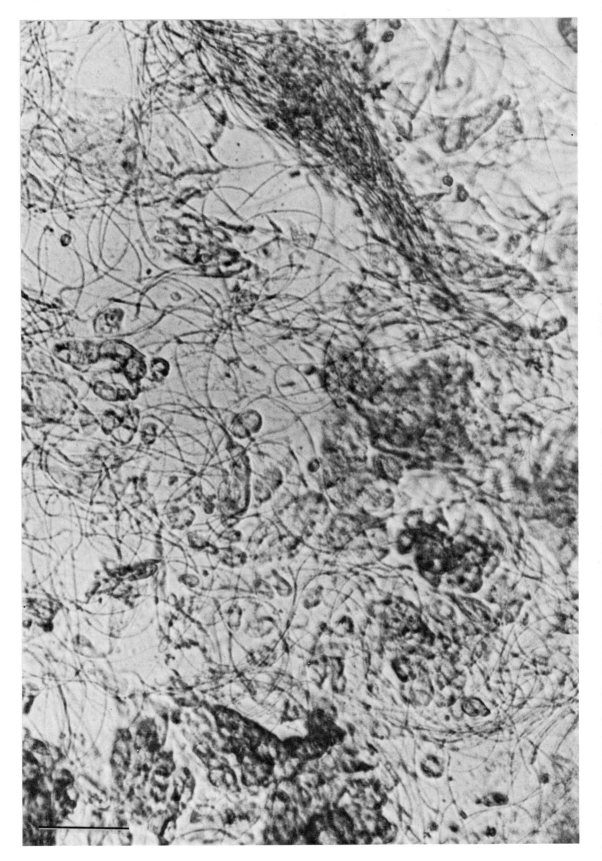

II.3

FIGURE II.4

ULTRASTRUCTURE DETAILS OF FRESH HAMSTER VAGINAL PLUG

The plug is in first phase. The larger part of the picture is occupied by intermixing mucous surfaces showing single membranelike density increase at the region of contact. Macrophage cell on bottom left of picture. Also apparent are macrophage cell processes.

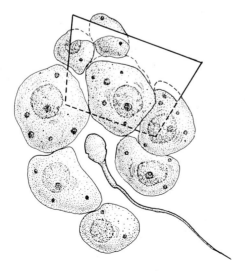

SPECIMEN

II.4. Hamster vaginal plug, 2–3 hours after mating. Veronal acetate-buffered 1% OsO$_4$; Epon 815; uranyl acetate ($\times$ 45,000). MA, macrophage cell.

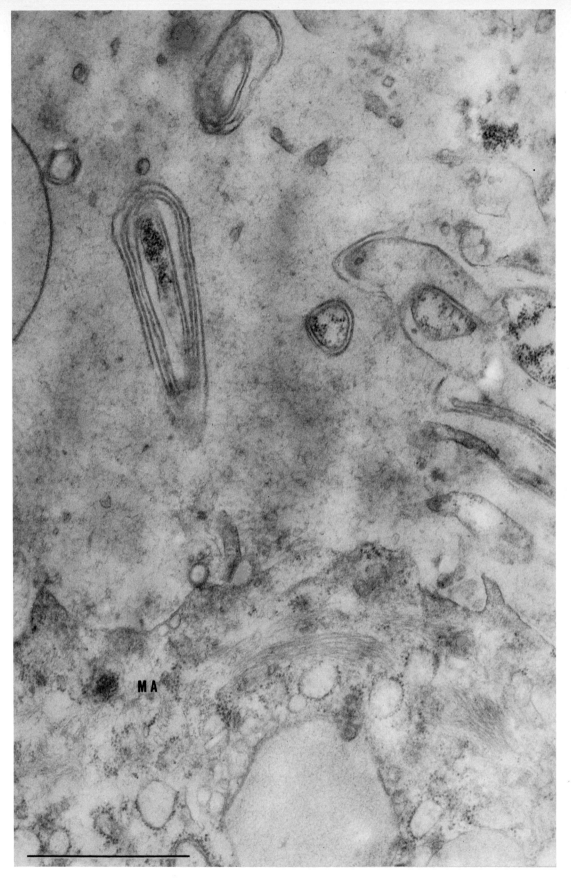

II.4

FIGURE II.5

HAMSTER VAGINAL PLUG, SECOND PHASE (photomicrograph)

In addition to spermatozoa, polymorphonuclear leukocytes and macrophage cells are in evidence and occupy the larger part of the picture. Observe dark, secretory granules, and irregular outline of cells.

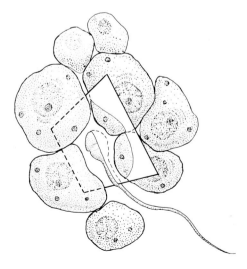

SPECIMEN

II.5. Hamster vaginal plug 6–7 hours after mating. Light micrograph, phase contrast (× 350).
MA, macrophage cell.

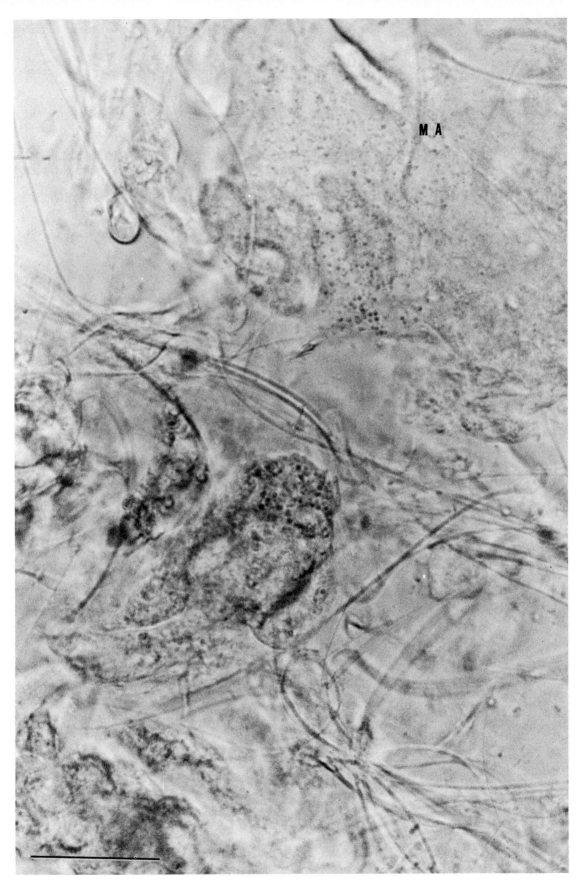

II.5

FIGURE II.6

HAMSTER VAGINAL PLUG, SECOND PHASE: ULTRASTRUCTURE

Macrophages and detached secretion droplets, also cross sections of sperm tail. The free-lying globules assumedly are packets of lysosomes which, in turn, contribute to the dissolution of the spermatozoon and the sperm head.

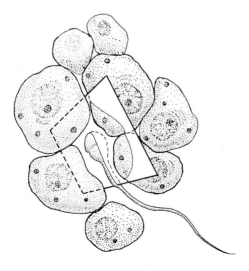

SPECIMEN

II.6. Hamster vaginal plug, 6–7 hours after mating. Phosphate-buffered 1% OsO₄; Maraglas; uranyl acetate (× 8,000).
L, lysosome; MA, macrophage cell.

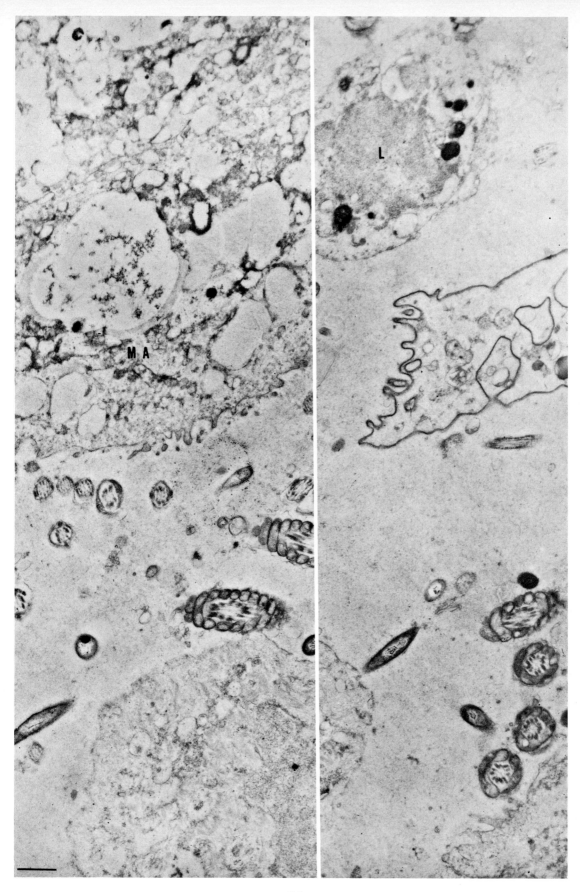

FIGURE II.7

HAMSTER VAGINAL PLUG, SECOND PHASE

In an area framed by two macrophages, mucous material surrounds spermatozoa (part of parasagittally cut sperm head and main piece visible).

Pinocytotic openings are present on the surface of macrophage cells, and the cellular processes are projecting into field. The irregular, circular, and elongated profiles are processes of macrophage cells. The electron density in some of them could be indicative of enzyme contents, most probably representing lysosomes. The round bodies within the macrophages are also probably lysosomes.

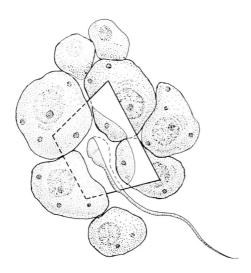

SPECIMEN

II.7. Hamster vaginal plug, 6–7 hours after mating. Phosphate-buffered 2% glutaraldehyde; Epon 815; uranyl acetate ($\times$ 12,000).
L, lysosome; MA, macrophage cell; MP, macrophage process.

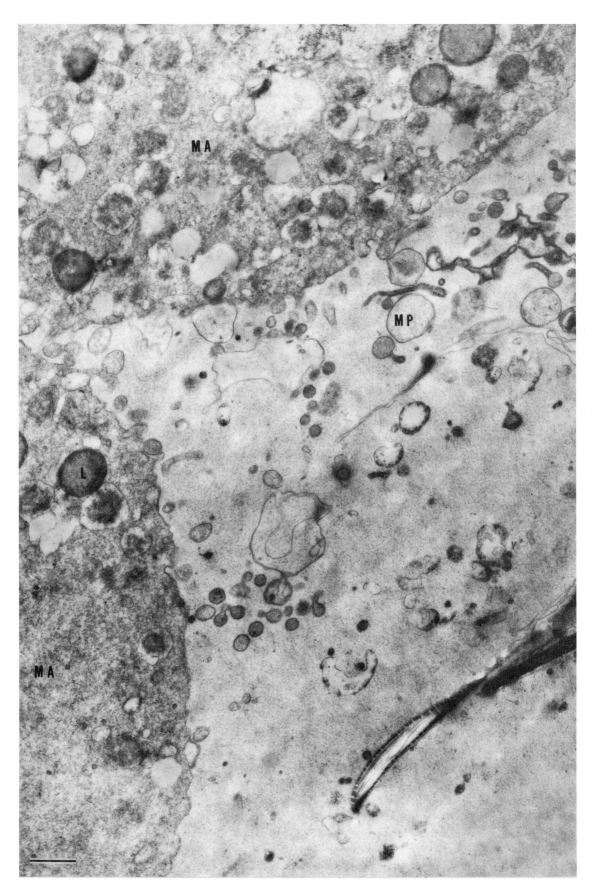

II.7

FIGURE II.8

HAMSTER VAGINAL PLUG, SECOND PHASE

Parasagittal section of sperm head surrounded with mucin layer. Parts of two macrophage cells, one containing residual bodies, are visible on picture. Spermatozoon head appears still intact in this picture although acrosomal cap appears greatly swollen. Cross sections of sperm tails are visible. Observe also membrane around the head which is filled with material of very low electron density, most probably originating from macrophage.

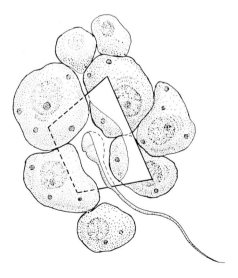

SPECIMEN

II.8. Hamster vaginal plug 6–7 hours after mating. Veronal acetate-buffered 1% OsO₄; Epon 815; uranyl acetate (× 16,000).

A, acrosome cap; MA, macrophage cell; RB, residual body.

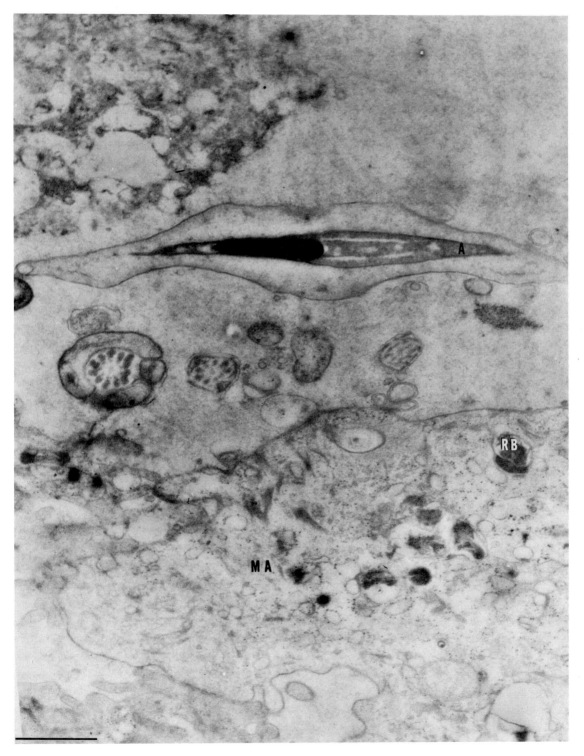

II.8

FIGURE II.9

HAMSTER VAGINAL PLUG, SECOND PHASE

Large lymphocytes, possibly monocytes, are surrounding spermatozoa, although not incorporating them. Sperm tails in enclaves of columnar cells.

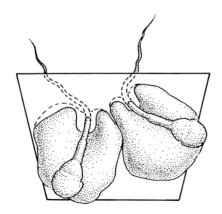

SPECIMEN

II.9. Hamster vaginal plug 9 hours after mating. Veronal acetate-buffered 1% OsO$_4$; Epon 815; uranyl acetate ($\times$ 28,000).

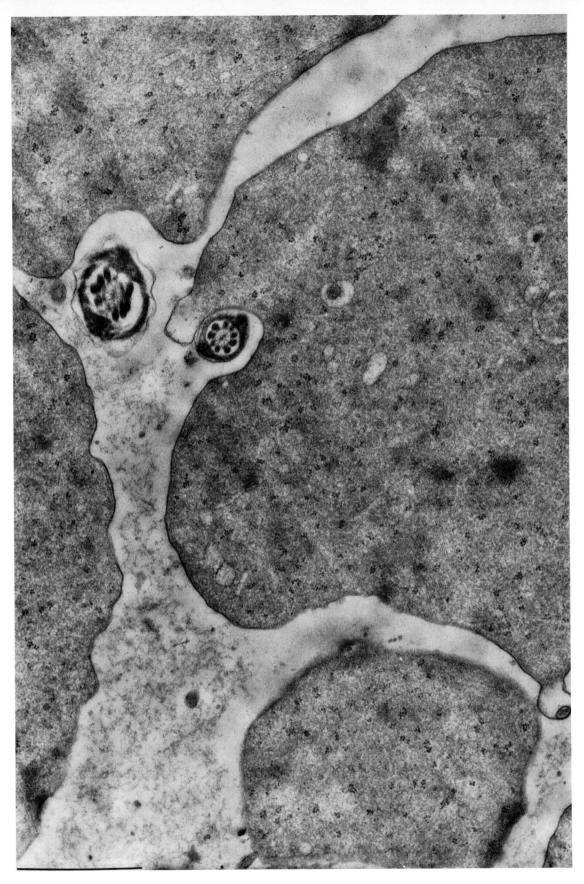

II.9

FIGURE II.10

SPERMATOZOON IN HAMSTER VAGINAL PLUG, SECOND PHASE

In addition to spermatozoon, macrophage cells are also in evidence, occupying the larger part of the electron micrograph. Dense granules and droplets on surface of macrophage cell can be observed.

Sperm head structure: Nucleus, acrosomal cap, subacrosomal layer are in evidence; apical body greatly enlarged; sperm head and cross section of numerous sperm tails surrounded by mucin.

Observe early changes in the hamster sperm head morphology which to some extent are also characteristic of capacitation changes observed in the uterus, e.g., loose cell membrane, greatly enlarged (and irregular) acrosomal cap, elongation in apical body.

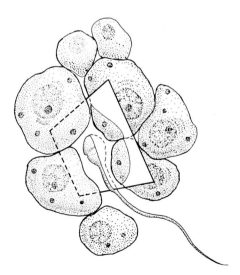

SPECIMEN

II.10. Hamster vaginal plug 6–7 hours after mating. Veronal acetate-buffered 1% OsO₄; Maraglas; uranyl acetate (× 28,000).
A, acrosome cap; AB, apical body; MA, macrophage cell.

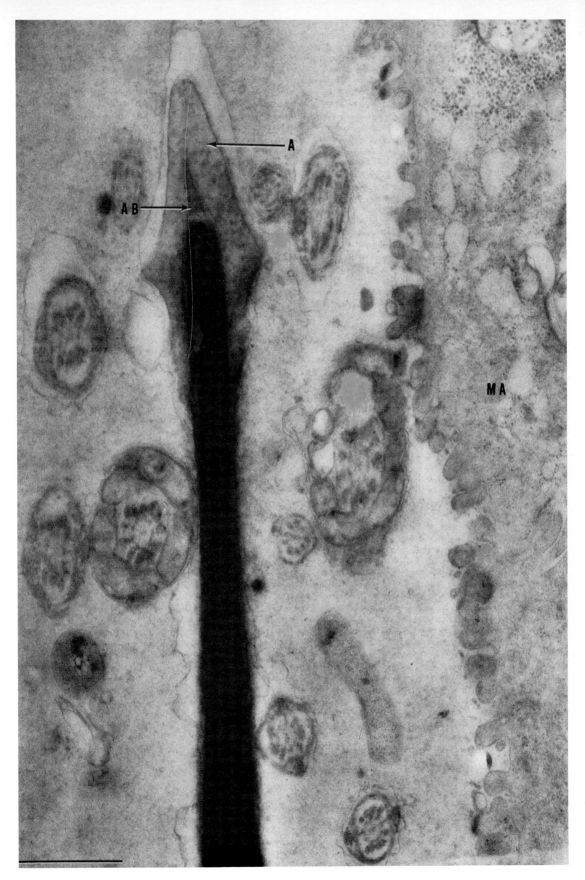

II.10

FIGURE II.11

HAMSTER VAGINAL PLUG, END OF SECOND PHASE: VAGINAL EPITHELIAL CELL

Some cytoplasmic vesicles and processes apparently are originating from the surface of vaginal epithelial cell; within the cell very fine fibrillae are observable.

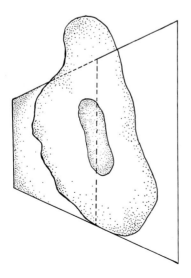

SPECIMEN

II.11. Hamster vaginal plug 7 hours after mating. Veronal acetate buffered 1% OsO_4; Maraglas; uranyl acetate ($\times$ 20,000).

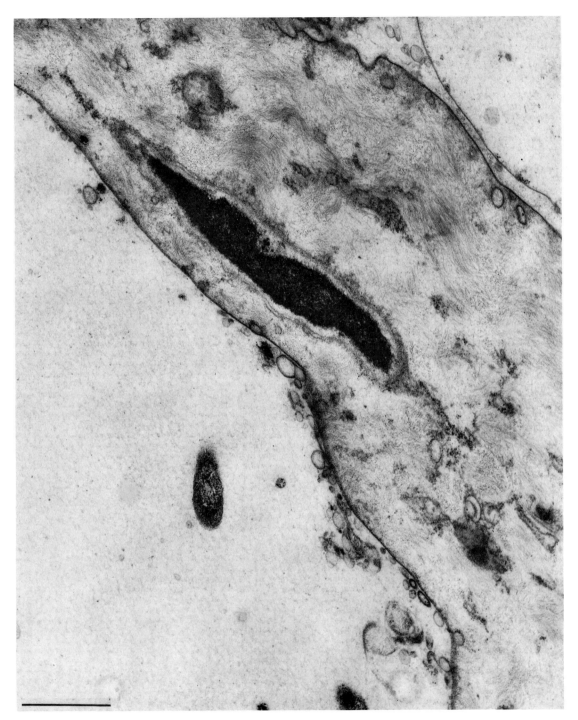

II.11

FIGURE II.12

LIGHT MICROGRAPH OF HAMSTER VAGINAL PLUG, THIRD PHASE

The plug apparently is composed of layers of dense, fibrous material (with occasional, trapped air bubbles in this picture).

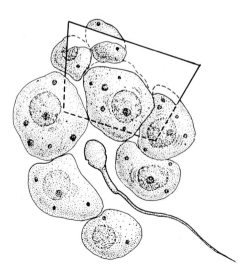

SPECIMEN

II.12. Hamster vaginal plug, 8–12 hours after mating. Phase contrast ($\times$ 1600). The bar represents $10 \, \mu$.

II.12

FIGURE II.13 AND II.14

LIGHT MICROGRAPHS OF A HAMSTER VAGINAL PLUG AT THE END OF THE THIRD PHASE

The solid plug is replaced by an elongated, sausagelike structure, which in advanced stages is empty in the center and shows only peripheral density. The peripheral wall (lower picture) is composed mostly of the intermixture of fibrous, mucous material.

SPECIMENS

II.13. Hamster vaginal plug 12 hours after mating, 1% Formalin fixation; paraffin embedded, hematoxylin-eosin ($\times$ 200).

II.14. Hamster vaginal plug 12 hours after mating. 1% Formalin fixation; paraffin embedded; hematoxylin-eosin ($\times$ 600). The bar represents 100 μ.

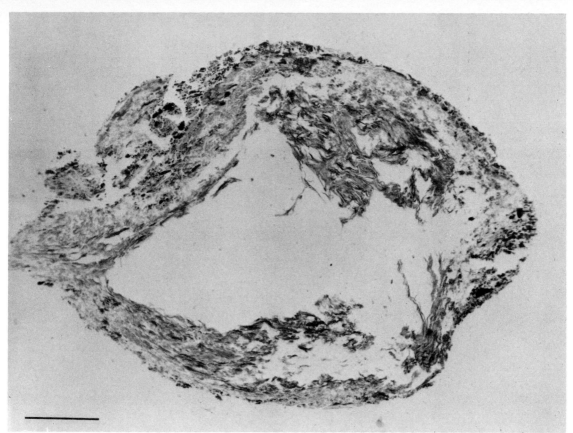

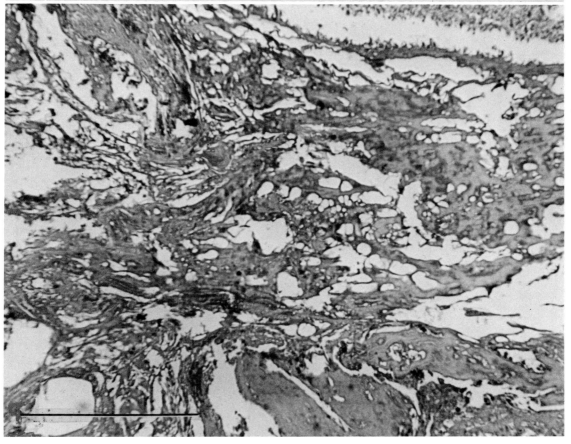

II.13 (↑)   II.14 (↓)

FIGURE II.15

HAMSTER VAGINAL PLUG, THIRD PHASE

With ultrastructural investigation, the dense plug appears to be composed of mucus, macrophages, and cell debris. This picture illustrates a macrophage cell. It is filled with a variety of cellular debris, various phagomes, and a spermatozoon. The head and midpiece of the sperm can be discerned.

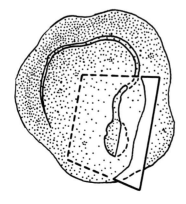

SPECIMEN

II.15. Hamster vaginal plug, 8–12 hours after mating. Veronal acetate-buffered 1% OsO₄; Epon 815; uranyl acetate ($\times$ 14,000).
PH, phagome; SP, spermatozoon.

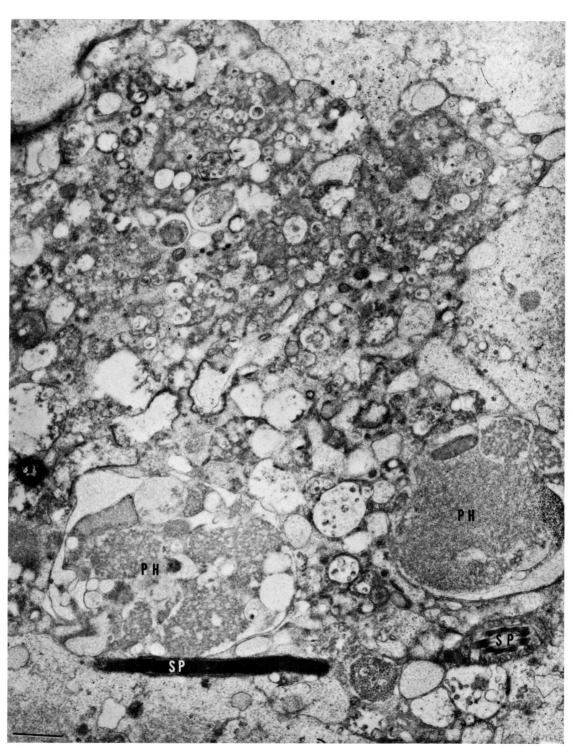

II.15

FIGURE II.16

LIGHT MICROGRAPH OF HAMSTER VAGINAL PLUG, FOURTH PHASE

The place of the dissolving plug is occupied by liquid which contains small groups of cells surrounded by dead spermatozoa attached to them.

SPECIMEN

II.16. Hamster vaginal plug, 14 hours after mating. Phase contrast ($\times$ 160). The bar represents 10 μ.

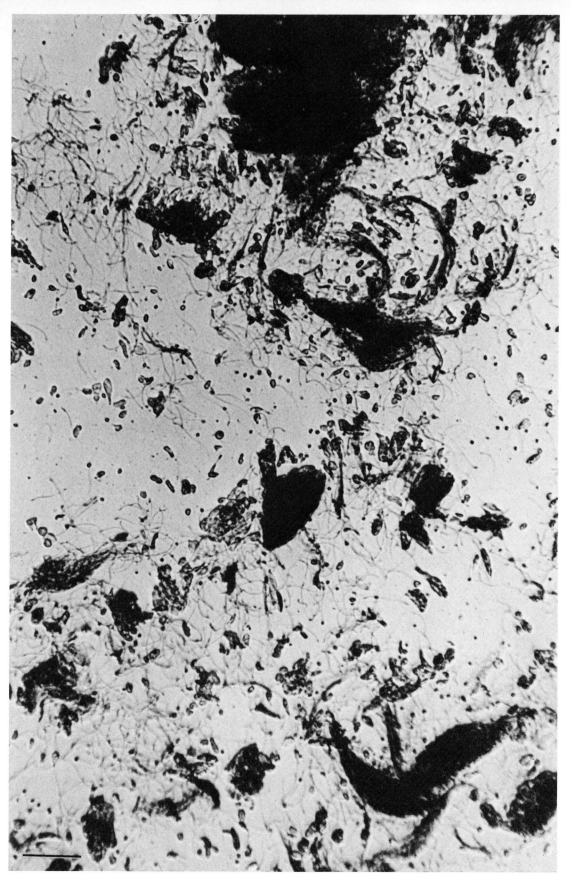

II.16

III

FROM OOCYTE
TO ZYGOTE

After careful consideration, it has been decided that in this chapter the organization of the textual and pictorial material should follow different courses. In order not to break the continuity of either the text or the pictorial history, the subchapters will follow different sequences. Namely, in the text, the morphology of the egg and cellular organelles is followed by the description of fertilization and the zygote. On the other hand, in the sequence of the pictorial material, after illustrating the cortex of the egg, the morphology of the penetrating sperm will be presented. This is followed by describing the process of incorporation and subsequently the ultrastructure of the other cell organelles.

Introduction

It has to be borne in mind that fertilization and related processes are in continuous flux. Therefore ultrastructure description of these phenomena is necessarily restricted to a given stage, or phase, of the flux in which the specimen has been fixed. The purpose of this introductory part is to give an overall view of the changes which occur in the freshly shed mammalian egg and subsequently take place in the zygote. Due to the nature of the subject and the approach, this description cannot be an all-encompassing study. Its main effort is to record the morphology of the postovulatory egg and of the zygote. It is not presented as an extensive review of all that has been written about the developing egg, since there are many articles on hand which do that.

A Brief Description of the Mammalian Egg as It Appears Under the Light Microscope

The egg of the Eutherian mammal is a round, globular structure alternating in size between 75 and 150 μ (Boyd and Hamilton, 1952). It is surrounded by two membranes. The proximal of the two is the cell membrane, also termed vitelline membrane, which has the regular (double) membrane structure. Within the vitelline membrane is the cytoplasm of the mammalian egg, which is also termed the vitellus, or vitelline material. As a rule, in the center of this is the nucleus.

This single cell is surrounded by a secondary membrane which is called the zona pellucida and is composed of a mucopolysaccharide-glycolipid matrix into which fine protein filaments are embedded. This is the only structure occurring in the mammalian body that is comparable to the chitin of the invertebrates and assumed to have no function aside from its rather atavistic protective activity. This is a product of the follicular cell secretion.

In certain mammals, e.g., the rabbit, if no fertilization has taken place within a given period, the aging egg is surrounded by a tertiary membrane. This is secreted by the oviduct epithelium and is referred to as the mucus coat. It has no observable function around the egg.

The sequence of morphological changes is as follows:

1. At the time of ovulation the oocyte nucleus is completing the first meiotic division and the first polar body is either in the process of discharge or has already separated. The vitelline membrane, which shows numerous microvilli, is abutting on the zona pellucida.

The mitochondria at the time of ovulation as a rule are rounded, have a dense filling, and cristae can be observed only on the periphery. Organized Golgi complex appears in the vicinity of the nucleus. In addition, a variety of smooth-walled cytoplasmic channels can be seen.

Cytoplasmic yolk bodies and lipids are present and, as a rule, fill out the smooth membrane covering.

2. Shortly after ovulation the vitelline material shrinks, and the microvilli temporarily disappear from the surface of the egg. However, their temporary absence is followed by the reestablishment of the cortical processes and the appearance of the cortical granules which approach the cell surface. The Golgi complex disappears, and mitochondrial morphology becomes irregular. At the same time, pinocytotic vesicles and pinocytotic channels become evident.

3. At the approach of the spermatozoon, the cortical villi apparently begin to move in the direction of the fertilizing spermatozoon. Although this reaction may occur on numerous loci (e.g., in the rabbit), it is fully developed only in the vicinity of one spermatozoon which becomes incorporated into the vitellus. In the rabbit the entry of the spermatozoon triggers the second meiotic division.

If no sperm is present, the cortical villi often incorporate one another in addition to the extraneous material which may lie in the vicinity of the vitelline membrane.

4. Following the entry of one spermatozoon into the egg, a cytoplasmic defense mechanism is activated. This apparently includes the disappearance of the cortical granules, a vitelline membrane reaction which, instead of incorporating, segregates the supernumerary spermatozoa and causes the expulsion of the second polar body.

Cellular function, as judged by the appearance of cellular organelles, is reestablished following fertilization. Characteristics are the sudden disappearance of cortical granules, changes in the outline and organization of the cytoplasmic villi, and the reestablishment of the usual mitochondrial shape with cristae projecting into the lumen of the organelle. The Golgi complex becomes localized again in the nuclear vicinity and is followed by a gradual disappearance of the yolk corpuscles.

FROM OOCYTE TO ZYGOTE

Light microscope studies have shown a decrease in the volume of the freshly shed egg following the expulsion of the polar bodies (Lewis and Wright, 1935; Hamilton and Laing, 1946; Boyd and Hamilton, 1952). Since the zona pellucida retains its size, the shrinkage of the vitellus causes an increase in the perivitelline area. However, this contraction in volume may be only partly responsible for the increase in the perivitelline area. The other could be a gradual dissolution of the proximal layer of the zona pellucida caused by an enzyme secreted by the egg.

Zona pellucida changes have often been described in the unfertilized rabbit egg. Namely, an external mucus coat is accumulating while the egg is passing through the oviduct, which is responsible for the greatly increased thickness of the zonal area (Bacsich and Hamilton, 1954).

Nucleus

The dictyate (or nuclear resting) phase in those oocytes which do not atrophy continues up to the preovulatory period. The first meiotic division in most animals is resumed a few hours before ovulation, but in the rabbit only at the time of ovulation (Pincus, 1936). The nucleus then continues with the diakenesis stage of the first meiotic prophase, and shortly after ovulation (following the completion of the first meiotic division), the first polar body is expelled.

Quite often, stacks of annulate lamellae may be observed in the nuclear vicinity originating from the nuclear membrane during the end of the dictyate period.

In the freshly shed rabbit egg the nucleus is surrounded by the nuclear envelope formed by double membranes which, at a few locations, still may show some nuclear pores.

For the purposes of this study, the morphology of the female pronucleus only will be considered. After completing the second meiotic division, the nucleus of the egg is referred to as the female pronucleus. It is a round or slightly oval structure which, following the detachment of the nuclear mass to form the second polar body, may have a slightly lobulated appearance. The membranes of the nuclear envelopes mostly are running at an uneven distance from one another. The karyoplasm has a low contrast filling in which filamentous and granular material can be observed. As a rule, close to the center of the female pronucleus is the major nucleolus. It measures up to $4\ \mu$ in diameter and is composed of electron-dense material. It consists of a combination of a reticular network and electron-dense granules. In most instances a number of additional nucleoli can also be observed. They measure up to $2\ \mu$ in size and occupy the periphery of the nucleus, often closely associated with the inner membrane of the nuclear envelope.

Although in the rabbit the nucleoli appear homogenous in density, in the rat (Sotelo and Porter, 1959) and in the human (Wartenberg and Stegner, 1960), a lighter center and denser periphery have been observed.

The passage of nucleoli or subcellular particles through the nuclear envelope of the mammalian egg has been repeatedly observed (Austin, 1961; Szollosi and Ris, 1963; Szollosi, 1965).

Cytoplasm

Ground Substance

The ground substance in the mammalian egg is essentially structureless and, following fixation for ultrastructure studies, fine filaments and granules (the usual concomitants of cytoplasmic structure) can be observed in it.

The Cell Membrane (or Vitelline Membrane) and the Cortex of the Egg

The cell membrane of the mammalian egg has the typical double membrane structure. At the time of ovulation the rabbit and particularly the hamster egg are covered by microvilli which are remarkably uniform in size and almost evenly spaced. Since electron microscope preparation techniques enable one to view only a small part of the surface of the egg, admittedly there is a valid question relating to the extent of the surface area covered by the villi.

There is a transitory period following ovulation when no villi are observed and the cell membrane is almost smooth. Subsequently, cytoplasmic processes resembling pseudopodia are formed at a period when the egg appears active in pinocytosis and phagocytosis. The cytoplasm of the egg appears quite labile and there is an evident cortical fluidity which apparently can be terminated in two ways, either by fertilization or by aging.

Since cellular structures are "frozen" following the use of fixatives, no actual movement can be observed in specimens studied with ultrastructure techniques, but from the material surrounded by these labile processes it is evident that phagocytosis is taking place. In addition to incorporating extraneous material, the pseudopodia may also incorporate one another. Openings of pinocytotic vesicles appear between them and continue into cortical channels located in the cytoplasm of the egg.

In eggs that have not been fertilized, after the lapse of some hours, the pseudo-podia are replaced by villi which assume identical length and width.

Individual microvilli show a denser periphery—in the vicinity of the cell membrane—and a lighter core. The center of the microvillus has a filamentous filling. The situation is somewhat similar in the pseudopodia.

In the vicinity of the cortical villi and pseudopodia, the dissolution of the zona pellucida often is apparent, which possibly may contribute to the size of the perivitelline area.

A change in cortical behavior is triggered by the approach of the spermatozoon. The sperm causes a so-called "cortical reaction" or "cortical wave formation" which is manifest by the greatly increased number of cytoplasmic cortical villi attempting to engulf the spermatozoon (Hadek, 1963a). That the cortex of the egg is an active participant in the incorporation of the spermatozoon is evident from the number of cytoplasmic processes and channels that suddenly appear on the egg's surface.

In the zygote of the rabbit, which is approached by supernumerary sperma-tozoa, glutaraldehyde fixation reveals cortical membrane "buds" which originate from the vitelline membrane. Somewhat similar processes, though far fewer in number, can be observed in osmium tetroxide-fixed eggs.

Changes on the surface of the egg following fertilization involve a decrease in the size and number of the processes and the complete disappearance of pseudopodia. The decrease in the size of the villi in the zygote is followed by the smoothing out of the surface in the cleaving egg. Once the early embryo reaches the blastocyst stage of development, regularly placed microvilli will reappear on the surfaces of both the inner cell mass as well as the trophoblast cells.

Although there is no morphological evidence to suggest either the presence or the nature of the new fertilization membrane, it is evident that it is made up of labile, proteinaceous material since resistance to the entry of supernumerary sperm in the rabbit zygote can be broken down by chemical (alcohol), and also by physical methods (elevation of the body temperature) (Austin and Braden, 1953).

CYTOPLASMIC LAMELLAR STRUCTURES

Endoplasmic Reticulum

Although the oocyte stained for light microscope study is remarkable for its strongly basophilic cytoplasm, strangely enough, membrane-attached endoplasmic reticulum (ER) is a rarity when the egg is studied with the electron microscope. Free ribose nucleic acid (RNA) has been observed in a variety of locations in most oocytes (Zamboni and Mastroianni, 1966a,b). However, neither their position nor their size is specific. The only exception is the oocyte of the guinea pig in which rough endoplasmic reticulum (ER) and a significant amount of free RNP particles appear to be present (Adams and Hertig, 1964). Consider also Szollosi (1967a) who observed rough ER in the hamster, rat, gerbil, and squirrel monkey oocytes.

Membranous profiles in the egg which resemble endoplasmic reticulum are stacks of annulate lamellae. They represent accumulations of vertically regimented cisternae (30 mμ to 50 mμ wide) which show densities most probably due to the presence of RNA at periodically repeating locations. Since their original descriptions by Afzelius (1956) and Swift (1956) in the sea urchin and amphibian oocyte respectively, the desquamation of annulate lamellae from the nuclear membrane has been observed to be characteristic of the follicular stages of oocyte development in the mammals also (Adams and Hertig, 1965; Baca and Zamboni, 1967). Although they originate from the nuclear membrane, their location in the freshly shed mammalian egg is not necessarily in the vicinity of the nucleus. As a matter of fact, annulate lamellae often can be observed in various locations within the cytoplasm, including the periphery of the egg. In the ectoplasm they are mostly associated with aggregates of vessels which may indicate that they participate in the formation of the vesicular foci.

A different kind of granular content is observed in the smooth-walled, round cytoplasmic bodies present in the rabbit and ferret eggs. They assumedly contain an inactive (nonfunctional) RNA and show very little change in content during the early life of the oocyte. [Similar structures have been observed by Zamboni and Mastroianni (1966a,b).]

Smooth Membrane Accumulations (Golgi Complex and Vesicular Aggregates)

The cytoplasm of the freshly ovulated mammalian egg contains numerous smooth-walled channels, lacunae, and canaliculi: well-identifiable elements of the Golgi complex which, as a rule, is located in the nuclear vicinity. In addition, numerous small vesicular foci are found dispersed throughout the cytoplasm of the egg.

During the postovulatory life of the rabbit and hamster egg, a gradual expansion of the smooth-walled vesicular system takes place. The Golgi complex, or elements which originated from it, appears to participate in several of the cell's physiological processes. As such, these elements can be observed to form small channels in the vicinity of the yolk bodies—apparently in the process of utilizing them. Further, many of the smooth-walled channels are in direct contact with pinocytotic openings on the surface of the cell, thus playing an active part in the metabolism of the egg. The Golgi complex has also been observed as a source of cortical granules (Szollosi, 1967b). Ultimately, enlarged channels may separate to form single membrane-bound bodies into which small, well-delineated vesicles bleb, possibly in the process of multivesicular body (MVB) formation.

Following fertilization, peripheral aggregates of smooth-walled vesicles and vessels are found in both the rabbit and hamster egg, often situated in the vicinity of the cell membrane. Under certain circumstances, these vesicular aggregates have been observed to expand into huge complexes which occupy a considerable part of the cortex of the egg.

Among rabbit eggs, excessive vesicular aggregations have been observed only on rare occasions (five out of several hundred). In these instances, the vesicles were of a variety of sizes and shapes and not very clearly demarcated from the other structural components of the egg. It is somewhat difficult to interpret whether the appearance of the vesicular aggregates is a rarely observed physiological phenomenon, or whether it is caused by steroid hormones which have a known effect on endoplasmic reticular hypertrophy, or possibly by an external agent's effect, e.g., phenobarbital, on cellular structure (Fawcett, 1966).

MITOCHONDRIA

There are many reports on mitochondrial morphology and related changes in the growing mammalian oocyte. At the time of ovulation, the mitochondria may assume a variety of shapes including hourglass (Hadek, 1965), dumbbell (Blanchette, 1961), and plain budding. Nevertheless, the majority of mitochondria in the ovulated mammalian egg are round or slightly oval cytoplasmic organelles which, as a rule, show a deviation from the typical mitochondrial morphology. In most instances they measure 0.1μ to 0.3μ in size, and their cristae are seen lying parallel with the mitochondrial wall. In addition, the mitochondrial lumen is mostly filled with a dense material that gives reason to assume the plausibility of mitochondrial metaplasia. Namely, the accumulation of dense material within the mitochondrial lumen, accompanied by changes in mitochondrial morphology (loss of cristae), creates the impression that the organelle is being transformed into a lysosome, or in other instances into microbodies.

In the developing mammalian egg, mitochondria have been observed to change their location—assumedly accommodating the areas in greater need of energy. For example, they can be observed in the vicinity of the nucleus in early development, but appear on the periphery, closely associated with the vitelline membrane, at the time of zona pellucida formation. While they are evenly dispersed in the freshly shed egg, they accumulate beneath the vitelline membrane soon after the commencement of its extrafollicular life.

SINGLE MEMBRANE-BOUND STRUCTURES

Lipid-Containing Structures

The cytoplasm of the egg is generously supplied with single membrane-bound structures. The simplest of these are the yolk bodies. Depending on the species, they occur essentially in two varieties: lipid droplets and proteinaceous yolk. The first are characterized by amorphous, deeply staining masses. The lipid bodies appear in several varieties, depending upon the species. For example, in the rabbit, they are structureless blebs. In the ferret, on the other hand, they may show a layering indicative of their gradual accumulation, i.e., somewhat similar to the process of myelin formation. These yolk particles show uneven peripheries. At places, peripheral depressions coincide with empty smooth-walled profiles sunken into their surface, possibly indicating the use or digestion of the material.

The most prevalent yolk enclosures in the rabbit egg are the single membrane-bound, round bodies. They are moderately dense, randomly dispersed within the egg, and show a somewhat higher concentration in the endoplasm than in the ectoplasm. These yolk bodies show a gradual decrease in volume in the post-ovulatory egg. Occasionally, the two types of yolk can be observed side by side. Similar membrane-bound cytoplasmic bodies measuring from $0.2\ \mu$ to $0.5\ \mu$ have been observed also in the human (Wartenberg and Stegner, 1960) and in the rat (Sotelo and Porter, 1959; Odor, 1960).

The Yolk Nucleus (or Balbiani Body)

The yolk nucleus is mentioned here because of the recent interest created by an article of Weakly (1967b). The name of yolk nucleus or "body of Balbiani" denotes the presence of a strongly osmiophilic cytoplasmic body. It was first described on the strength of light microscope studies in the oocyte of the spider (Wittich, 1845), and subsequently in a number of different animals (Balbiani, 1864, 1893; Munson, 1912). Anderson and Beams (1960) studied the "Balbiani body" in the guinea pig oocyte; their submicroscopic studies revealed it to be composed of single membrane tubules, channels and canaliculi, the typical components of the Golgi complex. Other studies, however, have revealed in the secondary follicles of the guinea pig (two or three layers of granulosa cells) unusual mitochondrial groupings around dense electron-scattering foci. This complex appears to partially surround the oocyte nucleus and was assumed to correspond to the yolk nucleus (Weakly, 1967b).

According to Weakly (1967b), three types of cell organelles (as recognized with the electron microscope) may give the impression of yolk bodies when studied with light microscope techniques: (1) whorls of rough or smooth ER; (2) massive accumulation of Golgi material; (3) densely packed mitochondria embedded in an electron-dense intramitochondrial substance. To these another type should be added; namely, (4) the stacks of annulate lamellae (Adams and Hertig, 1965).

Thus, while it is evident that the yolk body or Balbiani nucleus may be a histological entity, none such exists when studying the egg with ultrastructure techniques. Or, to be precise, utilizing contemporary electron microscope techniques, no such structure could be definitely identified with the yolk nucleus. One of the prerequisites of scientific observations is the ability to repeat it. Until this can be said about the yolk nucleus, final decision concerning its structure has to be postponed.

Cortical Granules

Cortical granules are round, single membrane-bound, electron-dense structures of almost uniform size (from $0.3\ \text{m}\mu$ to $0.5\ \text{m}\mu$), which derive their name from the fact that they first were observed in the cortex of (invertebrate) eggs. In the freshly ovulated mammalian egg they are located beneath the cell membrane; as a rule almost equidistant from one another. If fertilization occurs they disappear from the egg. On the other hand, if fertilization does not take place, they keep on accumulating until the egg disintegrates.

Cortical granules first were described in the sea urchin egg in which the ovum is limited by both the plasma and vitelline membrane (Moser, 1939; Endo, 1961a,b). Following sperm penetration, cortical granules ascend through the plasma membrane and unite with the vitelline membrane. It has been assumed that their functions are to trigger the fertilization reaction following sperm penetration, and to contribute to the elevation of the fertilization membrane, in order to prevent the entry of supernumerary sperm into the egg.

The existence of a layer of dense granules at the cortex of the mammalian egg in the hamster oocyte was first demonstrated with the phase contrast method by Austin (1956). Since these granules appeared similar to those in the invertebrates, the same name was applied. Cortical granules have been observed in the growing oocytes and tubal eggs of as diverse mammals as rabbits, guinea pigs, coypus, rats, mice, domestic pigs (Szollosi, 1967b) and rhesus monkeys (Hope, 1965).

Ultrastructure studies have shown that the cortical granules in the guinea pig, rabbit, golden hamster, and human evolve from the Golgi complex or related structures or areas (Adams and Hertig, 1964; Weakly, 1966; Szollosi, 1967a; Baca and Zamboni, 1967).

Histochemical studies coupled with ultrastructure observations being presented for the first time in this study, have indicated that the major component of the cortical granules may be acid phosphatase, although their rather neatly laid out position may suggest that their function is something akin to cell protection. Also, they may possibly be lysosomes. As lysosome granules, their function could be the destruction of the part of the sperm that is not needed for fertilization (that is, everything but the nucleus in the head). However, the proof of this theory has not yet been delivered since no recognizable cortical granule has been observed in the zygote in the vicinity of the disintegrating spermatozoon. Of course, the possibility may exist that the cortical granules themselves disintegrate in order to release the enzymes.

The disappearance of mammalian cortical granules following sperm penetration was thought to trigger the "zona reaction" of Braden *et al.* (1954) through the release of a chemical that makes the zona impermeable to succeeding sperm. While the contribution of cortical granules to the exclusion of supernumerary sperm in many mammals is a possibility, they certainly have a different function in the rabbit in which no "zona reaction" is evident and large numbers of spermatozoa penetrate the zona pellucida.

The other school of thought claims that cortical granules in mammals, just as in invertebrates, play an active role in the fertilization reaction. It is assumed that at the time of sperm penetration cortical granules become lodged in the perivitelline area, and following their dissolution their membrane joins the disrupted cell membrane in an effort to patch up the hole caused by the penetrating sperm. Some morphological evidence was produced to support this claim by the demonstration of cortical granules in the perivitelline area (Szollosi, 1967b). Further, it was also suggested that the chemicals they store may prevent the access of supernumerary sperm.

At this stage of our information, however, no real knowledge exists about cortical granule function in the mammalian egg. It would be logical to ascribe to the mammalian cortical granules a role akin to that in the invertebrate egg, e.g., formation of the fertilization membrane, but there is no definite proof for this.

Although there is no structure in the mammalian egg that could be compared morphologically to the fertilization membrane of the invertebrates (Endo, 1961a,b), a functional barrier to prevent superfecundation exists since the access of supernumerary sperm into the vitellus is hindered under normal physiological conditions. Some morphological evidence also was produced to support this claim by the demonstration of membrane elevation and blebbing in the fertilized rabbit egg (Hadek, 1966).

In fact, functional differences can be observed between the vitelline membrane of the oocyte and the cell membrane of the zygote: (1) the membrane of the egg apparently is a very labile membrane which readily sends forth processes into the perivitelline area; (2) it is closely associated with the cortical granules; (3) a large number of pinocytotic vesicles are present on its surface; and (4) it displays a readiness for attachment. On the other hand, in the membrane of the zygote (1) there apparently is very little lability; (2) the cortical granules are absent; and (3) there are very few pinocytotic vesicles. The extent to which dissolved cortical granules contribute to the membrane of the zygote is an unanswered question for the time being.

Multivesicular Bodies

Multivesicular body (MVB) is a widely used term designating a cell organelle observed with ultrastructure methods. It is mostly a circular or elliptical-shaped, smooth-walled, single membrane-bound cytoplasmic bag (measuring 0.1–0.6 μ), which contains an unspecified number of round vesicles. The vesicles within the multivesicular body, also smooth walled, are mostly circular, and vary in size and electron density. Structures which could be regarded as stages of MVB formation were observed. They apparently start with minute inpocketings into cytoplasmic channels. The next phase of development was the expansion of the cytoplasmic channel that contained the inpocketings, and the separation of the expanded part from the rest of the channel. As a result, cytoplasmic bags were formed which became filled with small circular profiles.

However, not infrequently, segregated vesicles also were observed in the lumens of mitochondria, thus the possibility of mitochondrial transformation into MVB's should also be considered.

Multivesicular bodies have been observed in many mammalian gametes, e.g., in all the developmental stages of the female gamete in the hamster (Odor, 1965); in the eggs of the mouse (Yamada et al., 1957), the rat (Franchi and Mandl, 1962; Odor, 1960; Sotelo and Porter, 1959), the monkey (Hope, 1965); in the ovum of the human (Wartenberg and Stegner, 1960) and of the rabbit (Hadek, 1965). Considering that they are usually found in the cortex of the egg in the vicinity of segrosome formation or foreign material incorporation, they possibly could be regarded as lysosomes.

PROTEINACEOUS STRANDS AND ISLANDS IN THE CYTOPLASM

The presence of proteinaceous strands in the cytoplasm of the developing hamster oocyte and postovulatory egg has been described by a number of authors (Hadek, 1966; Weakly, 1967a). These inclusions apparently have a high protein component since they disappear following trypsin digestion (Weakly, 1967a). To date, their origin remains unknown. They could be transformed cytoplasmic tubules which act as foci for the accumulation of additional protein particles. In their subsequent evolution the tubules lose their identity; the material becomes densely packed and hence assumes a somewhat crystalloid structure. The cytoplasmic strands disappear from the fertilized egg (two cell stage blastomeres) as well as from the aging oocytes. In the former they apparently become absorbed in the cytoplasm and possibly are used as a source of energy. In the latter they condense into well delineated needlelike densities, comparable to the proteinaceous crystalloid which has been observed in the egg of the human (Wartenberg and Stegner, 1960) and described in the blastocyst of the mouse (Alfert, 1950) and rabbit (Hadek and Swift, 1961b).

The Phenomenon of Fertilization and Related Topics

THE SPERM IN THE PERIVITELLINE AREA

The penetration of the rabbit spermatozoon through the zona pellucida apparently involves the distintegration of the acrosomal cap. As a result, when the spermatozoon reaches the vitelline membrane, there is only: (1) a ringlike remnant, the caudal extremity of the acrosomal cap [termed the equatorial region (Nicander and Bane, 1962a)], and (2) the subacrosomal (cytoplasmic) layer around the nucleus.

Following the disappearance of the acrosomal cap, the subacrosomal (cytoplasmic) layer seems to achieve a remarkable hypertrophy. This is particularly prominent in one location where it shows a ringlike thickening around the nucleus. This ring, or belt, usually is situated cranially from the equatorial region. Although the apical body, as a rule, is easily recognized at the apex of the nucleus, occasionally it may show the same density as the subacrosomal layer.

The sperm heads which have spent a considerable period in the perivitelline area appear to be gradually losing their subacrosomal sheath. This impression is gained from observing only a very thin subacrosomal layer around the sperm nucleus, or a layer of moderately dense droplets which apparently are in the process of disengaging from the subacrosomal layer.

Although some pictures are available which show the mammalian spermatozoon in the egg, our knowledge of mammalian sperm penetration is not comparable with our understanding of invertebrate fertilization. Therefore, the description of invertebrate sperm penetration is used as a pattern to which our present knowledge (or maybe assumption) will be compared.

In the sea urchin the acrosome plays an important role in fertilization (Colwin and Colwin, 1961). It is the outer acrosomal membrane of the sperm which establishes contact with the vitelline membrane of the invertebrate egg. Only after contact has been established will the inner acrosome membrane and the cell membrane (which is the inner membrane of the invertebrate egg) fuse and, following this, the content of the head (nucleus, etc.) practically pour into the egg (Colwin and Colwin, 1963). Thus the union of the two membranes joins the two gametes, and after sperm penetration has been completed this mosaic of membranes will surround the zygote.

Although the mammalian acrosome does not play a role comparable to that in invertebrates, nevertheless, in mammals, too, it is a mosaic of cell membranes (that of the egg and of the spermatozoon) which encloses the zygote (Szollosi and Ris, 1961).

The structure that remains in the mammalian sperm head following the disappearance of the acrosomal cap is not completely understood at present. It is not known whether one or two membranes remain following the disappearance of the acrosomal cap and subacrosomal layer. Sperm heads in the proximity of the vitelline membrane, even when denuded, are not the easiest objects to study with ultrastructure techniques. Thus, much remains for future studies, albeit with refined techniques.

THE ACT OF INCORPORATION (VARIETY OF INCORPORATIONS)

At the time the spermatozoon is ready for incorporation, it is devoid of its acrosomal cap and only the thin subacrosomal layer and apical body are present. It is not known which is the decisive factor that starts the incorporation reaction. Several spermatozoa could be present in the perivitelline area of the rabbit egg at the time the incorporation reaction starts, yet incorporation is restricted to one spermatozoon only. What attribute singles out one particular sperm remains unknown.

Actually, movements of the cortical pseudopodia can also be observed on the periphery of the unfertilized mammalian egg. Similarly, incorporation of extraneous material, or rather, demarcation of incorporated material often can be seen. Further, changes in oocyte outline, larger than usual outpocketings, are observable in the vicinity of practically every spermatozoon that reaches the vitelline membrane. In all instances but one, this cortical reaction stops. In the vicinity of one spermatozoon, however, the cortical reaction passes the point of no return, and from then on the incorporation reaction progresses according to a probably preset pattern.

The aforementioned implies that there is an innate cortical activity on the periphery of the mammalian egg that is accentuated and localized in the case of fertilization. The egg at the time of fertilization does not exhibit new functions, but it carries out certain of its established activities on a larger scale than previously. That the cytoplasm of the whole egg is participating in the reaction is evident from the spaces and areas, apparently empty vacuoles, that become evident in the cytoplasm of the egg and show connections with the outside.

A number of questions arise: for example, whether the apical body has any role in the cortical reaction; where is the point of no return; and how could one trigger a mammalian egg to induce a multiplicity of incorporations. Further, what stops a reaction that has already started?

POSTFERTILIZATION PHENOMENA

The cortical granules disappear practically immediately after the sperm has penetrated the egg.

Following fertilization in the rabbit, the cytoplasmic lipid and yolk granules disappear, and the mitochondria of the female gamete assume regular size and function again. The mitochondria of the penetrating spermatozoon apparently degenerate and dissolve. Cytoplasmic microbodies, which were present in large numbers in the freshly shed egg, also disappear from the zygote.

In the hamster egg the cytoplasmic strands persist only until blastomeres are formed.

The Prevention of Supernumerary Sperm Entry

Essentially two types of mechanisms are recognized in the mammalian egg for the prevention of supernumerary sperm entry. In the first type (characterized by the hamster, mouse, rat, etc.), after the passage of the first spermatozoon, assumedly some alteration is taking place in the zona pellucida's structure which prevents the penetration of succeeding or supernumerary spermatozoa through this secondary membrane. On the other hand, in the rabbit and a number of other animals (e.g., *Talpa europea*, the rocky mountain gopher, etc.), a number of spermatozoa can penetrate the zona pellucida but, under normal physiological conditions, only one spermatozoon gains access into the vitellus. Consequently, it is possible to observe in these eggs a number of spermatozoa on the surface of the egg which are located in the perivitelline area but which did not gain access to the vitellus. The mechanism which prevents the entry of supernumerary sperm into the egg is not precisely understood, although some morphological phenomenon which apparently keeps the excess sperm out has been described (Hadek, 1966).

In the second type then, a physicochemical change is taking place in the vitelline membrane which is comparable to the denaturalization of protein. This, in turn, prevents the entry of supernumerary sperm into the vitellus. For example, in the rabbit, in the vicinity of the spermatozoon to be incorporated, a large number of cortical villi and cortical disturbance are evident. This is manifest by the formation of a number of villi of various lengths and widths whose function it is to incorporate the spermatozoon; on the other hand, no villi are visible in the vicinity of the supernumerary spermatozoa, since the cortical reaction stops when the villi are still small. As a matter of fact, supernumerary sperm can lie practically on the vitelline membrane, yet a full-scale reaction will not develop. There are some minor surface elevations, some small villi appear, but not on a scale comparable to the phenomenon observed in the vicinity of the fertilizing or penetrating sperm.

To facilitate the actual sperm entry into the vitellus, it could be assumed that the apical body of the spermatozoon could have a localized effect on the vitelline membrane in its vicinity. This could produce a localized membrane dissolution, and the dissolved vitelline membrane (of the egg) and the dissolved subacrosomal membrane (of the spermatozoon) unite, thus facilitating the entrance of the sperm into the egg.

With regard to the exclusion of excess sperm from the egg, there are essentially two mechanisms which are assumed to function. The first of these is the immediate reaction which prevents the entry of a second spermatozoon. This "blocking" action is triggered immediately following the entry of the fertilizing gamete. Its surprising rapidity is assumed to be caused either by the dissolution or the disturbance of the cortical granules immediately beneath the vitelline membrane of the egg. According to that view, the dissolved cortical granules make the egg surface nonresponsive to subsequent spermatozoa. The second, latent and slower mechanism could be an immunological reaction on the part of the egg. Some experiments which challenge the immunological properties of the sea urchin egg have been performed. These studies have revealed a remarkable number of localized antigenic sites on the surface of the egg (Baxandall *et al.*, 1964a,b). An experiment was attempted while conducting this study on the immunological properties of the rabbit egg and zygote. In our experiment, rabbit antisperm antibodies have been prepared, and zygotes and unfertilized eggs have been challenged with ferritin-labeled antisperm antibodies. No conclusive result has been obtained thus far.

The assumption that the prevention of supernumerary sperm entry is a function akin to an immunological reaction probably depending upon a protein, is supported by the fact that the mechanism can be disturbed either by elevating the animal's temperature beyond the normal physiological range or through the administration of chemicals (Austin and Braden, 1953).

With regard to the morphological manifestations of preventing supernumerary sperm entry in rabbit zygotes which have been fixed with glutaraldehyde instead of osmium tetroxide, one can observe the emanation of thin-walled vesicles from the surface of the egg, apparently surrounding the supernumerary spermatozoa in the perivitelline area. Thus, the spermatozoa may trigger the elevation of membranous outpocketings from the surface of the mammalian zygote, which have the function of preventing supernumerary sperm entry.

Admittedly, a number of questions remain; for example, will this reactivity be changed by heat or alcohol or other treatment? Also, it is not known which physiological interference can extinguish it; nor how these cell membranes are related to the immunological processes, if in fact they are so related.

FIGURE III.1

DRAWING OF FRESHLY SHED EGG (Rabbit)

There is no perivitelline space between the egg and the zona pellucida. Some granulosa cells (part of the corona radiata) are still attached to the outer membrane (zona pellucida).

ER, endoplasmic reticulum; G, Golgi complex; M, mitochondria; MV, multivesicular bodies; N, nucleus; NO, nucleolus; RN, ribosenucleic acid-protein particle; RO, round bodies containing granular material (assumed RNA); SV, smooth-walled vesicles from smooth endoplasmic reticulum; Y, yolk bodies.

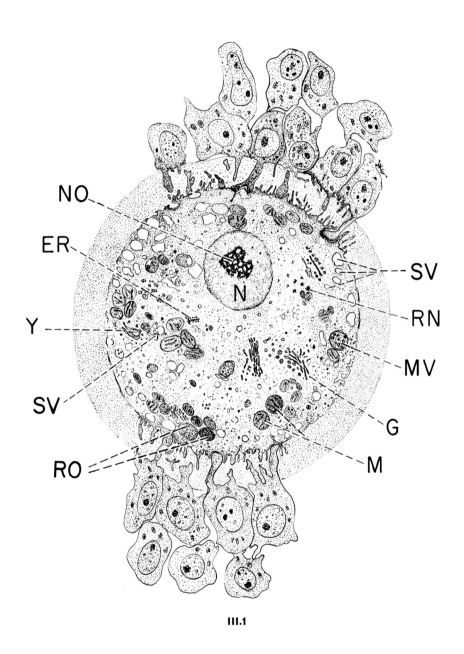

NO

ER

Y

SV

RO

N

SV

RN

MV

G

M

III.1

FIGURE III.2

RABBIT ZYGOTE SHORTLY AFTER FERTILIZATION

Three areas are evident in this micrograph. In the center is the egg, or ovum, surrounded by the vitelline membrane. It is separated from the zona pellucida (the outer, light ring) by a somewhat darker half-moon-shaped, perivitelline area. The outer layer of the zona pellucida is covered by a mucous layer.

The egg apparently is composed of the somewhat denser endoplasm and the lighter ectoplasm. The difference is due to the spherical shape of the egg: the periphery, being thinner, is transmitting more light than the center. The pronucleus is not visible yet. A number of signs indicate that the egg has been fertilized: (1) a number of spermatozoon profiles are visible in the perivitelline area, (2) two polar bodies are also visible (the larger presumably being the first one). This indicates the completion of the two meiotic divisions. The second division in the rabbit takes place only after fertilization.

Outside the perivitelline area one can observe the secondary and tertiary membranes. Two distinct layers are in evidence: an inner, more brilliant, zona pellucida, and an outer, less reflective, albuminous coat which has accumulated during the egg's passage through the oviduct (see also Bacsich and Hamilton, 1954). Some debris is attached to the egg, and possibly also two granulosa cells.

SPECIMEN

III.2. Rabbit zygote 18 hours after ovulation. Phase contrast ($\times$ 1000).
GC, granulosa cell; ML, mucous layer (around zona pellucida); P, polar body; PV, perivitelline area; SP, spermatozoon.

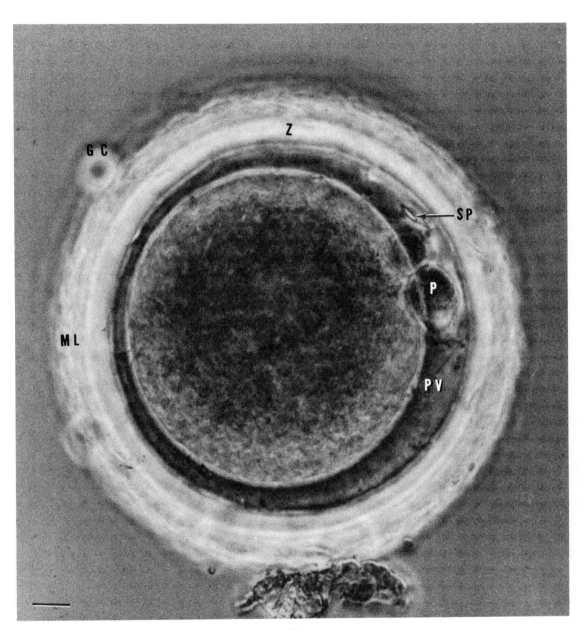

III.2

FIGURE III.3

OOCYTE AND GRANULOSA MICROVILLI IN HAMSTER EGG RECOVERED FROM GRAAFIAN FOLLICLE

The egg is in the lower part of the picture and granulosa cells on the upper part. The almost regularly placed microvilli originating from the oocyte have been cut at two levels in this section. The processes which originate from the granulosa cells are running in a haphazard direction. Oocyte villi contain cytoplasmic ground substance. Granulosa cell villi are somewhat denser and show some filamentous fillings. As yet only few pinocytotic vesicles are opening in the vitelline membrane. The dense layer on the surface of the egg, outside of the vitelline membrane, indicates a basal laminalike component (most probably polysaccharide) associated with the egg. In the egg, foci of smooth-walled endoplasmic reticulum and also mitochondria are visible. Some mitochondria show dumbbell shape, but a number of them already assume the circular appearance, which is the characteristic mitochondrial morphology in the freshly ovulated egg.

In this specimen the cortical granules are not present yet.

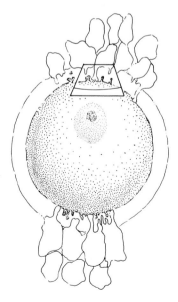

SPECIMEN

III.3. Hamster follicular oocyte. Veronal acetate-buffered 1% OsO_4; Epon 815; uranyl acetate ($\times$ 28,000).

GC, granulosa cell; GP, granulosa cell processes; MI, microvilli; PI, pinocytotic vesicle; VC, vesicular cytoplasmic aggregate.

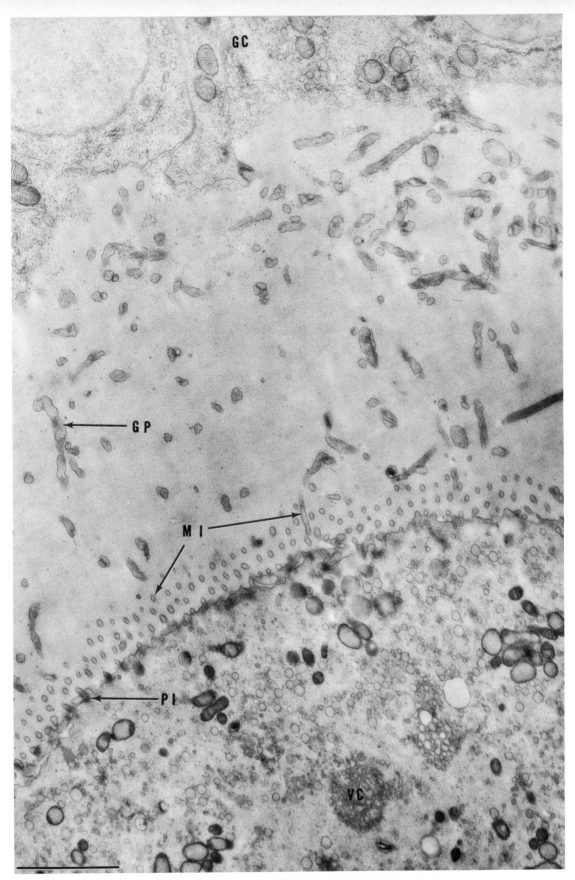

III.3

FIGURE III.4

THE DEVELOPMENT OF CORTICAL FLUIDITY

FRESHLY OVULATED RABBIT EGG, GRANULOSA CELLS STILL ATTACHED

The spermatozoon was observed outside of the granulosa cell (not visible on picture). Pseudopodialike processes instead of microvilli emanate from the surface. Some granulosa cell processes are lying along the surface of the egg.

Following ovulation, granulosa cell villi are either retracted or break off to be subsequently dissolved, possibly by multivesicular bodies, or to be sequestered. The villi of the egg also disappear for a short period, only to be followed by the emanation of cortical processes whose primary function assumedly is the incorporation of the sperm.

Within the cortex near the vitelline membrane, a large number of smooth, membrane-bound profiles are evident, some of them in the vicinity of pinocytotic vesicles, others possibly opening onto the surface of the egg.

On the surface there are two multivesicular bodies surrounded in a whorllike structure, apparently a forming segrosome. Within the cytoplasm of the egg, there is one multivesicular body and a number of mitochondria are evident; the mitochondrial cristae are aligned on the periphery and none are projecting into the lumen.

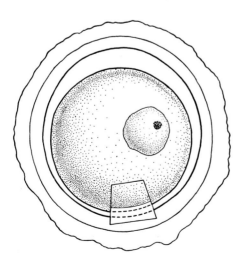

SPECIMEN

III.4. Rabbit egg 11 hours after mating. Veronal acetate-buffered 1% OsO_4; Epon 815; uranyl acetate ($\times$ 28,000).

GP, granulosa cell processes; M, mitochondria; MV, multivesicular body; PI, pinocytotic vesicle; VC, vesicular cytoplasmic aggregate.

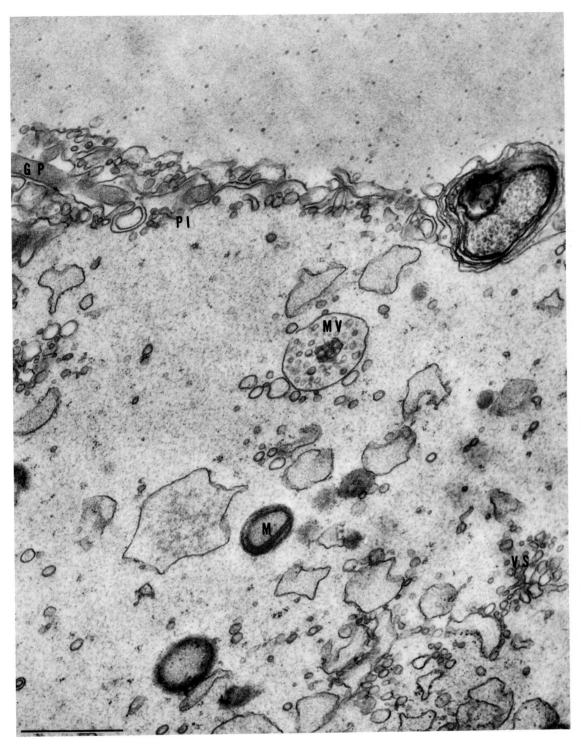

III.4

FIGURE III.5

THE DEVELOPMENT OF CORTICAL FLUIDITY

CORTEX OF FERRET EGG APPROACHING OVULATION

At the time of ovulation, the granulosa cell processes are either retracted or break off. The villi of the egg also disappear; thus, for a short period the egg presents an almost smooth surface. This picture shows the almost smooth surface of the ferret egg. Hardly any pinocytotic vesicle opens onto the egg's surface. In the cytoplasm irregularly shaped smooth membrane-bound vessels are close to the periphery of the egg. In addition, the cortex of the egg contains a number of single membrane-bound round bodies and mitochondria. In most mitochondria the cristae are thin and adhere closely to the mitochondrial wall.

There are apparent empty areas between the surface of the egg and the zona pellucida that could possibly indicate the dissolution of the zonal material. Therefore, the possibility that lytic enzymes from the egg may dissolve the zona pellucida should also be considered.

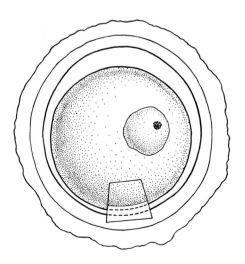

SPECIMEN

III.5. Ferret eggs at ovulation time after mating. Veronal acetate-buffered 1% OsO$_4$; Epon 815; uranyl acetate ($\times$ 24,000). M, mitochondria; Z, zona pellucida.

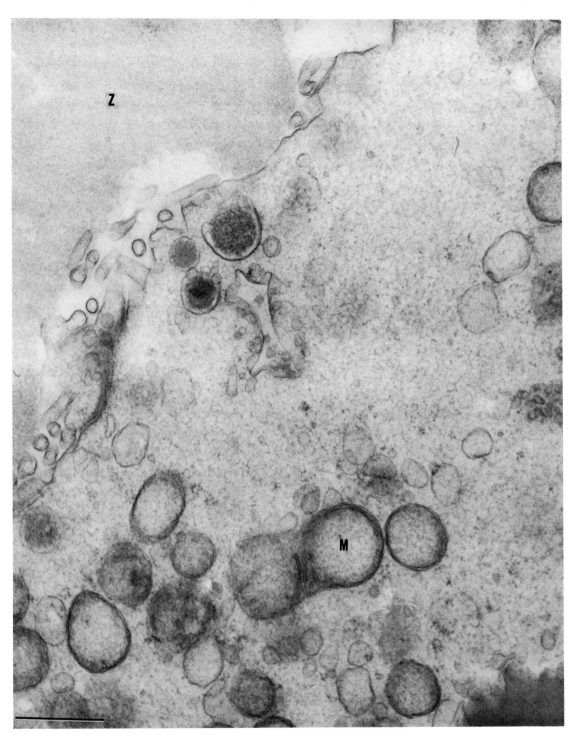

III.5

FIGURES III.6 AND III.7

VITELLINE SURFACE OF FERRET EGG

MEMBRANOUS SURFACE PROJECTION IN UNFERTILIZED RABBIT EGG

Surface of freshly shed, unfertilized ferret egg. A number of granulosa cell processes are still associated with the surface. Further, in this picture there are a number of round bodies containing granular material (inactive RNP), a few mitochondria, some of them appearing to bud while others are circular, with the cristae lying against the limiting membrane. In addition, a couple of irregular cortical granules are also visible.

Membranous villi from the surface of the rabbit egg project into perivitelline area. The egg is still in an actively incorporating phase, although signs of aging are the accumulating cortical granules. There are numerous pinocytotic vesicles in the vicinity of the surface, also a number of cortical granules are in evidence.

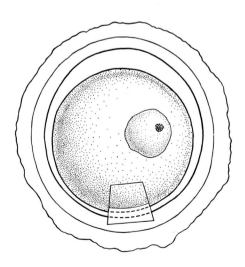

SPECIMENS

III.6. Ferret egg shortly after ovulation. Veronal acetate-buffered 1% OsO_4; Epon 815; uranyl acetate ($\times$ 22,000).

III.7. Unfertilized rabbit egg 8 hours after ovulation. Veronal acetate buffered 1% OsO_4; Epon 815; uranyl acetate ($\times$ 22,000).

CG, cortical granule(s); GP, granulosa cell processes; M, mitochondria; PI, pinocytotic vesicle.

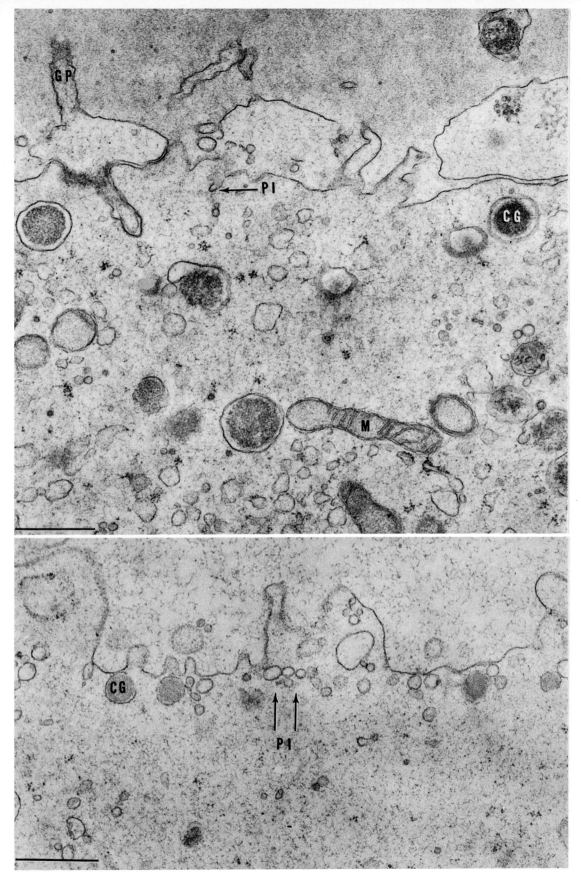

III.6 (↑)   III.7 (↓)

FIGURE III.8

CORTICAL FLUIDITY IN THE RABBIT EGG

CORTICAL VILLI PROJECTING INTO PERIVITELLINE AREA

Cytoplasmic processes projecting above the surface of the egg are incorporating one another. A profusion of smooth-walled, pinocytotic vesicles are opening between them. Of the three mitochondria, only in one are the peripheral cristae evident, in the other two, diffuse peripheral densities appear in addition to the lightly packed mitochondrial lumen. The possibility of mitochondrial metaplasia in the egg is a valid question.

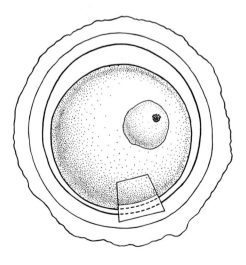

SPECIMEN

III.8. Rabbit egg 3–4 hours after ovulation. Veronal acetate-buffered 1% OsO_4; Epon 812; uranyl acetate ($\times$ 24,000).
M, mitochondria.

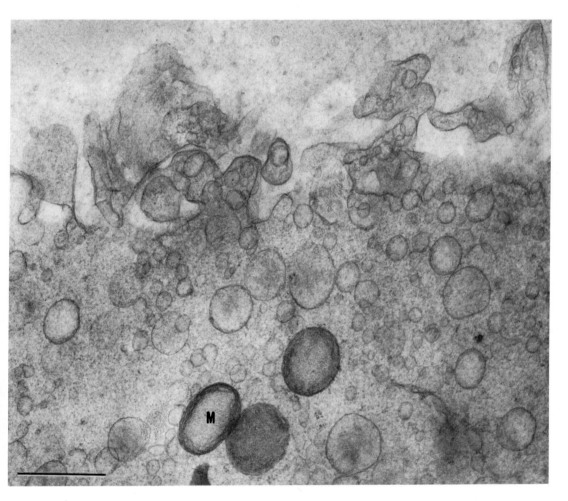

III.8

FIGURES III.9 AND III.10

THE DECREASE OF CORTICAL MOTILITY AND REESTABLISHMENT OF CORTICAL VILLI IN RABBIT EGGS

If the egg is not fertilized within the optimal time (1–4 hours in the rabbit) the cortical fluidity decreases and the villi reappear again as a rule accompanied by the cortical granules.

Within the cytoplasm large numbers of smooth membrane-bound profiles can be seen; some of them show varying densities, indicating cytoplasmic yolk. In addition, some mitochondria can be also observed (III.13), each of them showing dense, peripheral aggregation of villi and medium dense filling of the lumen, approaching the density of the nearby microbody. Cytoplasmic processes project and cortical, pinocytotic vesicles open onto the surface. There is the apparent accumulation of cortical granules.

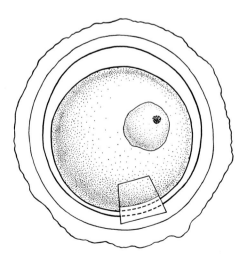

SPECIMENS

III.9. Rabbit egg. Veronal acetate-buffered 1% OsO_4; Epon 815; uranyl acetate ($\times$ 22,000).
III.10. Rabbit egg, after ovulation. Veronal acetate-buffered 1% OsO_4; Maraglas; uranyl acetate ($\times$ 22,000).
CG, cortical granule(s); M, mitochondria; PI, pinocytotic vesicle.

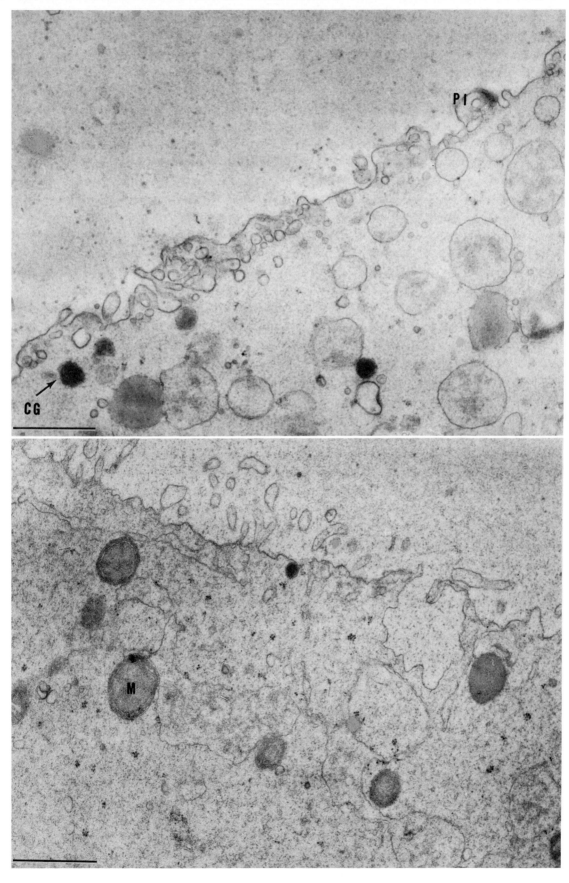

III.9 (↑)   III.10 (↓)

FIGURE III.11

CORTICAL VILLI IN UNFERTILIZED FERRET EGG

This is rather an atypical appearance of the ferret egg's surface. Large numbers of cytoplasmic villi are present. Between them is a lysosome possibly in the process of leaving the egg. One may observe the beginning accumulation of cortical granules. The cortex also contains smooth membrane-bound circular vesicles filled with granular material and some mitochondria with cristae lying closely against the mitochondrial membrane.

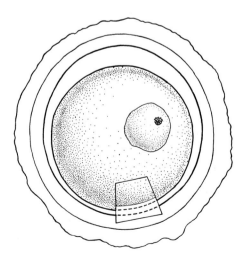

SPECIMEN

III.11. Ferret egg shortly after ovulation. Veronal acetate-buffered 1% OsO_4; Epon 815; uranyl acetate ($\times$ 22,000).

CG, cortical granule(s); L, lysosome; M, mitochondria; RO, round bodies (containing granular material: assumedly inactive RNA).

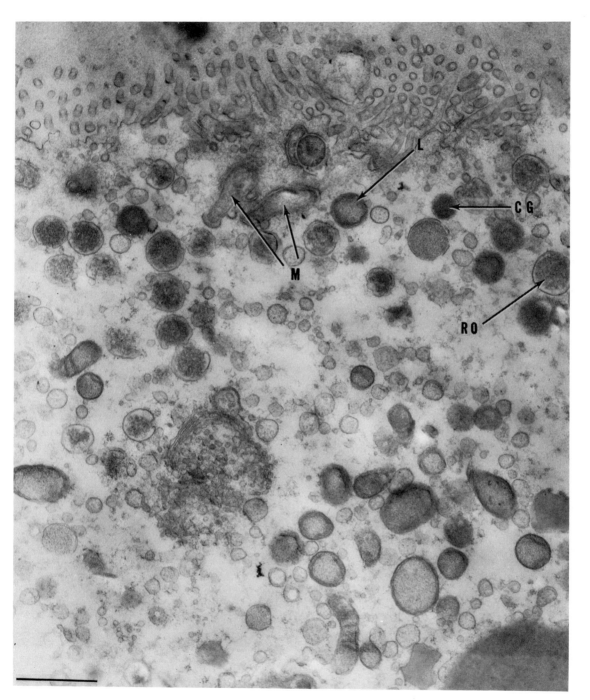

III.11

FIGURE III.12

COMMENCEMENT OF AGING

CORTEX OF RABBIT EGG SOME HOURS AFTER OVULATION

Four to six hours after ovulation microvilli take the place of pseudopodia, as one may observe on this rabbit oocyte. There is an accumulation of cortical granules in their typical locations, immediately beneath the vitelline membrane. In addition, mitochondrial metaplasia, lysosomes, and round bodies are in evidence.

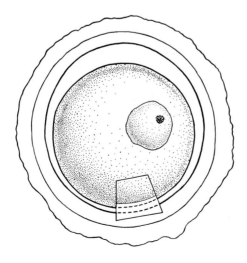

SPECIMEN

III.12. Rabbit egg. Veronal acetate-buffered 1% OsO_4; Epon 815; uranyl acetate ($\times$ 24,000).
CG, cortical granule(s); L, lysosome; M, mitochondria; RO, round bodies (containing granular material: assumedly inactive RNA).

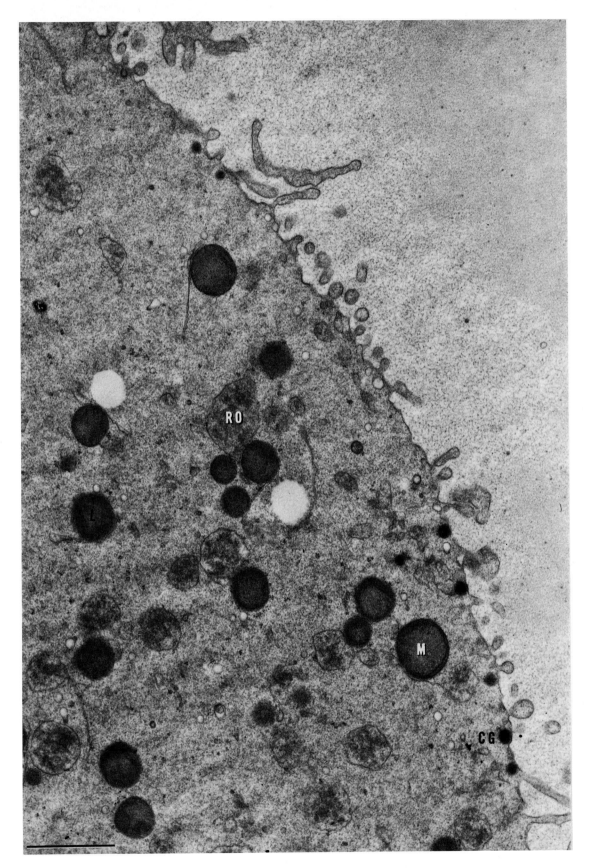

III.12

FIGURE III.13

AGING FERRET EGG

CORTEX OF FERRET EGG 8–10 HOURS FOLLOWING OVULATION

Ten hours after ovulation comparatively thin, cytoplasmic villi take the place of the cortical pseudopodia. No mitochondria can be recognized as such, their place apparently has been taken by various cortical bodies, e.g., lysosomes and microbodies. This picture also illustrates the density difference between the zona pellucida and perivitelline area. Observe that the latter has an apparently filamentous structure.

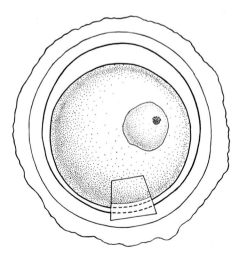

SPECIMEN

III.13. Ferret egg. Veronal acetate-buffered 1% OsO₄; Epon 815; uranyl acetate (× 13,000).
CG, cortical granule(s); PV, perivitelline area.

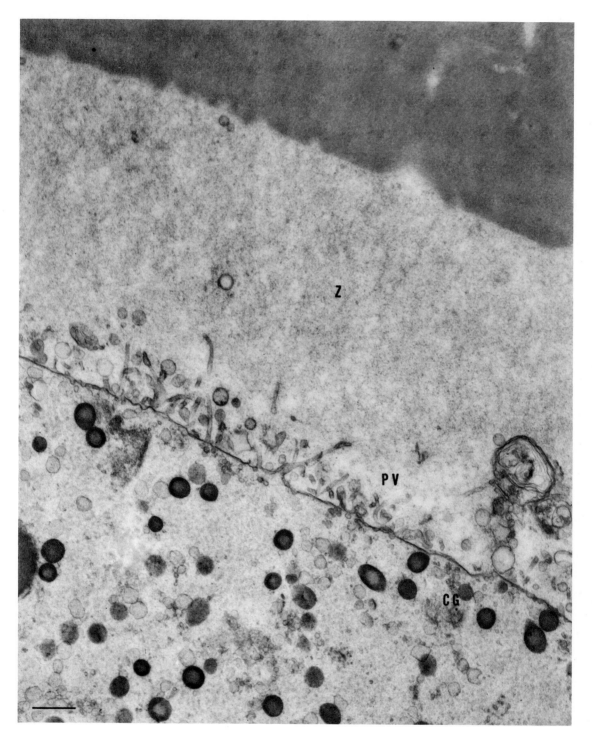

III.13

FIGURE III.14

CORTEX OF RABBIT EGG 72 HOURS AFTER OVULATION

The rabbit egg cannot be fertilized 72 hours after ovulation. One of the signs of the aging process is the accumulation of cortical granules beneath the vitelline membrane. These round granules are almost identical in size and are equidistant from one to another. The elapse of time in the unfertilized egg is marked by the gradual disorganization of the cell organelles. Thus 72 hours after ovulation the vitelline membrane has disintegrated and there is no barrier left between vitellus and perivitelline area. As a result vitelline material is lost into the perivitelline space. Indication of egg's outline in the accompanying picture is marked by cortical granules which remained aligned on a previous vitelline border.

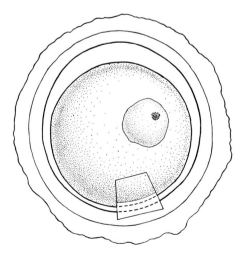

SPECIMEN

III.14. Unfertilized rabbit egg 72 hours after ovulation. Veronal acetate-buffered 1% OsO_4; Epon 812; uranyl acetate ($\times$ 34,000). CG, cortical granule(s).

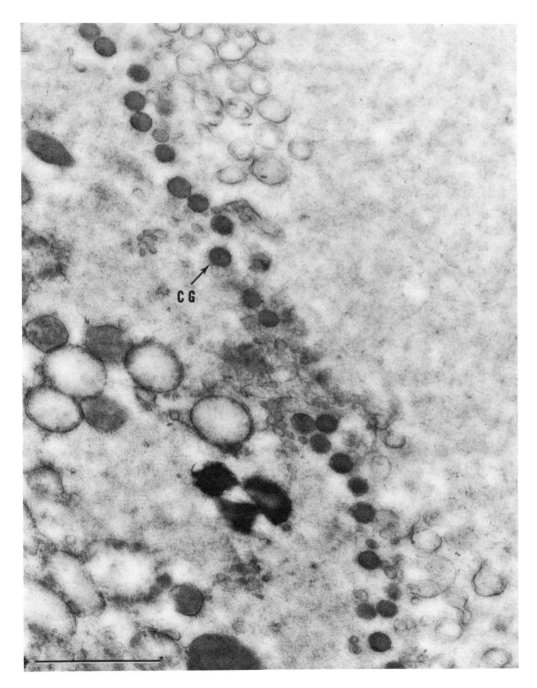

III.14

FIGURE III.15

THE PROCESS OF SPERM DENUDATION

SPERM HEADS IN VICINITY OF VITELLINE MEMBRANE IN RABBIT EGG

K_2MnO_4 fixation enhances membrane contrast. The islands around the two sperm heads represent the remnants of the acrosomal cap.

In addition, one can observe a circular, beltlike enlargement around the cranial third of both sperm nuclei. These are formed by the subacrosomal layers and have been observed in various sperm heads at diverse locations.

Pseudopodialike processes are apparent on the surface of the egg. Their small size indicates that these may be supernumerary sperms which arrived following penetration of the fertilizing spermatozoa.

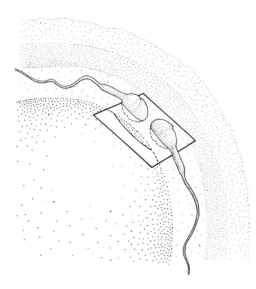

SPECIMEN

III.15. Rabbit egg 14 hours after mating. K_2MnO_4; Epon 812; lead acetate ($\times$ 22,000). A, acrosome cap; OO, oocyte: egg or zygote; S, subacrosomal layer.

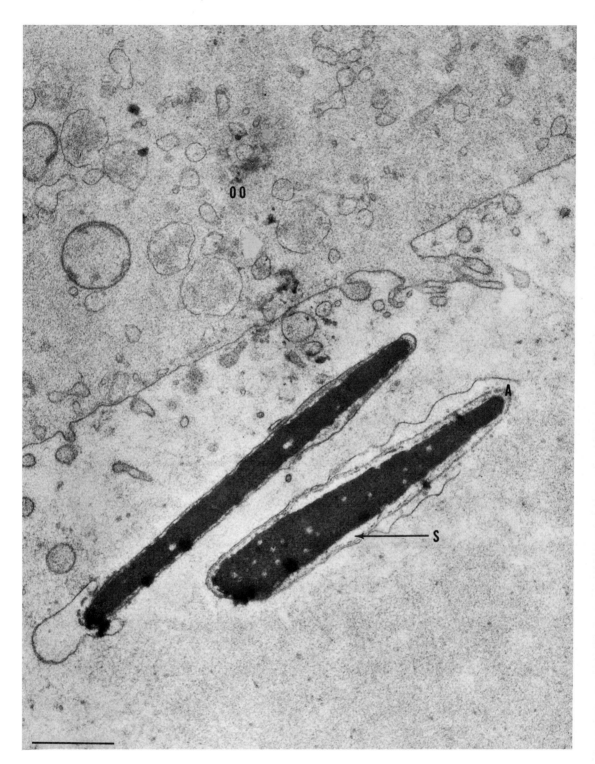

III.15

FIGURE III.16

THE PROCESS OF SPERM HEAD DENUDATION AT THE SURFACE OF THE VITELLINE MEMBRANE

Fingerlike processes (blebs) are seen budding from the surface of the sperm head, causing the complete disappearance of the acrosomal cap, excepting the equatorial region, which remains as a thin sleeve. Ringlike protuberance of subacrosomal layer can be well observed. [Some authors claim that the acrosomal layer also disintegrates to small globular units prior to the sperm penetration through the zona pellucida (Barros *et al.*, 1967).]

Following the disintegration of the apical body, the sperm nucleus is surrounded by the subacrosomal (cytoplasmic) layer only.

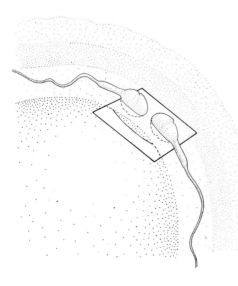

SPECIMEN

III.16. Rabbit egg 18 hours after mating. Veronal acetate-buffered 1% OsO$_4$; Epon 815; uranyl acetate ($\times$ 40,000).

AB, apical body; E, equatorial region (of sperm head); OO, oocyte: egg or zygote; PV, perivitelline area; S, subacrosomal layer.

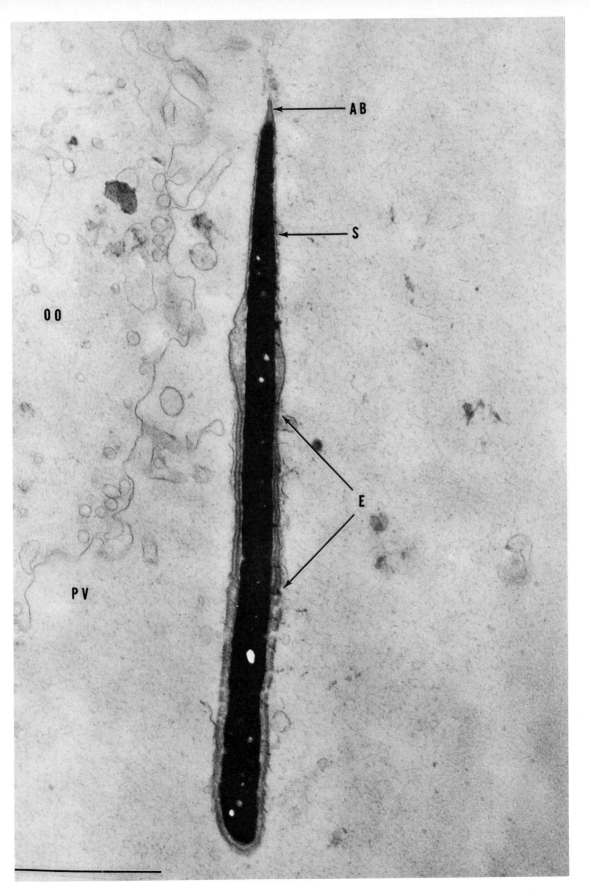

III.16

FIGURE III.17

THE PROCESS OF SPERM DENUDATION IN THE PERIVITELLINE AREA [the Disappearance of the Subacrosomal (Cytoplasmic) Layer]

RABBIT SPERM HEADS AND SECTIONS OF TAILS IN VICINITY OF VITELLINE MEMBRANE

The time relationship between the arrival of rabbit spermatozoon and the dissolution of the sperm head covering membranes hasn't been established yet. It appears that the subacrosomic (cytoplasmic) layer is effected only if the sperm has spent a considerable period in the perivitelline area. The acrosome cap has been shown either to dissolve into globules (Barros *et al.*, 1967), or into amorphous droplets (see previous pictures).

The process of the subacrosomal (cytoplasmic) layer dissolution is more advanced on this picture than in the previous micrograph. It is apparently forming small spherules, which are leaving the vicinity of the sperm head. The significance of the subacrosomal (cytoplasmic) disintegration has not been explained yet.

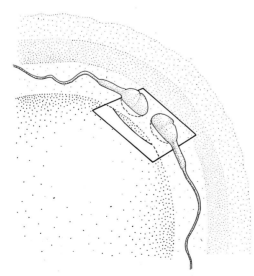

SPECIMEN

III.17. Rabbit egg 18 hours after mating. Veronal acetate buffered 1% OsO_4; Epon 812; uranyl acetate ($\times$ 24,000).

OO, oocyte: egg or zygote; S, subacrosomal layer.

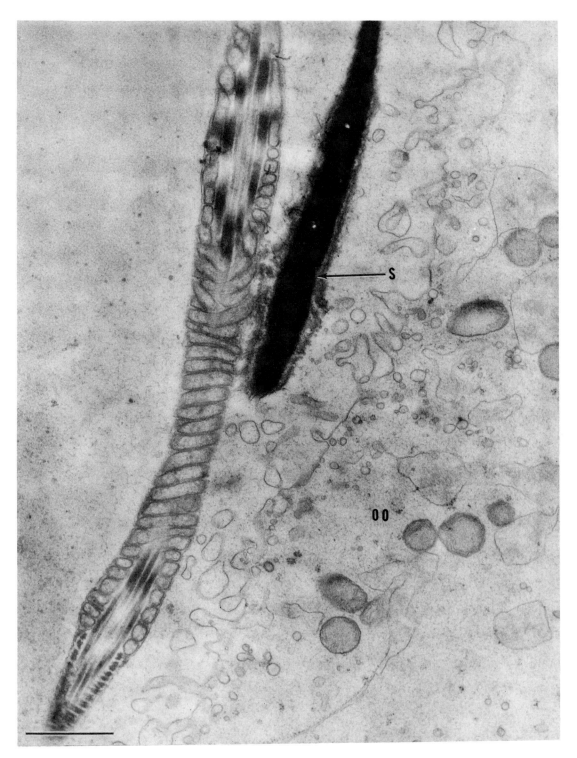

III.17

FIGURE III.18

DENUDED SPERM HEAD IN VICINITY OF VITELLUS

HEAD OF RABBIT SPERMATOZOON SURROUNDED BY VILLI OF VITELLINE MEMBRANE

Only a thin subacrosomal layer and the apical body are present. Actually, it is not known whether a complete denudation of the rabbit sperm head is a necessary prerequisite for incorporation into the vitellus. It is possible, however, that the apical body and perhaps the cytoplasmic layer also, act upon the vitelline membrane, causing localized lysis at spots where the two membranes (the vitelline and the sperm head) may meet and subsequently join one another (Colwin and Colwin, 1963; Szollosi and Ris, 1961).

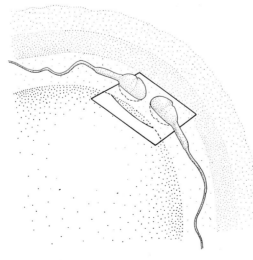

SPECIMEN

III.18. Rabbit egg, 20 hours after mating. Veronal acetate-buffered 1% OsO_4; Epon 812; uranyl acetate ($\times$ 60,000).
AB, apical body; VS, vitelline surface or vitelline membrane.

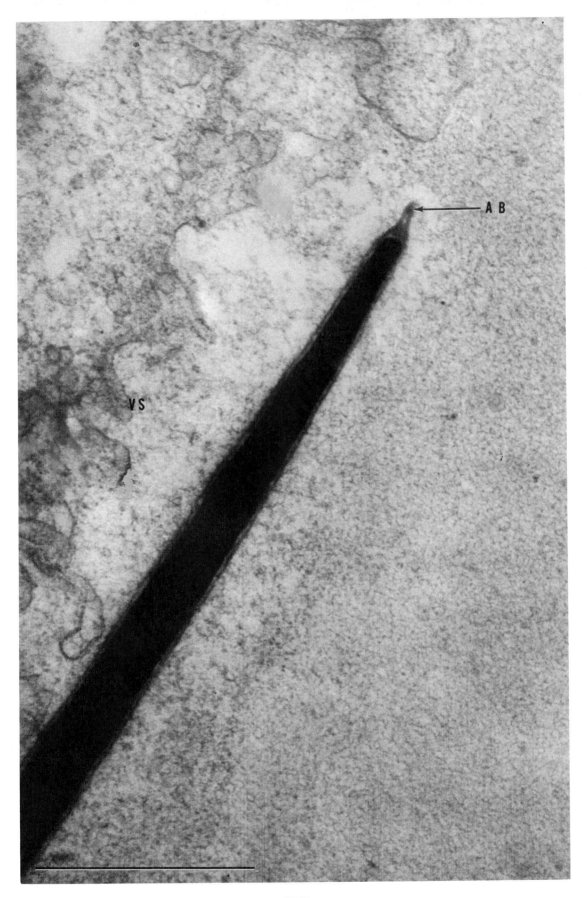

III.18

FIGURES III.19 AND III.20

THE (POSSIBLE) START OF SPERM INCORPORATION

RABBIT SPERM HEAD LYING ON VITELLINE MEMBRANE

According to some observations (Szollosi and Ris, 1961), the rat sperm sinks sideways into the egg. However, the incorporation of the spermatozoon into the egg is preceded by the union of the two membranes in forming a mosaic. This picture shows the localized dissolution of the membrane around the sperm head at loci where contact is established with the vitelline membrane.

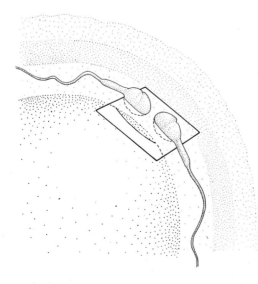

SPECIMENS

III.19. Rabbit ovum 18 hours after mating. Veronal acetate-buffered 1% OsO_4; Epon 812; uranyl acetate ($\times$ 22,000).
III.20. Rabbit ovum 18 hours after mating. Veronal acetate-buffered 1% OsO_4; Epon 812; uranyl acetate ($\times$ 56,000).
OO, oocyte: egg or zygote; VS, vitelline surface or vitelline membrane.

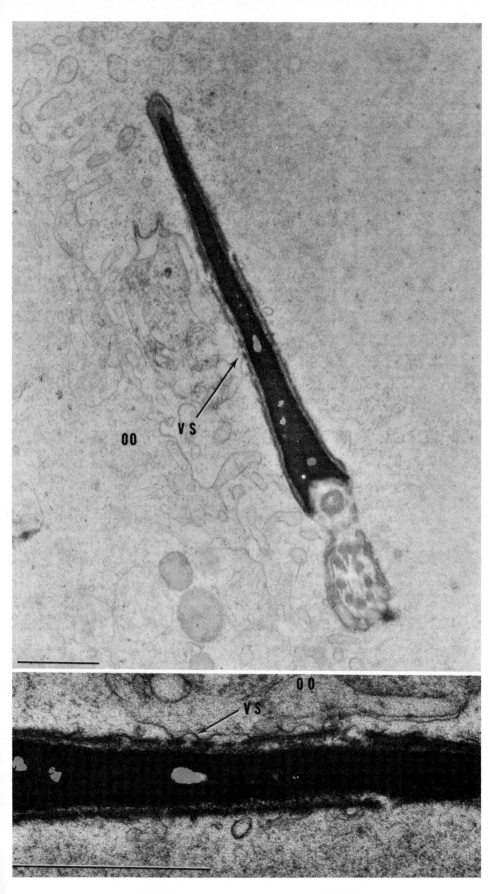

III.19 (↑)   III.20 (↓)

FIGURE III.21

PHENOMENON OF SPERM INCORPORATION

SPERMATOZOON ON THE SURFACE OF RABBIT EGG

It is hard to perceive the thin cytoplasmic layer at the apex and around the caudal aspect of the nucleus. This denuded sperm head is being surrounded on one side by a number of vitelline processes. Because of the number and irregularity of these oversize cortical villi, one may assume that the sperm on the electron micrograph may be the one which is going to be incorporated into the vitellus.

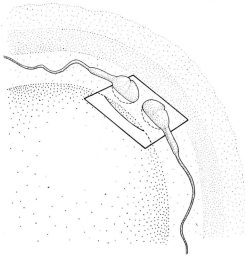

SPECIMEN

III.21. Rabbit ovum 18–19 hours after ovulation. Veronal acetate-buffered 1% OsO₄; Epon 812; uranyl acetate ($\times$ 80,000).
VS, vitelline surface or vitelline membrane.

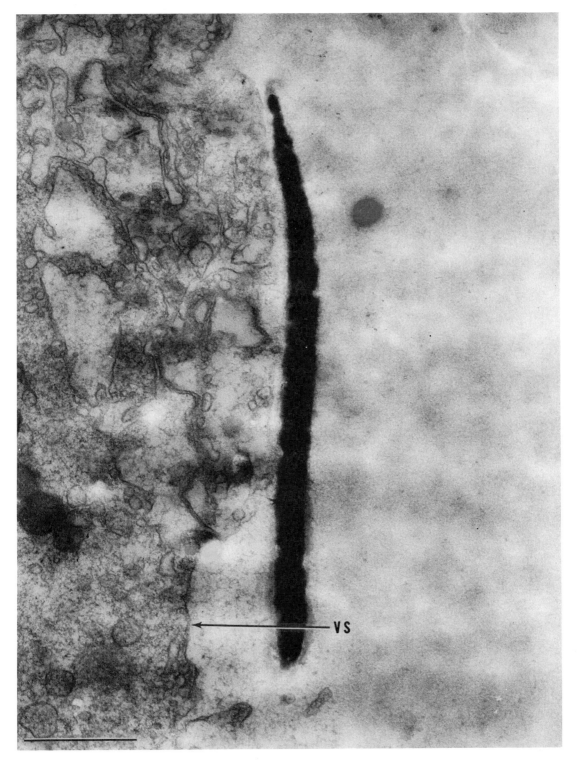

III.21

FIGURE III.22

INCORPORATION OF SPERM OF RABBIT IN VITELLUS OF RABBIT EGG

Rabbit sperm head apparently in the process of sinking into vitellus of egg. Denuded sperm head (nucleus) in this instance is still in the perivitelline area. The sperm head is surrounded by the cytoplasmic villi of the egg.

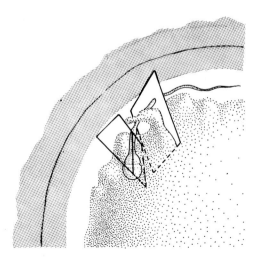

SPECIMEN

III.22. Rabbit egg 19 hours after mating. Veronal acetate-buffered 1% OsO$_4$; Epon 815; uranyl acetate ($\times$ 45,000).

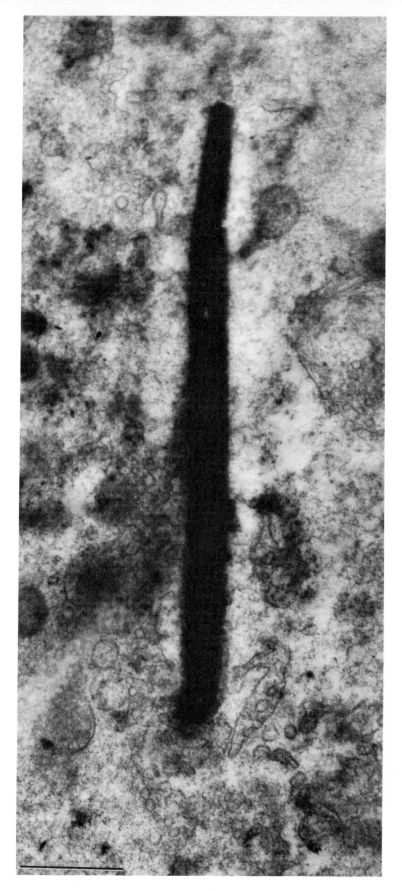

III.22

FIGURE III.23

RABBIT SPERM INCORPORATION

RABBIT SPERM TAIL AMIDST VITELLINE PROCESSES

Electron micrograph shows rabbit sperm tail in the vicinity of the vitelline surface surrounded by large number of vitelline processes. Observe cortical granules, vacuoles in the huge pseudopodialike processes around filamentous end of spermatozoon's tail.

This and the previous picture would suggest that spermatozoon incorporation occurs in a process of cytoplasmic upwelling (or cortical wave) akin to the fertilization cone formation in the invertebrates, during which the cortical villi of the egg incorporate the spermatozoon.

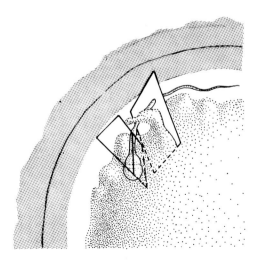

SPECIMEN

III.23. Rabbit egg 19 hours after mating. Veronal acetate-buffered 1% OsO_4; Epon 815; uranyl acetate ($\times$ 30,000).

OO, oocyte: egg or zygote; SP, spermatozoon; VP, vitelline (cytoplasmic) processes.

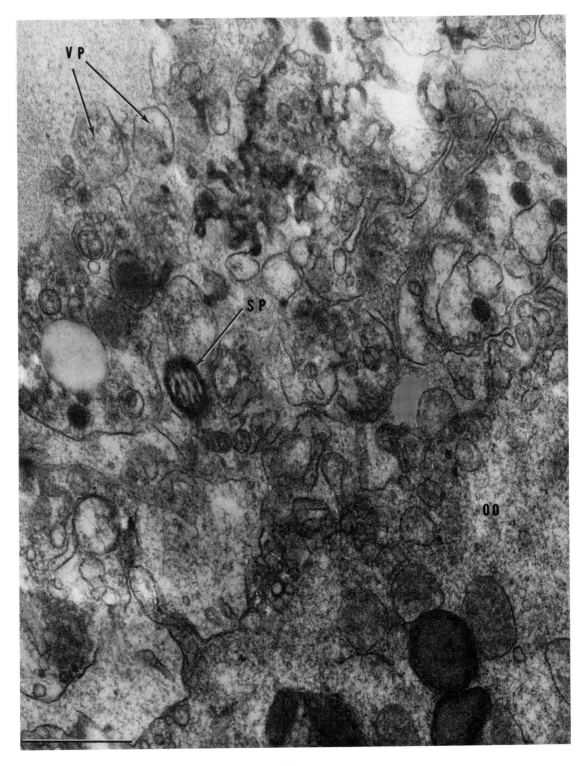

III.23

FIGURE III.24

FRESHLY INCORPORATED SPERM HEAD

TRANSVERSE SECTION OF RABBIT SPERM HEAD IN VITELLUS

Freshly incorporated sperm head in oocyte cytoplasm. Rabbit sperm in the cortex of the egg is apparently surrounded by finely granular cytoplasmic matrix, also by smooth membranous profiles. The outer layer of the sperm nucleus is apparently in the process of forming fine, threadlike processes, which are running perpendicularly to the surface of the nucleus (evident on the apex). In addition, some delicate vesiculation is also evident at the apex of the sperm head.

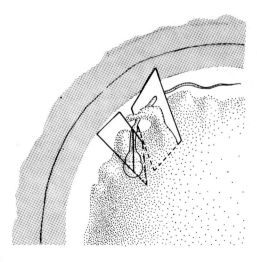

SPECIMEN

III.24. Rabbit egg 20 hours after mating. Veronal acetate-buffered 1% OsO_4; Epon 812; uranyl acetate ($\times$ 22,000).

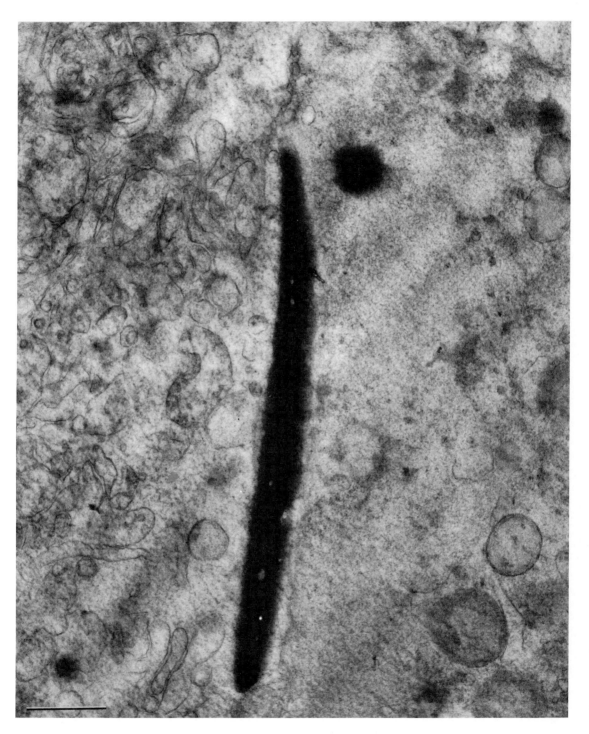

III.24

FIGURE III.24A

PENETRATING SPERMATOZOON

While the apical part of the sperm head is still outside the egg, the rest of the head and the neck are already within the vitellus. Fused vitelline and spermatozoon cell membrane are evident within the egg. Dispersion of nuclear material into peripheral filamentous component around a dense central core is well observable. Another remarkable aspect of this picture is the homogeneity of the vitelline material in the vicinity of the incorporated sperm nucleus and the absence of cellular organelles.

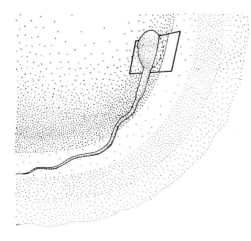

SPECIMEN

III.24A. Polyspermic hamster egg, fertilized *in vitro*. Glutaraldehyde fixation post osmicated (× 25,000).
E, Equatorial region in sperm; N, nucleus; PV, perivitelline areas; VS, vitelline surface or vitelline membrane; arrow, fused cell membranes of egg and spermatozoon.
Courtesy of Dr. C. Barros and Dr. L. E. Franklin.

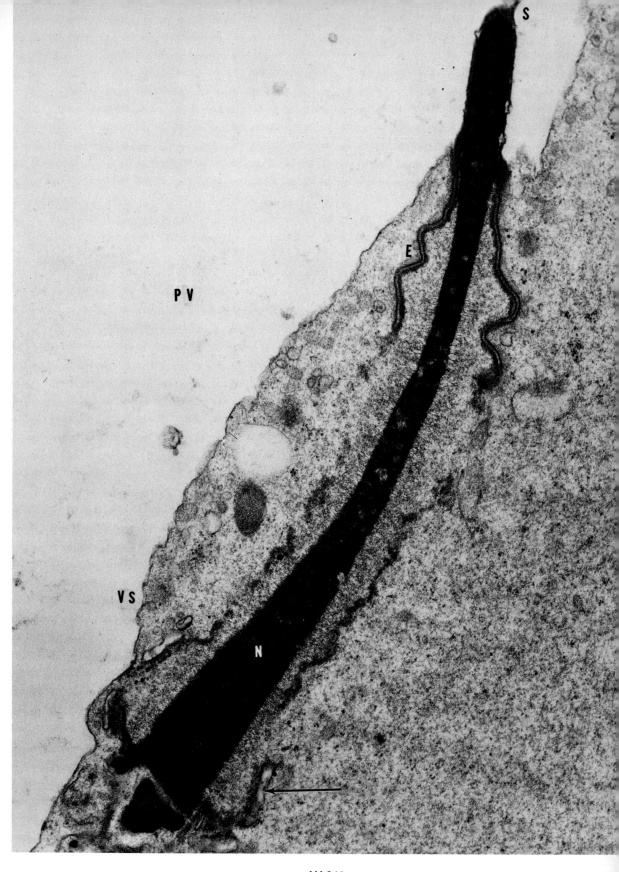

S

E

PV

VS

N

III.24A

FIGURE III.24B

SPERMATOZOON WITHIN THE EGG

Sperm head and midpiece can be observed within the egg in vicinity of the vitelline membrane. Fused cell membranes of egg and spermatozoon are visible around apical part of incorporated sperm. There is no membrane apparent about the mid or caudal part of the sperm nucleus, nor around the spermatozoon's midpiece.

The beginning separation of the nucleus into peripheral filamentous, and central, dense core is evident.

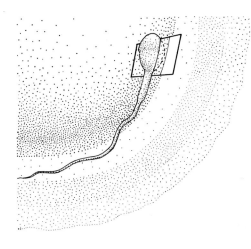

SPECIMEN

III.24B. Fertilized rat egg. Veronal acetate buffered 2% OsO_4; methacrylate ($\times$ 15,000). MS, Mitochondrial spiral (around midpiece of sperm tail); N, nucleus; VS, vitelline surface or vitelline membrane; Z, zona pellucida.
Courtesy of Dr. D. G. Szollosi and Dr. H. Ris.

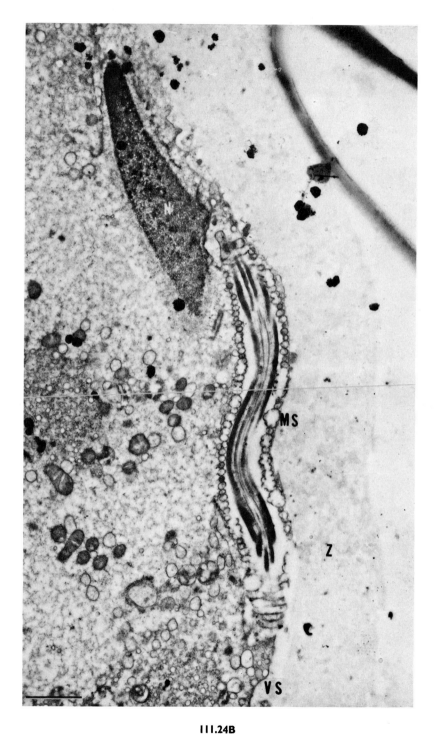

III.24B

FIGURES III.24C AND III.24D

DISPERSAL OF NUCLEAR MATERIAL IN PENETRATING SPERM HEAD

Figure III. 24C. At the time of its entrance, the sperm head already shows beginning dispersal into peripheral filamentous material, while the part which is outside of egg is still dense. This may indicate the possibility that absence of the covering membranes may trigger the dispersal.

Figure III. 24D. Further support is lent to this hypothesis by this partially penetrated sperm head. The nucleus in the anterior two-thirds of head where the membranes are absent already shows the filamentous dispersal, while the posterior aspect, which is still surrounded by membranes, is still compact.

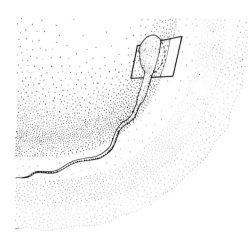

SPECIMENS

III.24C. Polyspermic hamster egg, fertilized *in vitro*. Glutaraldehyde fixation post-osmicated (× 25,000).

III.24D. Polyspermic hamster egg, fertilized *in vitro*. Glutaraldehyde fixation post-osmicated (× 25,000).

C, cell membrane; N, nucleus; PV, perivitel-line area; arrow, fused sperm cell membrane and vitelline membrane.

Courtesy Dr. C. Barros and Dr. L. E. Franklin.

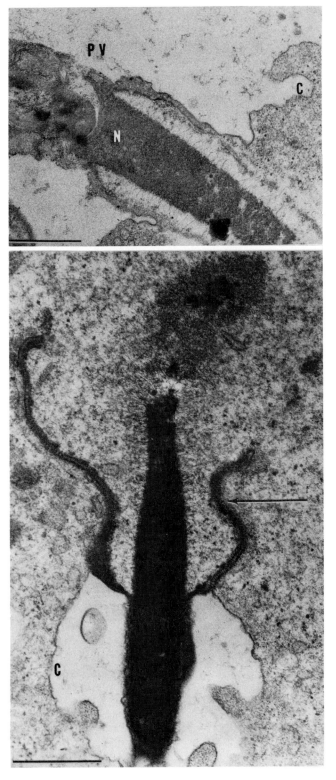

III.24C(↑)   III.24D(↓)

FIGURE III.25

FORMATION OF MALE PRONUCLEUS

CROSS SECTION OF RABBIT SPERM HEAD SHORTLY AFTER PENETRATION INTO THE EGG

Transformation of the sperm head into the male pronucleus involves the rearrangement of the nuclear material. Following the rounding of the sperm head, the male gamete apparently develops a central light and a peripheral dense area before the male pronucleus is fully formed. A moderate sunburst effect emanating from the sperm head is evident on this picture. These filaments are apparently originating from the surface of the male.

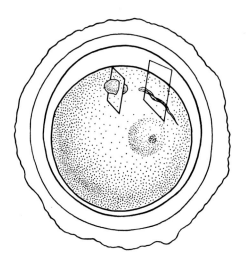

SPECIMEN

III.25. Rabbit zygote, 20–22 hours after mating. Veronal acetate-buffered 1% OsO₄; lead acetate (× 30,000).

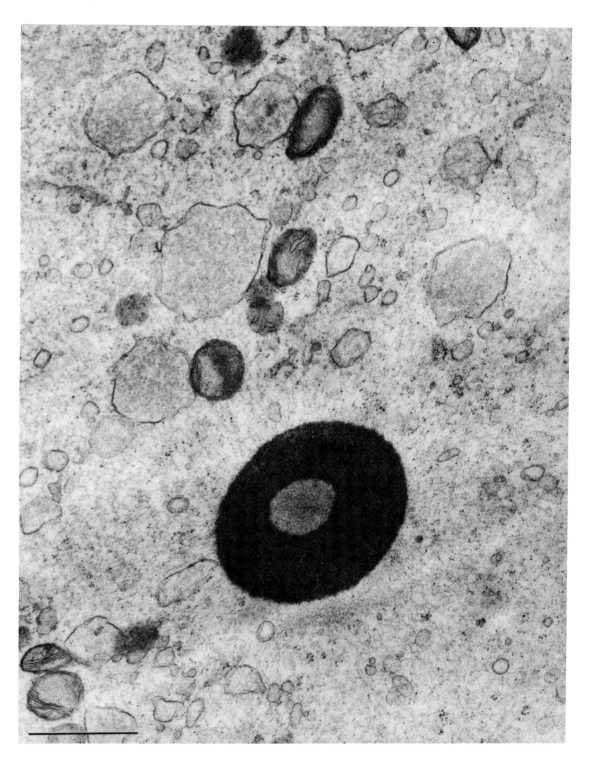

III.25

FIGURES III.26 AND III.27

SPERM TAIL IN HAMSTER EGG

*OBLIQUE SECTION THROUGH SPERMATOZOON TAIL IN CORTEX OF
HAMSTER ZYGOTE*

After sperm incorporation the surface of the egg becomes even and most of the villi disappear. Although the whole spermatozoon is incorporated into the egg, it is only the head which contributes to the formation of the male pronucleus. The tail has no role to play—with the possible exception of the centriole. (Its fate is not known for the time being.)

Following the spermatozoon's arrival into the egg, the organelles which surround the sperm tail undergo degenerative changes. These pictures demonstrate the tail of the hamster sperm still surrounded by the male mitochondria. However, soon after fertilization gradual degenerative changes set in, which apparently start with the accumulation of a dense focus in the lumen of the mitochondria which is subsequently replaced by vesicles or vacuoles. A number of vacuolar sequestrations are visible. In some cases evolving multivesicular bodies also can be observed in the vicinity of the remnants of the sperm tail, indicating the possibility of mitochondrion transformation into multivesicular body.

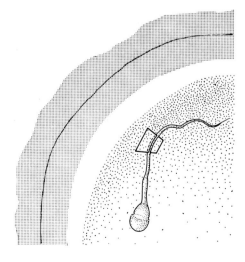

SPECIMENS

III.26. Hamster zygote assumedly 10 hours after mating. Phosphate-buffered 2% glutaraldehyde, postosmicated; Epon 815; uranyl acetate ($\times$ 32,000).

III.27. Hamster zygote assumedly 10 hours after mating. Phosphate-buffered 2% glutaraldehyde, postosmicated; Epon 815; uranyl acetate ($\times$ 32,000).

M, mitochondria; PF, peripheral rough fibers (in spermatozoon's tail); PV, perivitelline area; VS, vitelline surface or vitelline membrane.

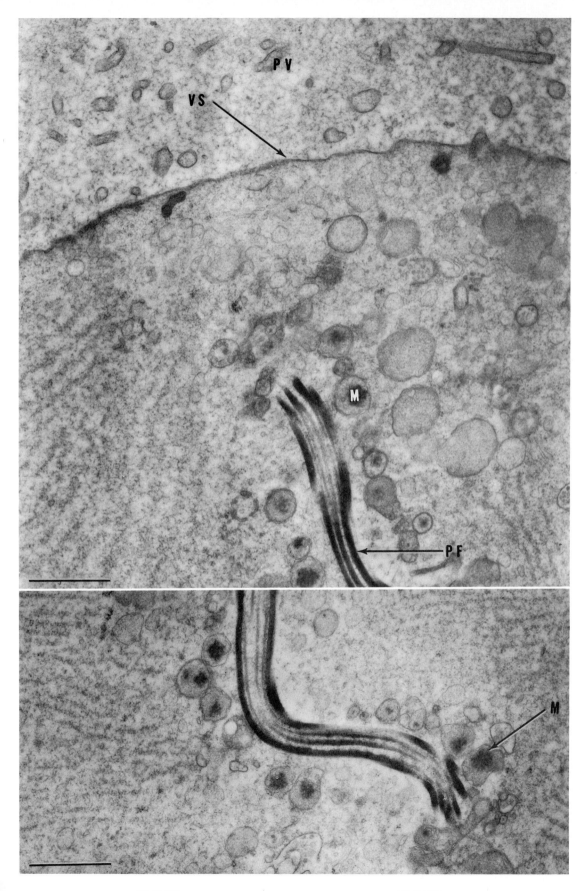

FIGURES III.28 AND III.29

GRADUAL DISORGANIZATION OF MALE MITOCHONDRIA IN VITELLUS

CORTEX OF RECENTLY FERTILIZED HAMSTER EGG

Hamster sperm tail (midpiece) within the vitellus is surrounded by large, round profiles, many of them mitochondria. Assumedly they are mitochondria of the male, although, at least in this stage, some similarity seems to exist between the mitochondria of the two gametes. In addition there are a number of intermediary forms (some resembling lysosomes, others microbodies) which may indicate that these structures represent the gradual degeneration of the male mitochondria. A number of empty profiles associated with the morphology of multivesicular bodies are also apparent and may indicate the possibility of mitochondrial transformation into multivesicular bodies.

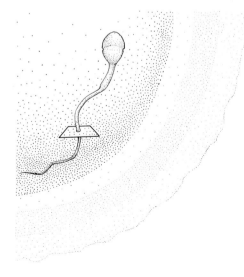

SPECIMENS

III.28. Hamster zygote. Phosphate-buffered 1% OsO₄; Epon 815; uranyl acetate (× 30,000).

III.29. Hamster zygote. Veronal acetate-buffered 1% OsO₄; Epon 815; uranyl acetate (× 14,000).

M, mitochondria; MV, multivesicular body; SP, spermatozoon.

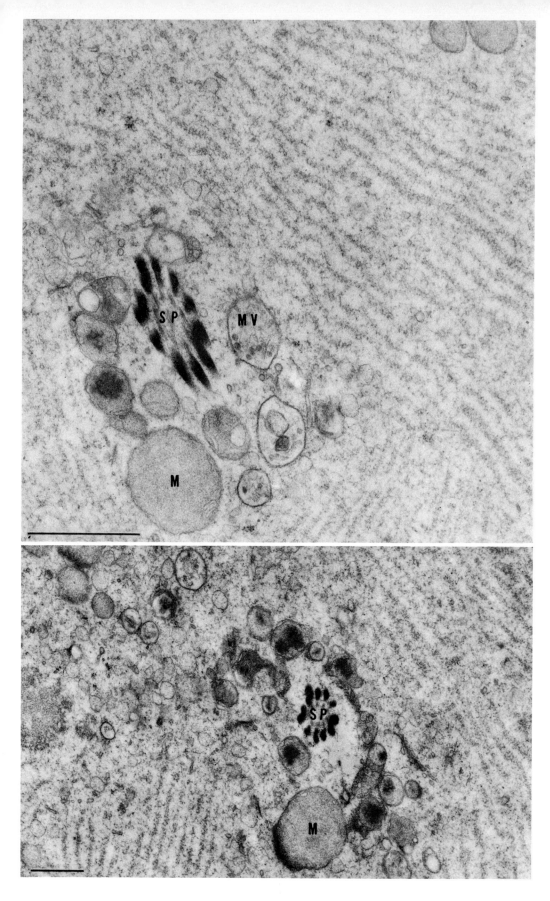

III.28 (↑)   III.29 (↓)

FIGURE III.30

DISINTEGRATING HAMSTER SPERMATOZOON TAIL

CORTICAL AREA IN HAMSTER ZYGOTE

Disintegrating spermatozoon tail in vicinity of a bilobed dense body (arrow)—microbody?—which may be a transformed mitochondria.

Disorganized cytoplasmic droplets are visible in the perivitelline area, which represents remnants from the separation of the second polar body. Remarkably enough, excepting the bilobed structure, no lysosomes are observed in the vicinity of the spermatozoon tail.

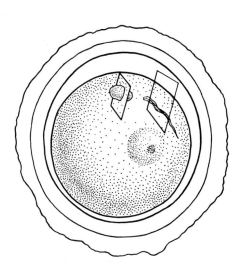

SPECIMEN

III.30. Hamster zygote. Phosphate-buffered 2% glutaraldehyde, postosmicated; Epon 815; uranyl acetate (× 22,000).

PV, perivitelline area; SP, spermatozoon; arrow, bilobed mitochondria or possibly microbody.

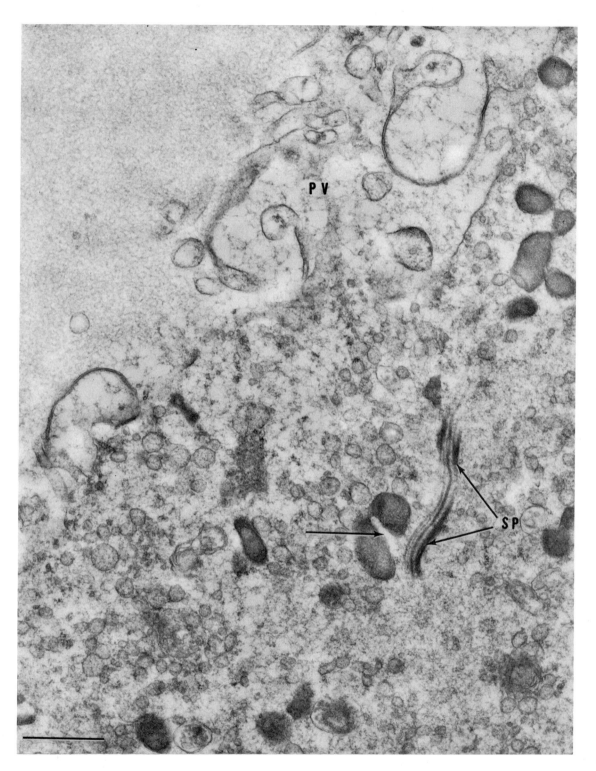

III.30

FIGURE III.31

SUPERNUMERARY SPERM OF RABBIT ON VITELLINE SURFACE OF EGG

There are essentially two factors which may keep the sperm out of the egg: (1) previous fertilization, (2) the age of the egg. The latter occurs when the egg is too old to respond to the sperm.

From the absence of pseudopodia on the surface of the rabbit egg and by its replacement with smaller, cytoplasmic villi, it is assumed that these are supernumerary spermatozoa, which have not been incorporated. The reasons for this statement are as follows: There are no cortical granules present, which indicate either that the egg is freshly ovulated, or that it is fertilized. If it was a recently ovulated egg, then some granulosa cell processes would still be in evidence, which on this occasion are missing. On the other hand, if it had passed the period of fertilizability, then cortical granules would be in evidence. Consequently, a spermatozoon has probably already penetrated.

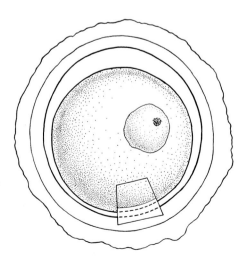

SPECIMEN

III.31. Rabbit egg. Veronal acetate-buffered 1% OsO₄; Epon 815; uranyl acetate (× 14,000).

VS, vitelline surface or vitelline membrane; Z, zona pellucida.

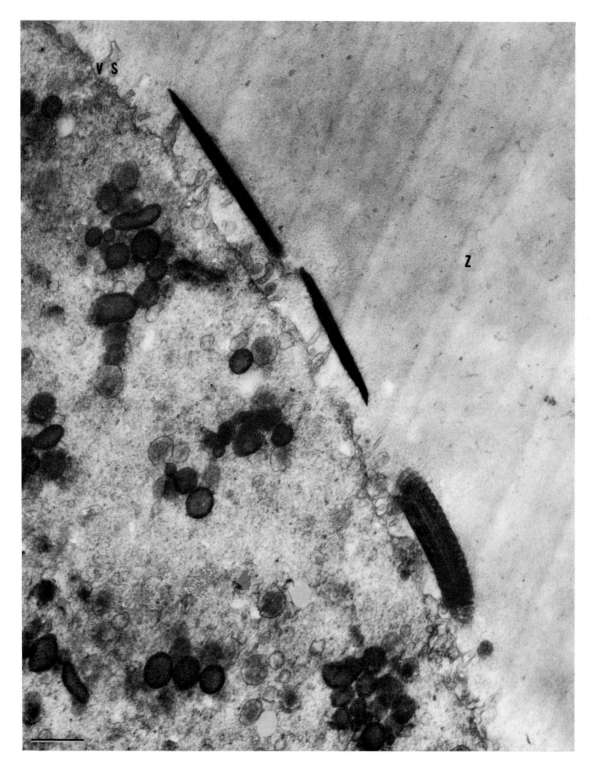

III.31

FIGURES III.32 AND III.33

VITELLINE SURFACE FUNCTION AND EXCLUSION MECHANISM

SURFACE OF PENETRATED RABBIT EGG

Aldehyde fixation reveals to a greater extent than osmium, additional structures and possible functions associated with the vitelline membrane. This, and the subsequent pictures illustrate outpocketings and blebbings of the vitelline membrane. Some of these blebs apparently contain well-delineated, membranous enclosures, whose function for the time being is conjectural, but which could be enzyme pods. These could perform a variety of tasks, among others: dissolving the zona pellucida or the material in the perivitelline area. In the rabbit zygote the elevated membrane has been observed to become closely associated with supernumerary spermatozoa in the perivitelline area, and this membrane may serve to hinder the penetration of the supernumerary sperm into the zygote.

Figure III.32 demonstrates cortical membrane elevation.

Figure III.33 shows the association of elevated cortical membrane with spermatozoon.

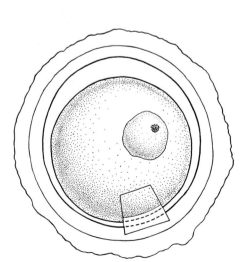

SPECIMENS

III.32. Rabbit zygote. Phosphate-buffered 2% glutaraldehyde, postosmicated; Epon 812; uranyl acetate (× 22,000).

III.33. Rabbit zygote. Phosphate-buffered 2% glutaraldehyde, postosmicated; Epon 812; uranyl acetate (× 22,000).

EM, elevated membrane (or vitelline membrane bleb) on surface of egg; PV, perivitelline area; SP, spermatozoon; Z, zona pellucida.

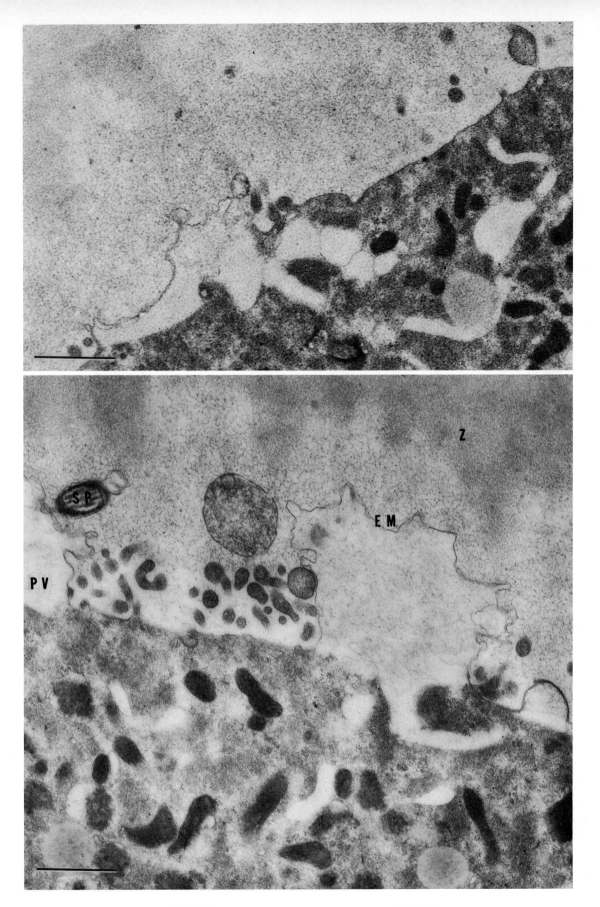

III.32 (↑)   III.33 (↓)

FIGURES III.34 AND III.35

VITELLINE SURFACE FUNCTION AND SUPERNUMERARY SPERM EXCLUSION MECHANISM

SUPERNUMERARY SPERM EXCLUSION MECHANISM ON EGG SURFACE IN PERIVITELLINE AREA OF RABBIT ZYGOTE

Vitelline membrane blebs projecting from the surface of the egg contain well-delineated single-membrane enclosures, possibly enzyme pods. Theoretically speaking, these could have one or several functions, e.g., dissolving the zona pellucida, neutralizing the subacrosomal layer around the sperm head, excluding the supernumerary sperm, etc.

Membranous cortical outpocketings originating from the vitelline membrane of the egg, one with well-observable stalk approaches tail of spermatozoon. Such cortical outpocketings, as a rule, become associated with supernumerary spermatozoa located in the perivitelline area. In this particular case membrane is in vicinity of tail.

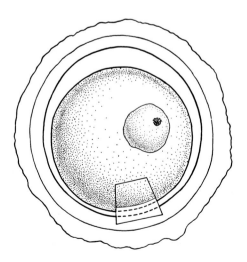

SPECIMENS

III.34. Rabbit zygote. Phosphate buffered 2% glutaraldehyde, postosmicated; Epon 812; uranyl acetate (× 22,000).
III.35. Rabbit zygote. Phosphate-buffered 2% glutaraldehyde, postosmicated; Epon 812; uranyl acetate (× 22,000).
EM, elevated membrane (or vitelline membrane bleb) on surface of the egg.

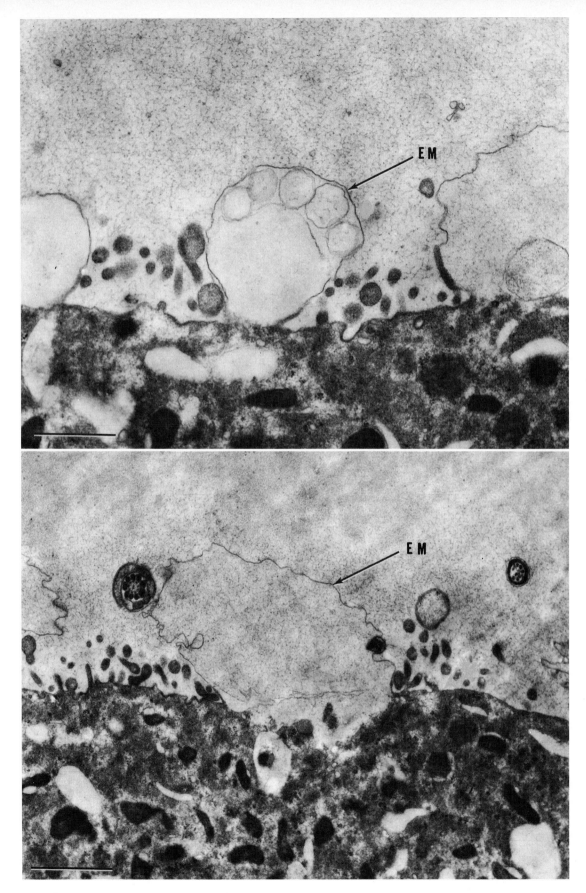

III.34 (↑)   III.35 (↓)

FIGURE III.36

SUPERNUMERARY SPERM EXCLUSION MECHANISM

Membranous cortical outpocketings (arrow) partially surround the sperm tail. Actually one could assume a number of various stimuli which could trigger membranous elevations. For example, it could be a process akin to an immunological reaction, or it could be an activity resembling the function of a macrophage. Again, blebs could originate without any further stimulation and accidentally meet and incorporate the supernumerary spermatozoon.

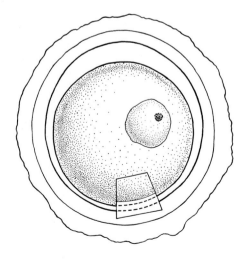

SPECIMEN

III.36. Rabbit zygote. Phosphate-buffered 2% glutaraldehyde, postosmicated; Epon 812; uranyl acetate (× 22,000).

SP, spermatozoon; VS, vitelline surface or vitelline membrane; arrow, membranous cortical outpocketings.

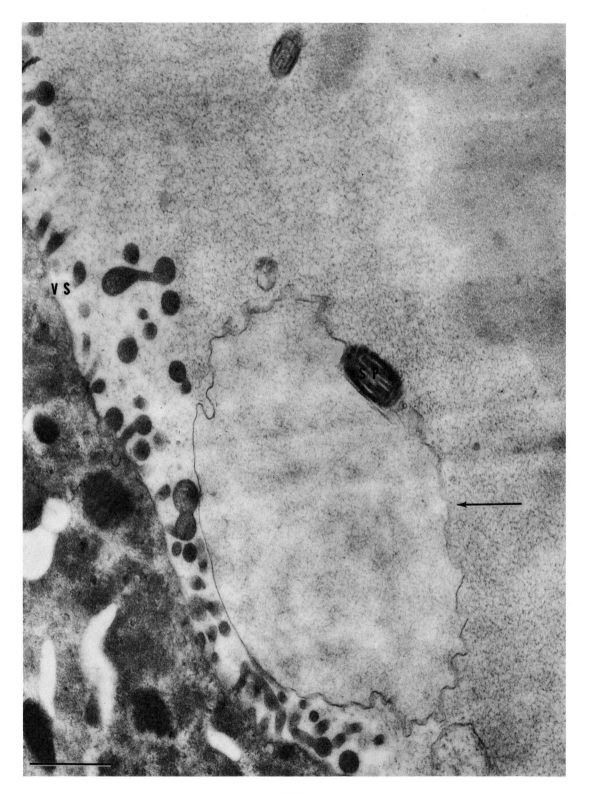

III.36

FIGURES III.37 AND III.38

SUPERNUMERARY SPERM EXCLUSION MECHANISM

CORTEX AND PERIVITELLINE AREA OF PENETRATED RABBIT EGG

Rabbit egg 18 hours after mating. Spermatozoon tail in the perivitelline area being surrounded by smooth (arrow) membrane. Spermatozoon is almost completely enclosed, in a way "sequestered" from the egg by the bleb.

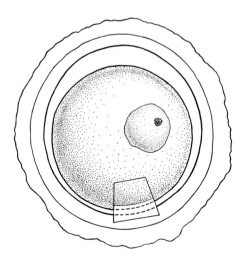

SPECIMENS

III.37. Rabbit egg. Phosphate-buffered 2% glutaraldehyde, postosmicated; Epon 812; uranyl acetate ($\times$ 22,000).

III.38. Rabbit egg. Phosphate-buffered 2% glutaraldehyde, postosmicated; Epon 812; uranyl acetate ($\times$ 22,000).

SP, spermatozoon; VS, vitelline surface or vitelline membrane; arrow, smooth membrane and sperm tail.

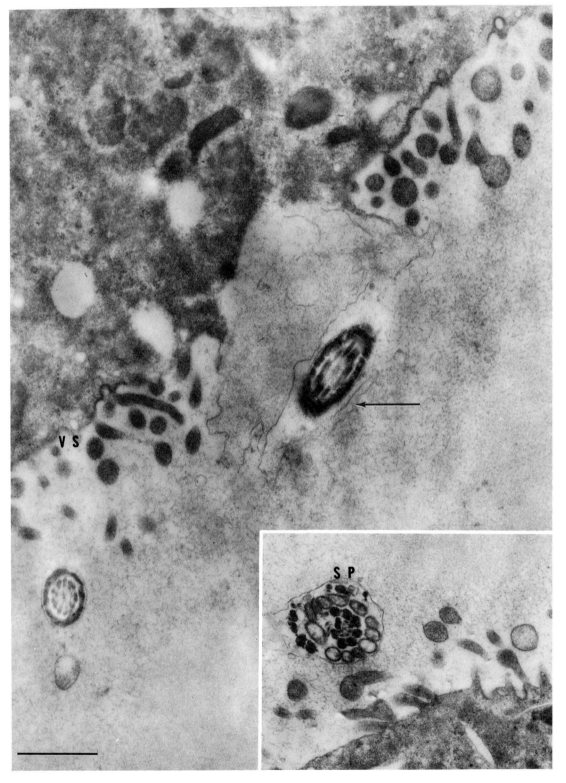

III.37 (↑)   III.38 (↓)

FIGURE III.39

VITELLINE MATERIAL IN PERIVITELLINE AREA

*PERIVITELLINE AREA OF HAMSTER ZYGOTE SHORTLY AFTER INCORPORATING
SPERMATOZOON*

Vigorous cytoplasmic movements in mammalian eggs are often accompanied by the escape of cytoplasmic material into the perivitelline area. This material may become separated by the surface movement of the pseudopodia, or escape at the time of the polar body extrusion. It could also be separated at the time of sperm incorporation, and ultimately following cleavage division. This picture shows the surface of the golden hamster egg in which irregular blebs of cytoplasmic material appear above the vitelline membrane. Some of this material is already surrounded by a membrane (arrow), while others apparently are still undelineated. It is assumed that sooner or later all of the loose, unincorporated cytoplasmic material will be surrounded by membranes and form segrosomes.

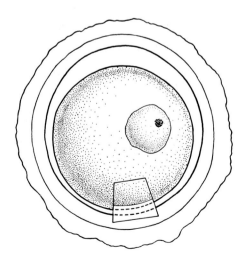

SPECIMEN

III.39. Hamster zygote. Phosphate-buffered 2% glutaraldehyde, postosmicated; Epon 815; uranyl acetate (× 12,000).
CB, cytoplasmic blebs (originating from the egg, lying free in perivitelline area); arrow, escaped cytoplasmic material in perivitelline surrounded by membrane.

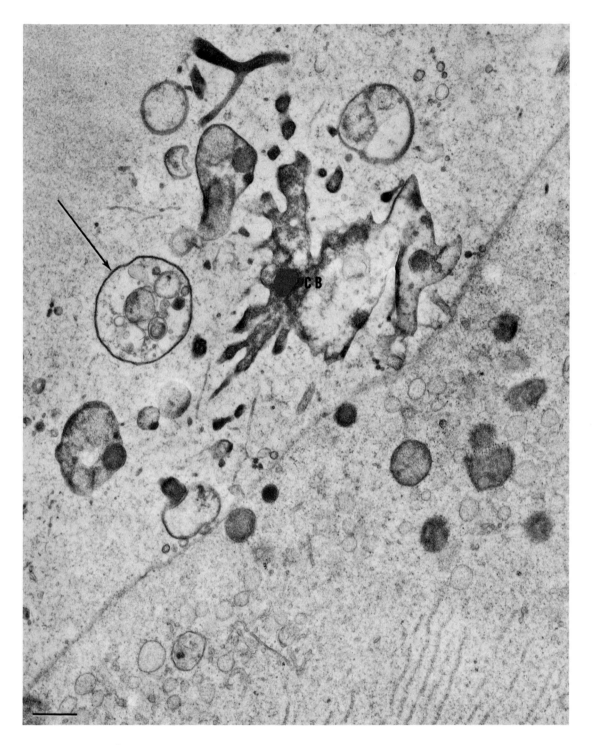

III.39

FIGURE III.40

HAMSTER POLAR BODY AND ZYGOTE

PERIVITELLINE AREA OF HAMSTER ZYGOTE

The first polar body in the rabbit and in the hamster separates from the oocyte at the time of ovulation; the second polar body separates following the penetration of spermatozoon. The polar body shown in the electron micrograph opposite is situated in the perivitelline area between the vitelline membrane and the zona pellucida. It is always surrounded by a cell membrane, which is present also on this occasion. The nuclear mass, as a rule, is well delineated by the nuclear envelope. On occasions, however, there is only an electron-dense mass present within the cytoplasm. In the accompanying picture one may observe mitochondria, a number of smooth membrane vesicles, cortical granules, microsomes, etc. In other instances, however, there are practically no cell organelles present, and the polar body consists mainly of structureless, cytoplasmic material.

In some instances polar bodies have been observed to perform regular cellular functions, that is to say to synthesize DNA, to form pseudopodia or microvilli on their surface; and further, to incorporate material, and to form phagomes. In exceptional circumstances polar bodies undergo a second meiotic division. However, none was observed in this study.

On this picture a hamster first polar body can be observed with a delineated nuclear mass, a profusion of cytoplasmic organelles, mitochondria, and smooth-walled vesicles. In addition, regularly dispersed cortical granules are present in the polar body while only a few are present in the zygote.

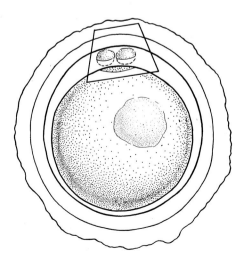

SPECIMEN

III.40. Hamster egg. Veronal acetate-buffered 1% OsO_4; Epon 815; uranyl acetate ($\times$ 8,000). CG, cortical granule(s), P, polar body; VS, vitelline surface or vitelline membrane.

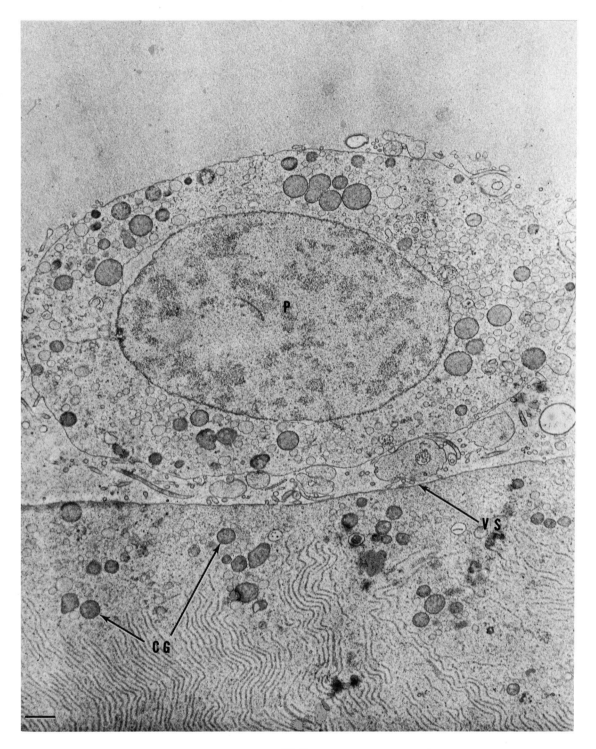

III.40

FIGURE III.41

POLAR BODY IN RABBIT ZYGOTE

PERIVITELLINE AREA OF RABBIT ZYGOTE

This picture shows one whole polar body and part of another. The zygote is situated on the right. There are two membrane-enclosed masses within the polar body, the lower one containing islands of dense material, apparently of nuclear origin. In addition to the nuclear material mitochondria, and smooth-walled vesicles are also present. Cortical granules, still present in the polar body while absent from the zygote, can be observed beneath the cell membrane in a location corresponding to their position in the egg.

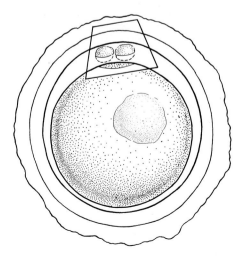

SPECIMEN

III.41. Rabbit zygote. Phosphate-buffered 2% glutaraldehyde, postosmicated; Epon 812; uranyl acetate (× 12,000).
P, polar body; arrow, cytoplasmic enclosure (segrosome?).

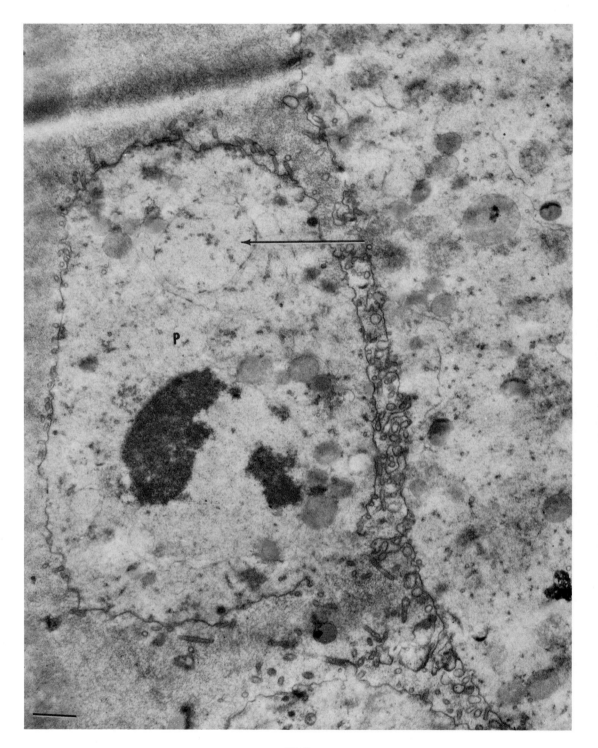

III.41

FIGURE III.42

POLAR BODIES IN RABBIT EGG

TWO POLAR BODIES SITUATED WITHIN THE PERIVITELLINE AREA OF RABBIT ZYGOTE

Visible on this picture are the vitelline membrane, and the polar bodies. It is also evident that the texture of the perivitelline area differs significantly from that of the zona pellucida (in the upper right of the picture). Two nuclei are present in the lower polar body, indicating that a separation of the nuclear mass has taken place, no doubt as the result of the second meiotic division. Consequently, this is the first polar body, and the upper one is the second. Further support is lent to this hypothesis by the presence of a large number of cortical granules in the lower polar body, whereas there are only very few present in the upper one.

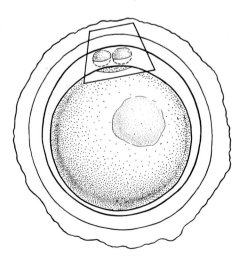

SPECIMEN

III.42. Rabbit zygote 14 hours after ovulation. Veronal acetate-buffered 1% OsO_4; Epon 815; uranyl acetate ($\times$ 8,000).

CG, cortical granule(s); PV, perivitelline area; VS, vitelline surface or vitelline membrane; Z, zona pellucida.

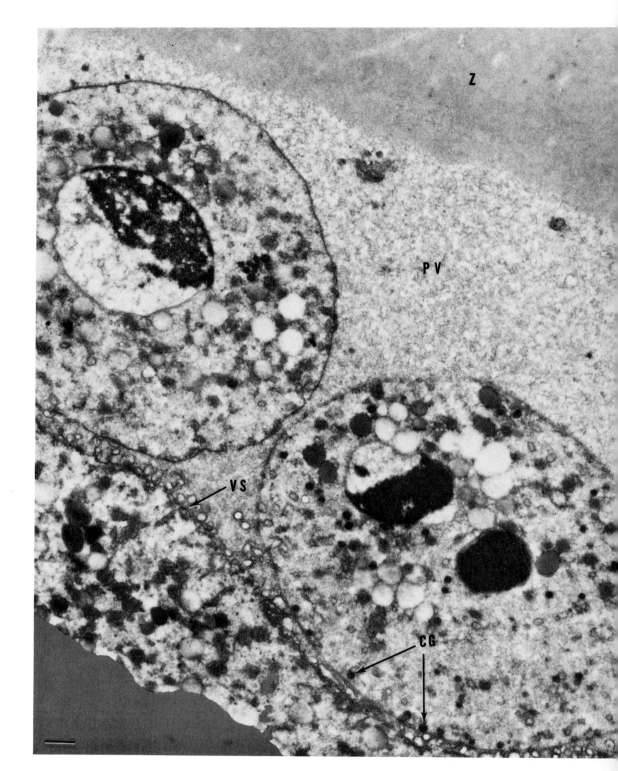

III.42

FIGURES III.43 AND III.44

NUCLEOLUS IN THE RABBIT OOCYTE AT THE TIME OF OVULATION

III. 43.   The nucleus in the freshly shed egg is surrounded by a nuclear envelope in which an inner and an outer element are well discernible. As a rule, a number of nucleoli containing RNP are closely associated with the nuclear envelope. (The karyoplasmal filaments contain the DNA). Golgi complex and annulate lamellae are in the juxtanuclear area of the newly shed egg.

III. 44.   Nucleolus at the nuclear membrane. The Golgi complex occupies practically the whole juxtanuclear area. Mitochondria are also present. They have dense lumen and peripheral cristae.

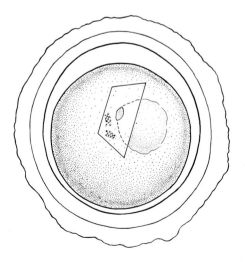

SPECIMENS

III.43. Rabbit egg; veronal acetate-buffered 1% OsO$_4$; Epon 812; uranyl acetate ($\times$ 30,000).

III.44. Rabbit egg; veronal acetate-buffered 1% OsO$_4$; Epon 812; uranyl acetate ($\times$ 22,000).

AN, annulate lamellae; G, Golgi complex; NO, nucleolus.

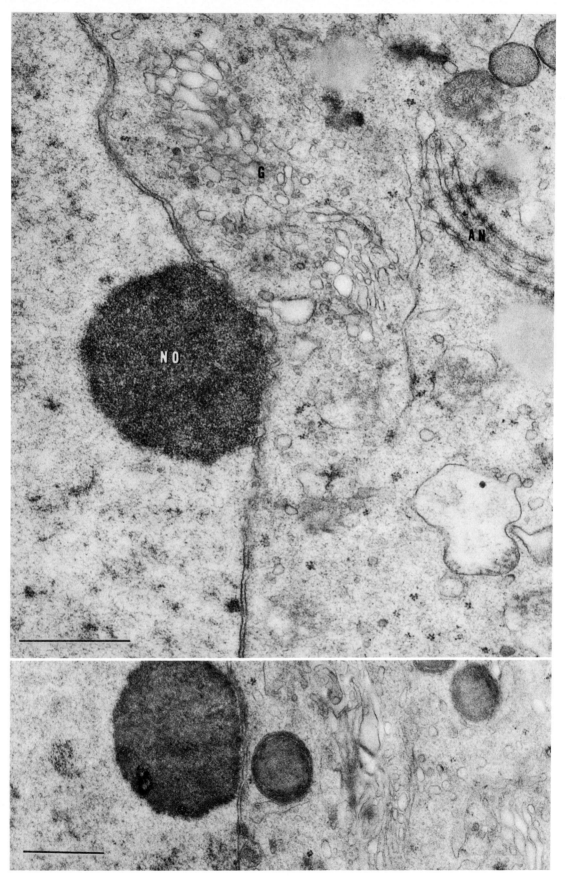

III.43 (↑) III.44 (↓)

FIGURE III.45

FEMALE PRONUCLEUS IN HAMSTER EGG

Hamster oocyte nucleus shortly after penetration of the spermatozoon; nucleus is almost completely round and is surrounded by a distinct nuclear membrane. In the center there is one major nucleolus, which is well delineated from the surrounding karyoplasm. In addition, two nucleoli of dense chromatin material are visible. Mitochondria and smooth channels in juxtanuclear region.

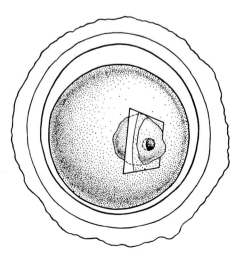

SPECIMEN

III.45. Hamster egg (zygote). Phosphate-buffered 2% glutaraldehyde; Epon 815; uranyl acetate (× 10,000).
NO, nucleolus.

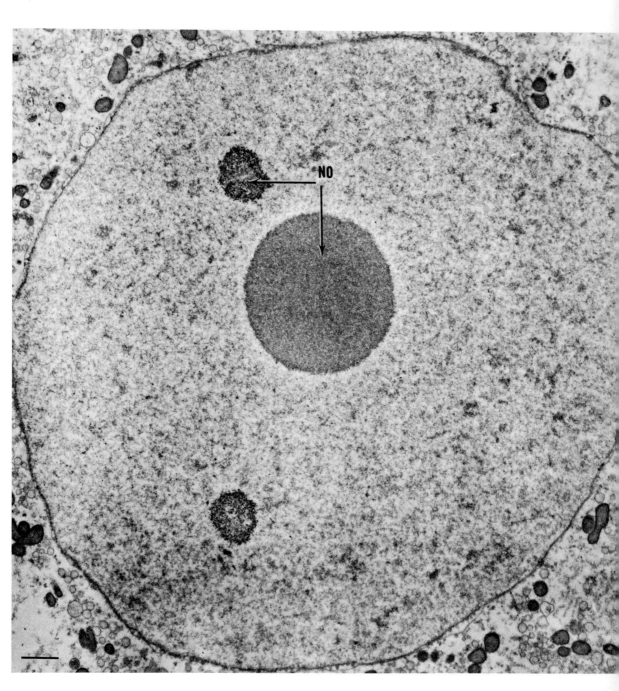

NO

III.45

FIGURE III.46

MALE AND FEMALE PRONUCLEUS IN HAMSTER EGG

Female pronucleus and a smaller nuclear mass are visible in this picture. Both of them show irregular outline. In the pronucleus, one major nucleolus and seven smaller nucleoli are visible. Only two nucleoli are visible in the second nuclear mass, which is considerably smaller in size. In the vicinity of the pronucleus, mitochondria and some cytoplasmic strands (to be discussed in greater detail later) are visible.

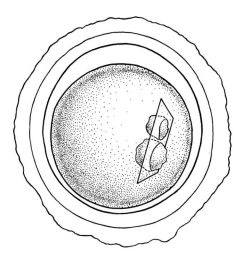

SPECIMEN

III.46. Hamster egg. Veronal acetate-buffered 1% OsO_4; Epon 812; uranyl acetate ($\times$ 4,000). CS, cytoplasmic strands; PN, pronucleus.

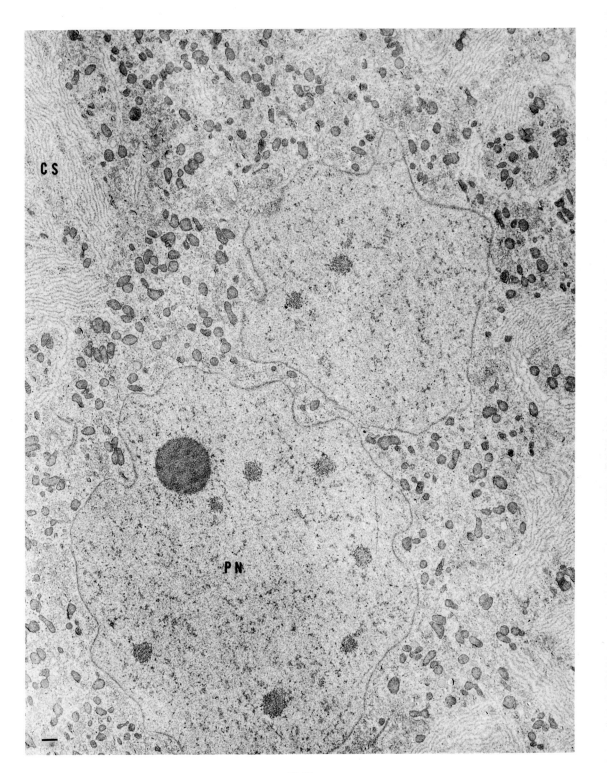

III.46

FIGURES III.47–III.49

ANNULATE LAMELLAE IN RABBIT AND HAMSTER EGG

The similarity between the three pictures is the presence of annulate lamellae. These are composed of flat cisternae in which one can observe the accumulation of periodically repeating densities filling the space between the two opposing membranes.

Considering that in the mammalian egg at the time of ovulation no cytoplasmic RNP is observed with the electron microscope—a result contradicted by light microscopic observations—one wonders whether the densities accumulating on the annulate lamellae could be RNP particles and the annulate lamellae a replacement for the rough ER. The rest of the ribosomes assumedly are accumulated in nonactive form in round, single membrane-bound structures.

Annulate lamellae originate from the nuclear membrane and gradually move away from the nucleus. As a rule, one may observe several stacks in the cytoplasm. Subsequently they disintegrate into small tubular elements.

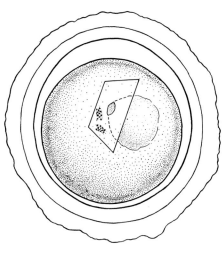

SPECIMENS

III.47. Rabbit egg. Veronal acetate-buffered 1% OsO$_4$; Epon 812; uranyl acetate ($\times$ 22,000).

III.48. Rabbit egg. Veronal acetate-buffered 1% OsO$_4$; Epon 812; uranyl acetate ($\times$ 12,000).

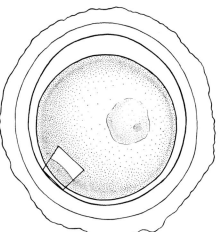

III.49. Hamster egg. Veronal acetate-buffered 1% OsO$_4$; Epon 812; uranyl acetate ($\times$ 15,000).

AN, annulate lamellae; M, mitochondria.

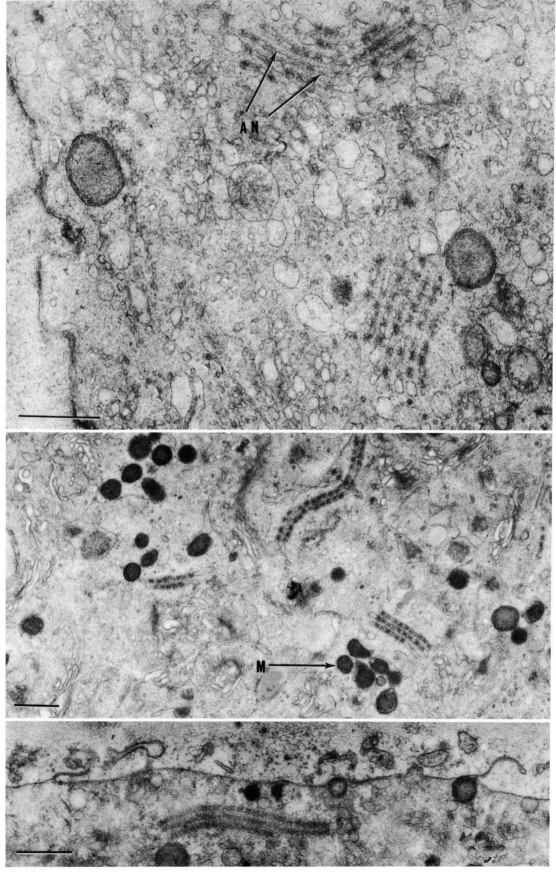

III.47 (↑)   III.48 (↔)   III.49 (↓)

FIGURES III.50 AND III.51

METAPLASIA OF MITOCHONDRIA AND GRANULAR BODIES

ENDOPLASM IN PERINUCLEAR AREA OF FERTILIZED RABBIT EGG

The upper picture shows four mitochondria. In two of them, secondary enclosures are forming within the mitochondrial lumen, while in two others irregular densities appear. It is plausible that through enzyme accumulation accompanied by changes in mitochondrial ultrastructure, not only the mitochondrial morphology but also its function may change, thus, forming lysosomes and microbodies at a time when the cell needs them to a far greater extent than functioning mitochondria.

Below. The life of annulate lamellae is restricted to a comparatively short period of the gamete's life. Another depository of RNP material may be the round bodies that contain granular material. These round structures were not observed in the process of being utilized. They were rather stable in appearance and content unless fertilization took place. Then their content has disappeared into the cytoplasm of the egg. With regard to their function, they could represent RNP particles (in an inactive form), since no rough endoplasmic reticulum is present in the egg around the time of ovulation.

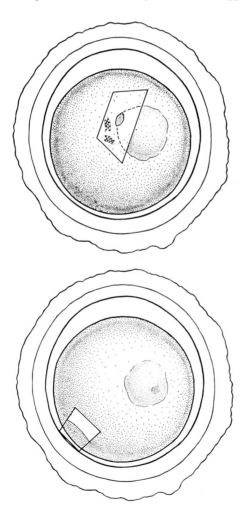

SPECIMEN

III.50, III.51. Rabbit egg 20 hours after mating. Veronal acetate-buffered 1% OsO_4; Epon 815; uranyl acetate ($\times$ 32,000).

N, nucleus; RO, round bodies (containing granular material: assumedly inactive RNA).

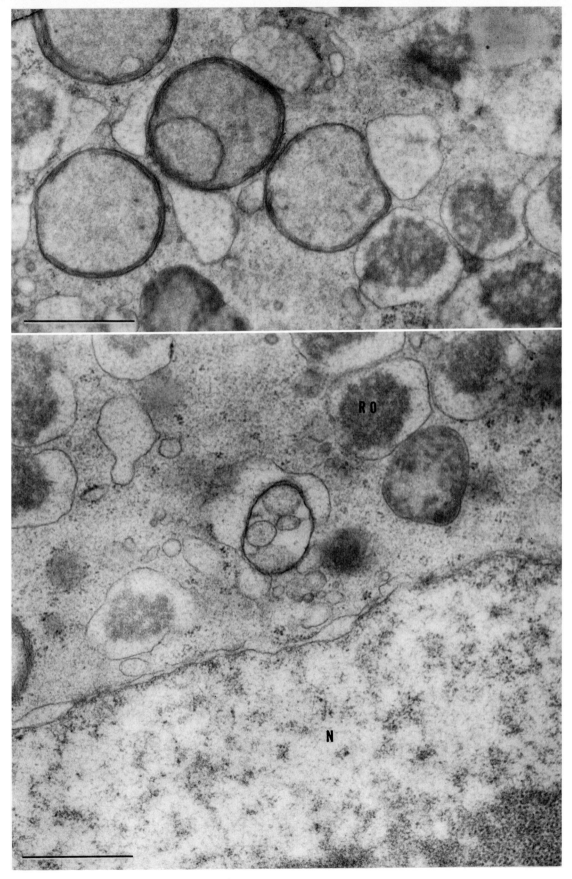

III.50 (↑)   III.51 (↓)

FIGURE III.52

GOLGI COMPLEX IN RABBIT OOCYTE

RABBIT EGG RELEASED FROM VESICULAR FOLLICLE ASSUMEDLY SHORTLY BEFORE OVULATION

In this picture one may see the nuclear envelope and the Golgi complex in juxtanuclear position. The outer elements of the Golgi complex are large-size vesicles. In the vicinity of the nucleus, two types of cytoplasmic bodies are visible. One is a denser type with darker peripheral outline, the other is a lighter. The denser type of cytoplasmic bodies in most instances are either mitochondria, in which after careful consideration one can observe the cristae, or lysosomes, or possibly microbodies. The lighter ones are either yolk bodies or bodies containing inactive RNA. Compare the Golgi complex in this specimen with that visible on Fig. III.55. Increase in the size of the Golgi complex appears to be related to the lapse of time since ovulation.

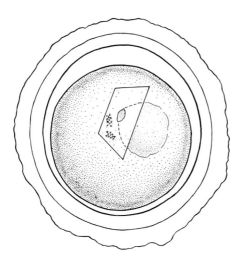

SPECIMEN

III.52. Follicular rabbit oocyte. Veronal acetate-buffered 1% OsO_4; Epon 812; uranyl acetate ($\times$ 22,000).
G, Golgi complex; N, nucleus.

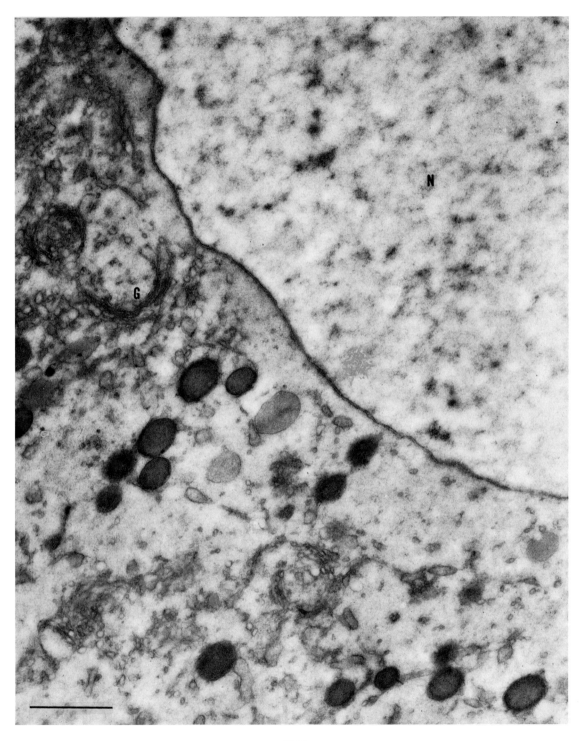

III.52

FIGURE III.53

CORTICAL VESICULAR AGGREGATES IN RABBIT EGG

Shortly after ovulation, accumulations of smooth-walled, cytoplasmic vesiculae appear in the periphery of the rabbit egg. Thus, besides the centrally placed Golgi complex, peripheral accumulations of vesicular structures are also taking place. These could be derived from smooth endoplasmic reticulum since elements of the Golgi complex, as a rule, cannot be observed at the border of the cell. In this picture of an unfertilized egg, there is a cortical accumulation of smooth-walled vesicular foci quite close to the vitelline membrane. Some of the larger, outer elements appear to show continuity with pinocytotic vesicles. In addition, cortical granules, mitochondria, possibly lysosomes and also some bodies containing inactive RNA can be observed.

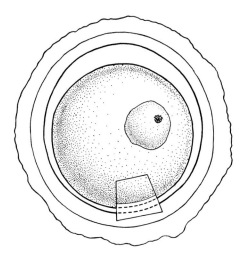

SPECIMEN

III.53. Rabbit egg. Veronal acetate-buffered 1% OsO₄; Epon 812; uranyl acetate ($\times$ 22,000).

M, mitochondria; RO, round bodies (containing granular material: assumedly inactive RNA); VC, vesicular cytoplasmic aggregate; VS, vitelline surface or vitelline membrane.

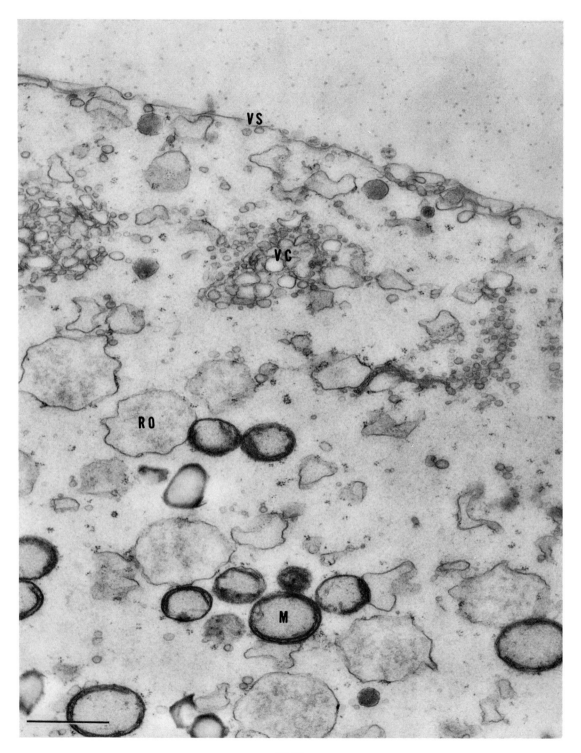

III.53

FIGURE III.54

CORTICAL VESICULAR AGGREGATES (1)

CYTOPLASM OF FERRET EGG

Aggregates of smooth-walled vesicles appear in the vicinity of the yolk bodies. Some of the vesicles seem to penetrate into the outer layer of the yolk, indicating the possibility of its utilization by the egg.

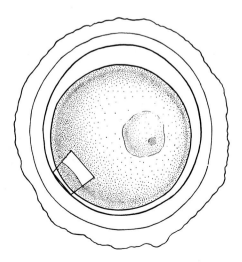

SPECIMEN

III.54. Freshly ovulated ferret egg: Veronal acetate-buffered 1% OsO$_4$; Epon 812; uranyl acetate ($\times$ 22,000).
VC, vesicular cytoplasmic aggregate; Y, yolk bodies.

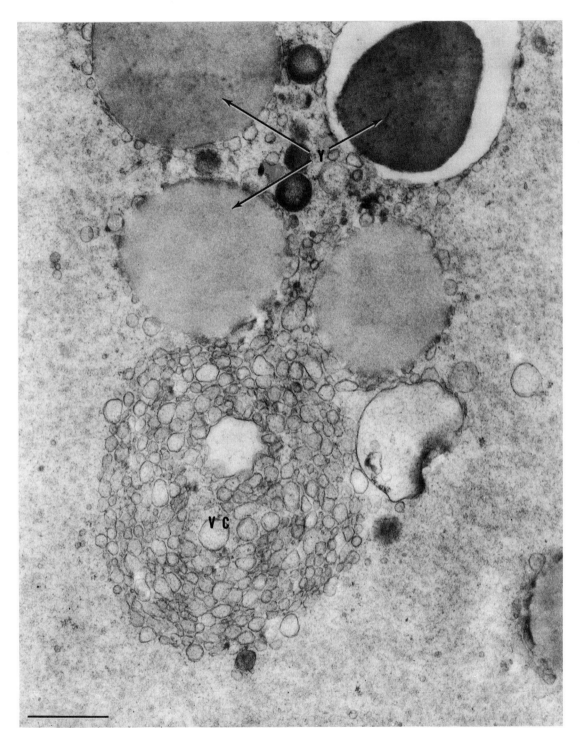

III.54

FIGURE III.55

CORTICAL VESICULAR AGGREGATES (2)

ECTOPLASM IN THE FERRET EGG

Vesicular aggregates may occur in different sizes and complexity, also within the same species. Their structure—complexity—may be related to the length of the postovulatory life of the egg. In the ferret such aggregates are often in the vicinity of yolk corpuscles, indicating a relation to their metabolism.

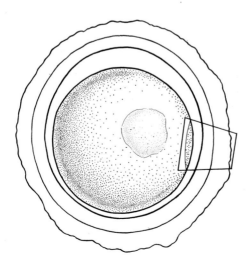

SPECIMEN

III.55. Ferret egg: Veronal acetate-buffered 1% OsO_4; Epon 812; uranyl acetate ($\times$ 22,000).

VC, vesicular cytoplasmic aggregate; Y, yolk bodies.

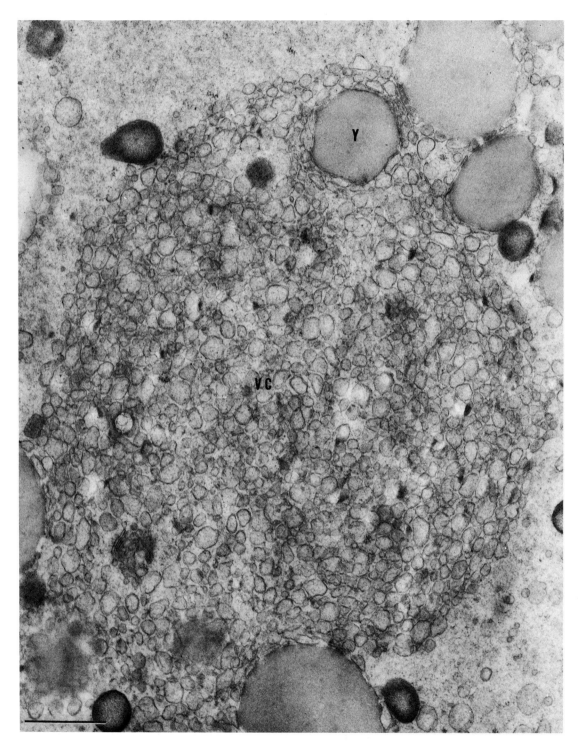

III.55

FIGURE III.56

CORTICAL VESICULAR AGGREGATES IN UNFERTILIZED RABBIT EGG (1)

Cortical vesicular aggregates have been observed in the eggs of all the species investigated. In addition to the rather inconspicuous loci shown in a previous illustration (III.54), hypertrophied areas could also be observed in some of the rabbit eggs. This electron micrograph shows such an aggregate in the cortex of the unfertilized rabbit egg.

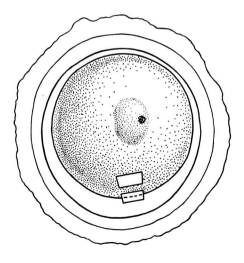

SPECIMEN

III.56. Rabbit egg 30 hours after mating. Veronal acetate-buffered 1% OsO_4; Epon 815; uranyl acetate ($\times$ 30,000).
PV, perivitelline area; VC, vesicular cytoplasmic aggregate; Z, zona pellucida.

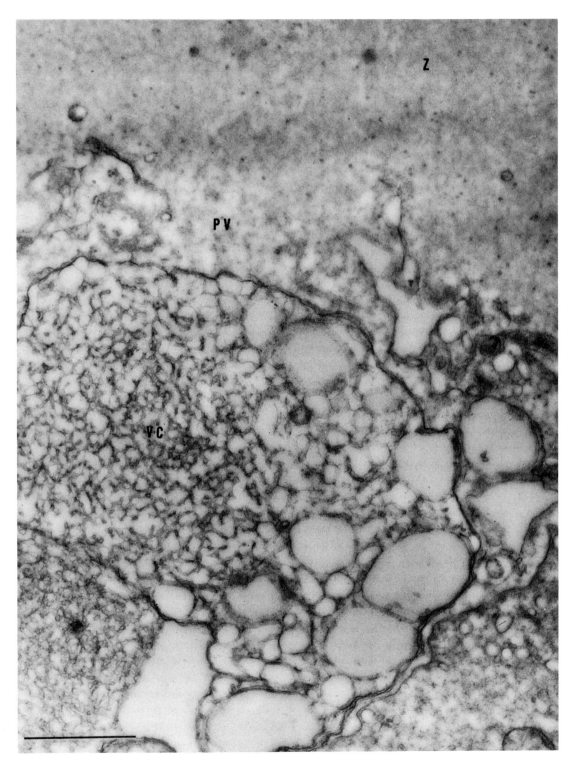

III.56

FIGURE III.57

CORTICAL VESICULAR AGGREGATES IN UNFERTILIZED RABBIT EGG (2)

Under certain conditions, vesicular aggregates in the cortex of unfertilized rabbit egg appear to assume a separate growth of their own.

Vesicular aggregates may enclose comparatively large areas of the cytoplasm, possibly representing a use of the vitellus in order to prolong the egg's existence. It is rather difficult to interpret the morphology of such structures. However, it appears that following the primary groupings, secondary membranous associations take place until it is impossible to determine which was the primary structure.

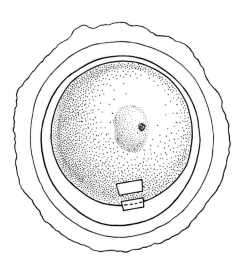

SPECIMEN

III.57. Rabbit egg 34 hours after mating. Veronal acetate-buffered 1% OsO$_4$; Epon 815; uranyl acetate ($\times$ 44,000).

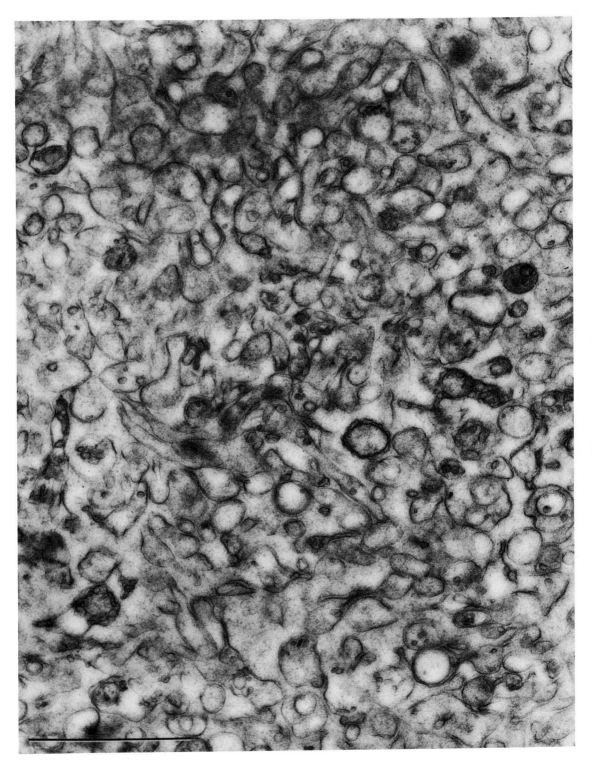

III.57

FIGURE III.58

MITOCHONDRIA IN CORTEX OF RABBIT EGG

CORTEX OF EGG DURING SMOOTH PERIOD

The possibility that mitochondria are labile cell organelles which on occasion may assume a variety of shapes and structures should be borne in mind.

In the egg of the rabbit, mitochondria at the time of ovulation appear circular, cristae tightly lying on the mitochondrial membrane. In addition, on the strength of various observations, the possibility of mitochondrial metaplasia—the ability of the mitochondria to form other cell organelles—also appears plausible, at least in the mammalian egg. Admittedly, the structures are always closely related, e.g., lysosomes and microbodies, both circular and like the mitochondria showing high acid phosphatase content. As the accompanying electron micrograph demonstrates, as a rule the mitochondrial lumen accumulates dense filling. Thereafter, if no fertilization takes place, the mitochondria apparently may become a lysosome or a microbody. On the other hand, in fertilized eggs, its morphology reverts to the customary appearance (e.g., elongated with cristae pointing into the lumen). This picture shows a comparatively large number of mitochondria; also, empty smooth-walled vesicles, and some granular bodies.

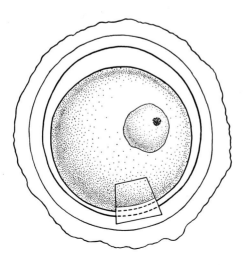

SPECIMEN

III.58. Rabbit egg approximately 3 hours after ovulation. Veronal acetate-buffered 1% OsO_4; Epon 815; uranyl acetate ($\times$ 22,000).

M, mitochondria; RO, round bodies (containing granular material: assumedly inactive RNA).

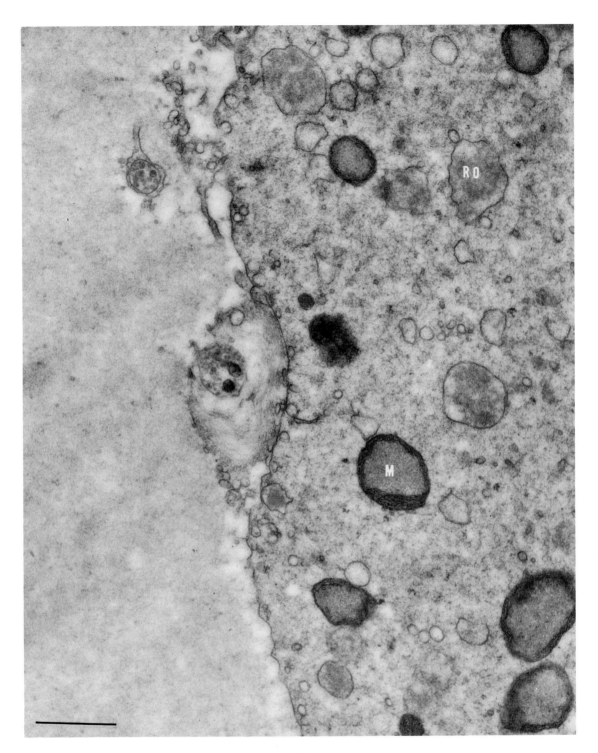

III.58

FIGURE III.59

MITOCHONDRIA IN ECTOPLASM, FERRET EGG

CORTEX OF EGG OBTAINED FROM THE VESICULAR FOLLICLE OF THE FERRET

In the egg of the rabbit, mitochondria at the time of ovulation appear circular, cristae tightly lying on the mitochondrial membrane. In the ferret egg, the majority of mitochondria appear in the transitory stage, indicative of mitochondrial budding, e.g., hourglass and dumbbell shapes. In addition, one also can observe lipid type yolk characterized by irregularly shaped dense bodies surrounded by a number of small, smooth tubules.

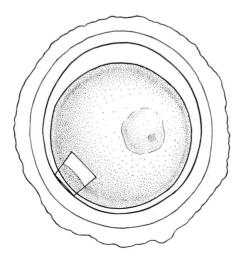

SPECIMEN

III.59. Ferret egg from vesicular follicle. Veronal acetate buffered 1% OsO_4; Epon 812; uranyl acetate ($\times$ 22,000).
M, mitochondria; MB, microbodies.

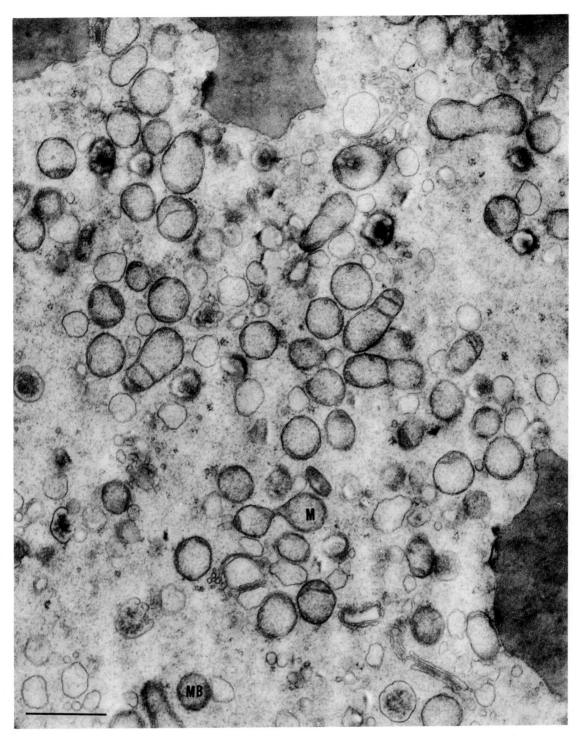

III.59

FIGURE III.60

CHANGING MITOCHONDRIAL STRUCTURE IN RABBIT ZYGOTE

In the rabbit egg following penetration of the sperm, there is a gradual reestablishment of the mitochondrial structure toward the more familiar morphology observed in somatic cells.

It is evident from these pictures that the cristae are gradually beginning to project again into the lumen of the mitochondria. This return to the usually observed morphology occurs parallel with the gradual disappearance of granular material from the irregularly circular cytoplasmic bodies (inactive RNA?).

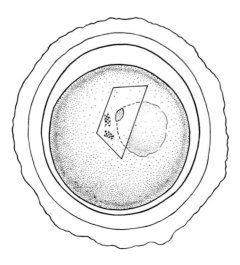

SPECIMEN

III.60. Rabbit zygote. Veronal acetate-buffered 1% OsO_4; Epon 815; uranyl acetate ($\times$ 24,000).

M, mitochondria; RO, round bodies (containing granular material: assumedly inactive RNA).

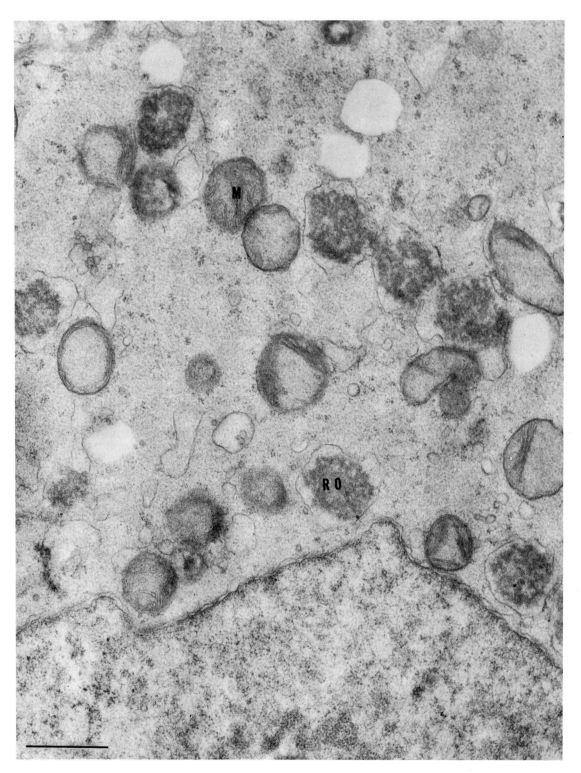

III.60

FIGURE III.61

CORTICAL GRANULES AND THEIR ORIGIN

CORTEX OF HAMSTER EGG

The name "cortical granule" has been associated with small, round electron-dense bodies which are almost identical in size and situated beneath the vitelline membrane at the cortex of the egg. They are doubly refractile in unfixed preparations (Austin, 1961), and in the unfertilized egg they are almost equidistant from one another. In this electron micrograph only two of the round structures are cortical granules, the other two (arrow) apparently are on their way to their location and probably will undergo some changes yet (become smaller and denser).

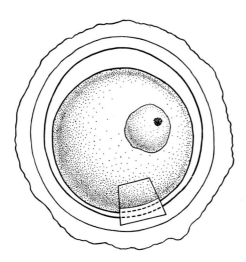

SPECIMEN

III.61. Freshly ovulated hamster egg. Veronal acetate-buffered 1% OsO_4; Epon 815; uranyl acetate ($\times$ 22,000).

CG, cortical granule(s); arrow, cortical granules, round structures which assumedly will become cortical bodies.

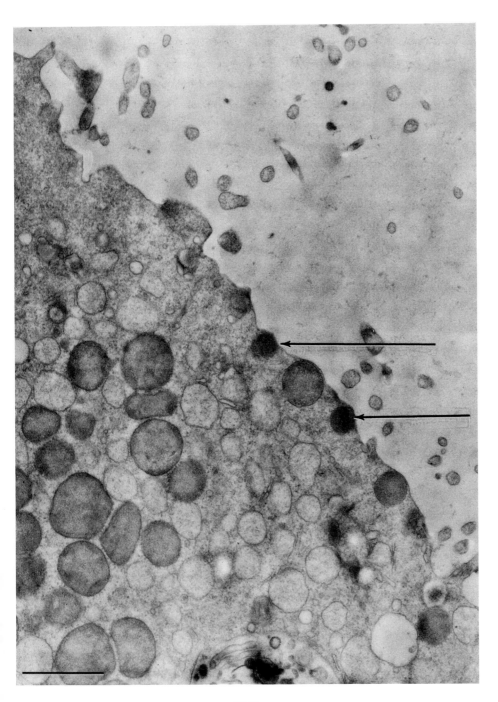

III.61

FIGURE III.62

CORTICAL GRANULES AND THEIR ORIGIN

JUXTANUCLEAR AREA IN RABBIT EGG

Cortical granules are originating from the Golgi area by gradual detachment of small, dense bodies. The circular bodies at the time of their formation assumedly already show the morphological characteristics of cortical granules: e.g., single membrane cover, dense filling, size, etc.

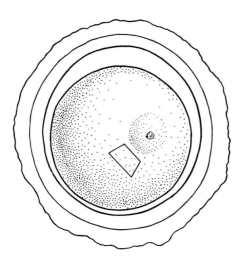

SPECIMEN

III.62. Unfertilized rabbit egg 16 hours after ovulation. Veronal acetate-buffered 1% OsO₄; Epon 815, uranyl acetate (× 22,000). Arrow, cortical granule.

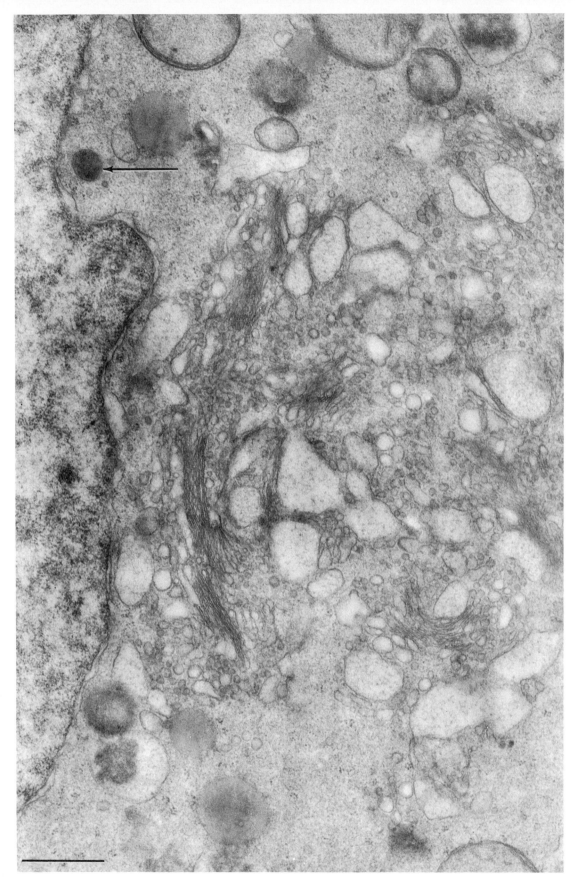

III.62

FIGURE III.63

CELLULAR ORGANELLES IN CORTEX OF HAMSTER EGG

CORTICAL AREA IN UNFERTILIZED EGG

It has been shown that in the early postovulatory period, pseudopodialike processes are projecting from the oocyte surface. Later they are replaced by microvilli, which in the unfertilized egg become similar in size.

In this typical hamster egg, pseudopodia are present in addition to a large number of pinocytotic vesicles, which is characteristic of an active egg immediately after ovulation. In addition, one can observe the beginning accumulation of cortical granules, which itself is indicative of the postovulatory age of the ovum. As a rule, their location is immediately below the vitelline membrane, which enables one to recognize them easily. They are round, almost identical in size, and the increase in their number bears a relationship to the age of the egg. Also, large numbers of very dark microbodies are evident in the cytoplasm of this oocyte. Apparently unconnected fibrils can be also observed in the cytoplasm, which could represent remnants of spindle fibers from the first meiotic division.

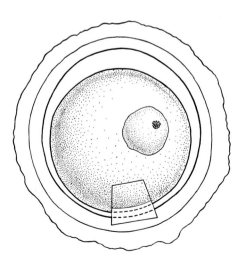

SPECIMEN

III.63. Hamster egg. Veronal acetate-buffered 1% OsO$_4$; Epon 812; uranyl acetate ($\times$ 22,000).
CG, cortical granule(s); MB, microbodies; arrow, pinocytotic vesicle.

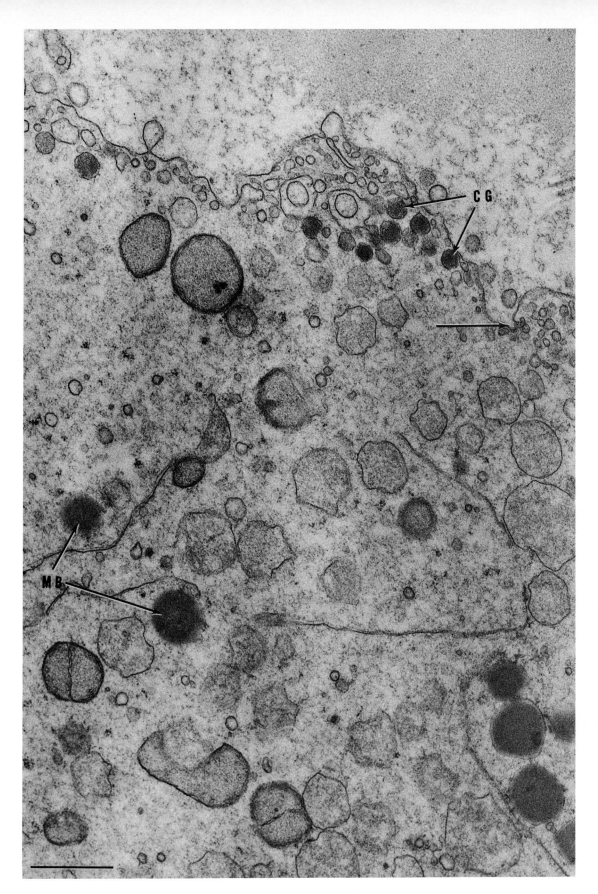

III.63

FIGURE III.64

HISTOCHEMICAL REACTION IN CORTICAL GRANULES

TRANSVERSE SECTION OF RABBIT EGG TOWARD POLE

    In an effort to establish the possible nature of the cortical granules, a histochemical test for the presence of acid phosphatase was performed on unfertilized eggs. As it is evident from the opposite picture, cortical granules show a strong acid phosphatase reaction.

    A much lower intensity is observable in the mitochondria and other organelles in the oocyte. In this rabbit oocyte, cortical granules are accumulated on the periphery of the egg. The densities in the perivitelline area are mostly artifacts.

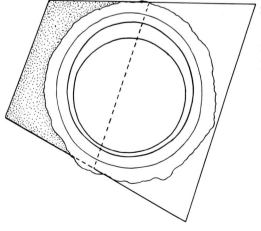

SPECIMEN

III.64. Rabbit egg. Gomori acid phosphatase; 2% glutaraldehyde; postosmicated; Epon 812 ($\times$ 4,000).
M, mitochondria.

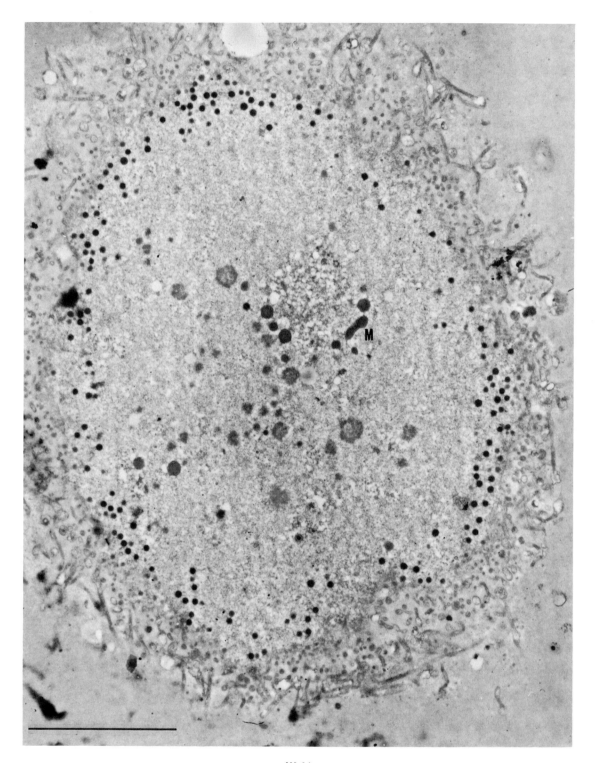

III.64

FIGURE III.65

ACID PHOSPHATASE REACTING ELEMENTS IN MAMMALIAN EGG

A QUADRANT OF AN UNFERTILIZED RABBIT EGG

Cortical granules in the periphery are reacting with an almost even intensity. The acid phosphatase-containing elements within the vitellus are mitochondria and microbodies.

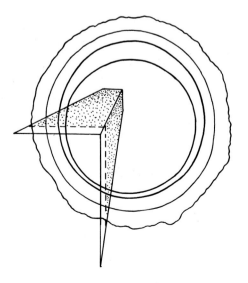

SPECIMEN

III.65. Rabbit egg. Gomori acid phosphatase; glutaraldehyde; postosmicated; Epon 812 (× 12,000).

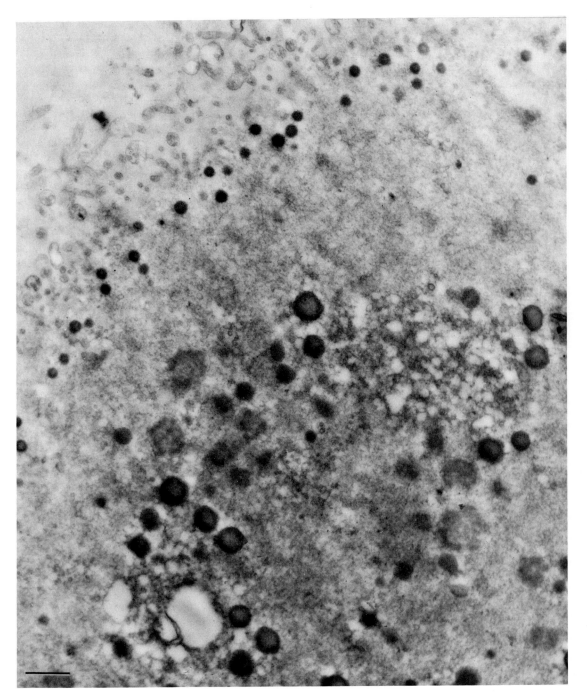

III.65

FIGURE III.66

CORTICAL GRANULES IN THE PERIVITELLINE AREA

CORTEX OF RABBIT EGGS

During fertilization, or due to cortical movements, or to aging, cortical granules may become displaced in the perivitelline area. However, as a rule, they always remain closely associated with the vitelline surface. Certain authors have claimed that the function of the cortical granules may be the reparation of the vitelline membrane defects, which occur when the spermatozoon penetrates the egg.

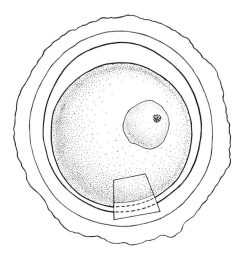

SPECIMEN

III.66. Rabbit egg. Veronal acetate-buffered 1% OsO$_4$; Epon 812; uranyl acetate ($\times$ 30,000).

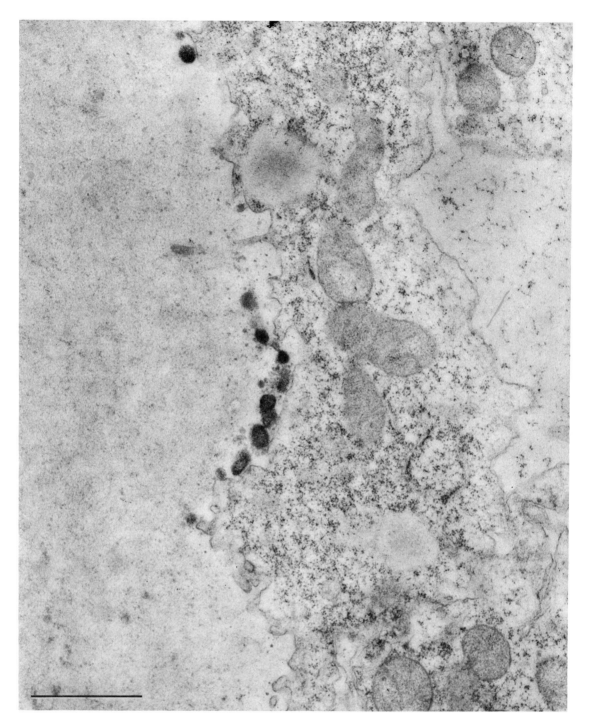

III.66

FIGURES III.67 AND III.68

FOREIGN BODY DELINEATION ON THE SURFACE OF THE EGG

PERIVITELLINE AREA OF FRESHLY OVULATED HAMSTER EGG

Material which finds its way through the zona pellucida and becomes lodged in the perivitelline area apparently is either incorporated or segregated.

These pictures illustrate the type of extracellular cytoplasmic segrosomes which can be observed in the perivitelline area of the hamster egg. Figure III.69 represents a membrane-bound, cortical enclosure in which smooth vesicles and oval profiles are visible. They could be granulosa cell processes which were not retracted and subsequently were surrounded by the vitelline membrane.

Figure III.70 represents segrosome formation at an advanced stage. In this particular case only a couple of granulosa cell processes are observable in the vicinity of the extra cytoplasmic bodies. Apparently, the material left behind is first surrounded by membranous whorls, and subsequently enclosed by the cell membrane.

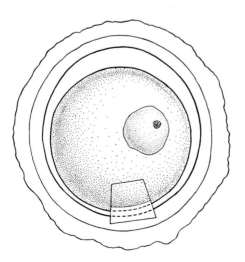

SPECIMEN

III.67, III.68. Hamster egg. Veronal acetate-buffered 1% OsO$_4$; Epon 812; uranyl acetate ($\times$ 22,000).

VS, vitelline surface or vitelline membrane.

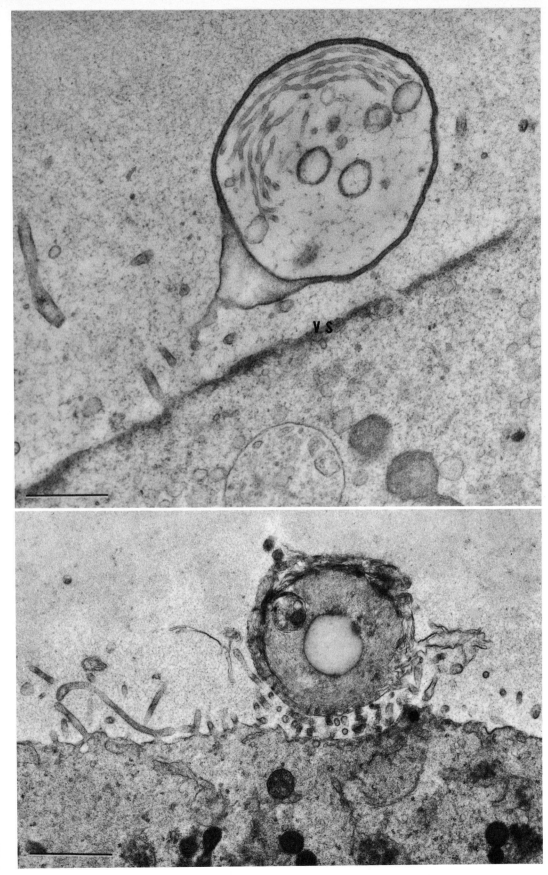

V S

III.67 (↑)   III.68 (↓)

FIGURES III.69 AND III.70

THE FORMATION OF EXTRACELLULAR SEGROSOME IN THE PERIVITELLINE AREA OF THE RABBIT EGG

CORTICAL AREAS OF FRESHLY SHED, AS YET UNFERTILIZED, RABBIT OVA

In the process of segrosome formation it is usually a lysosome or a multivesicular body which is first associated with a foreign body that is on the surface of the egg. This subsequently is surrounded by thin membranes, originating from the vitelline surface, which segregate the foreign body.

In Figure III.69 the multivesicular body is being surrounded by the membranes.

In Figure III.70 membranes and cytoplasmic processes are surrounding an already segregated focus.

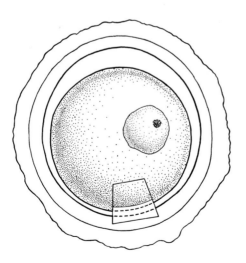

SPECIMEN

III.69, III.70. Rabbit egg. Veronal acetate-buffered 1% OsO₄; Epon 812; uranyl acetate (× 22,000).

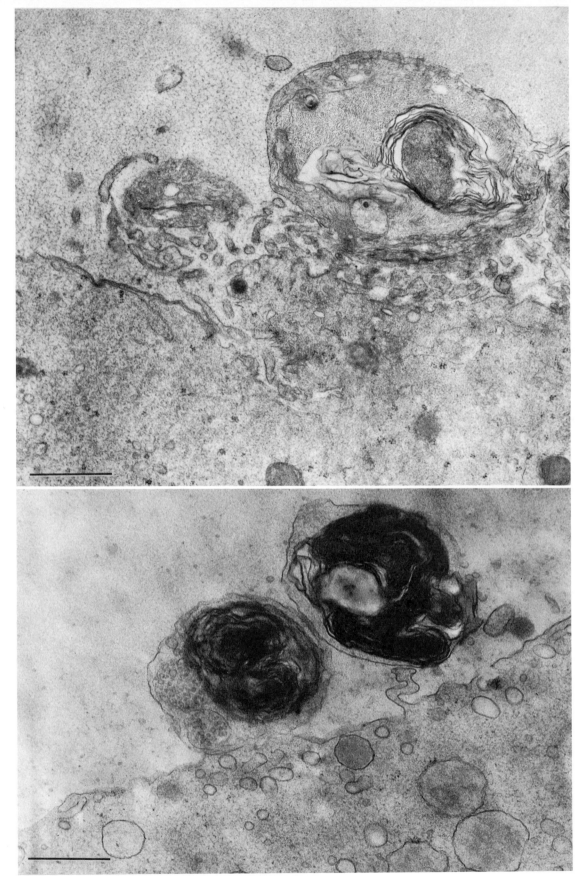

III.69 (↑)   III.70 (↓)

FIGURE III.71

YOLK IN THE MAMMALIAN EGG

CYTOPLASM OF RABBIT EGG SHORTLY AFTER OVULATION

Potassium permanganate (K_2MnO_4) fixation mostly affects membranous organelles within the cell. In this particular picture, in addition to mitochondria and microbodies, lipid bodies are also present. They are characterized by irregular outline and great variations in size. The latter often shows a dense periphery and an empty lumen from which the material has apparently been dissolved. There are also observable a number of dense, mostly round structures, the microbodies.

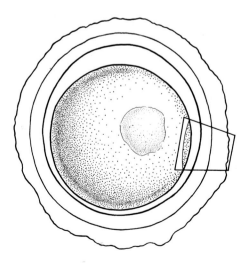

SPECIMEN

III.71. Rabbit egg $16\frac{1}{2}$ hours after mating. K_2MnO_4 fixation; Epon 812 ($\times$ 16,000). LP, lipid bodies (yolk); M, mitochondria; MB, microbodies.

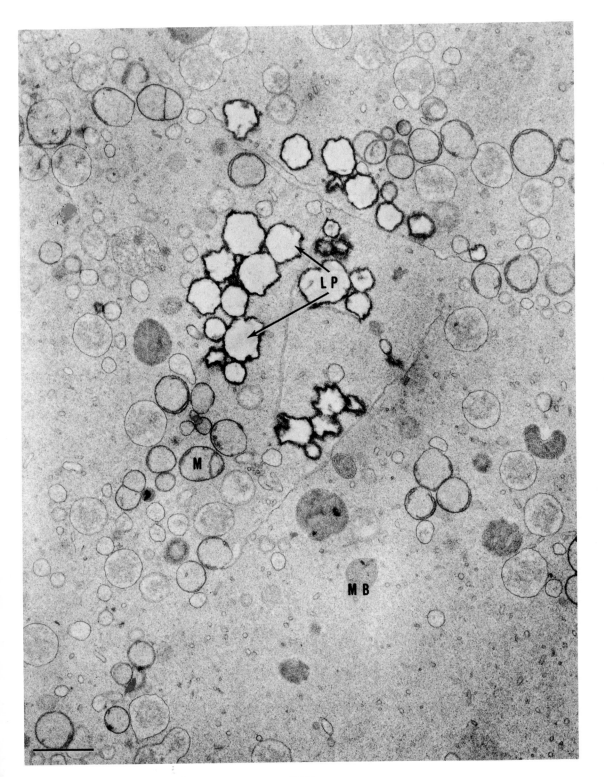

III.71

FIGURE III.72

YOLK IN MAMMALIAN EGG

ECTOPLASM OF FRESHLY OVULATED FERRET EGG

These circular yolk bodies in the ectoplasm of freshly ovulated ferret egg assumedly represent lipid and protein. In addition to showing the apparent skeleton, membrane whorl, they also show the possible method of its utilization. In this particular picture the yolk bodies appear to have whorllike skeletons around which the material has accumulated. These structures are delineated by single smooth membranes, and outside of this smooth vesicles are present, occupying depressions on the surface possibly responsible for their utilization.

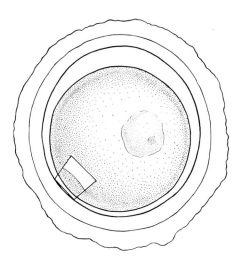

SPECIMEN

III.72. Freshly ovulated ferret egg. Veronal acetate-buffered 1% OsO_4; Epon 815; uranyl acetate ($\times$ 22,000).

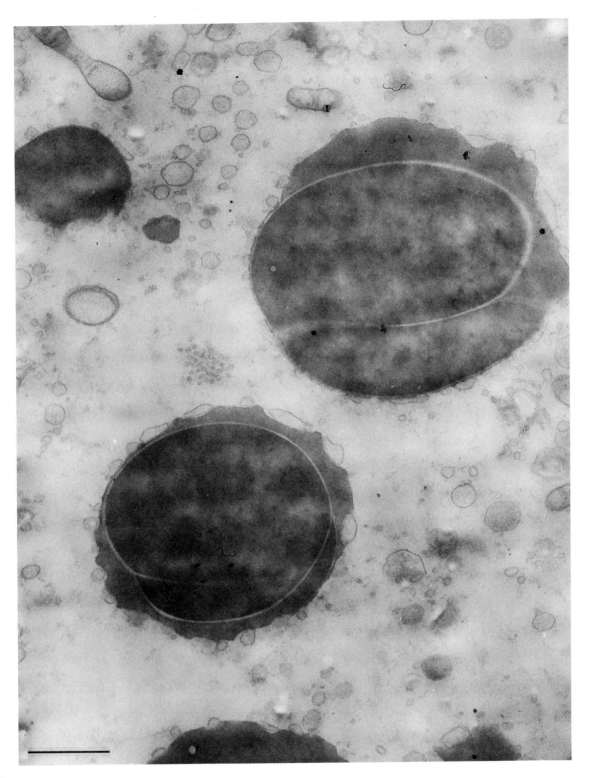

III.72

FIGURE III.73

YOLK BODIES IN RABBIT EGG

CYTOPLASM OF RABBIT EGG

Amorphous dark bodies possibly containing glycolipid are often observed in the rabbit egg. They are surrounded by a smooth membrane, and small channels are found in indentations on their surface.

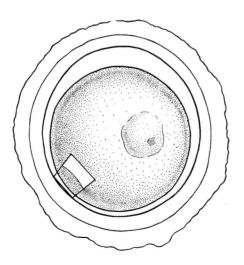

SPECIMEN

III.73. Rabbit egg 8 hours after ovulation. Veronal acetate-buffered 1% OsO_4; Epon 812; uranyl acetate ($\times$ 24,000).

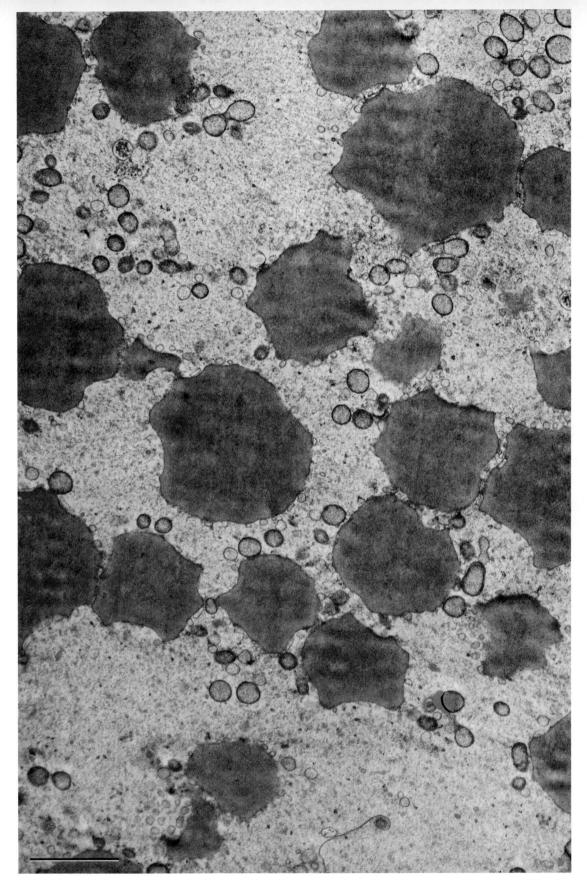

III.73

FIGURE III.74

YOLK IN MAMMALIAN EGG

ECTOPLASM OF FERRET EGG

The most frequently encountered yolk bodies in the unfertilized ferret egg are the apparently structureless, diffuse, lipid enclosures. They may occur in a variety of sizes and shapes and are characterized by moderate density. They are surrounded by smooth membrane channels, which could be the cytoplasmic mechanism for metabolizing the lipid.

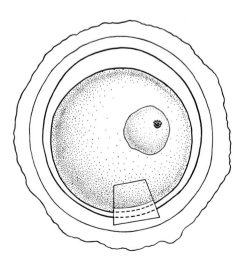

SPECIMEN

III.74. Freshly ovulated ferret egg. Veronal acetate-buffered 1% OsO₄; Epon 815; uranyl acetate (× 33,000).

VS, vitelline surface or vitelline membrane; Y, yolk bodies.

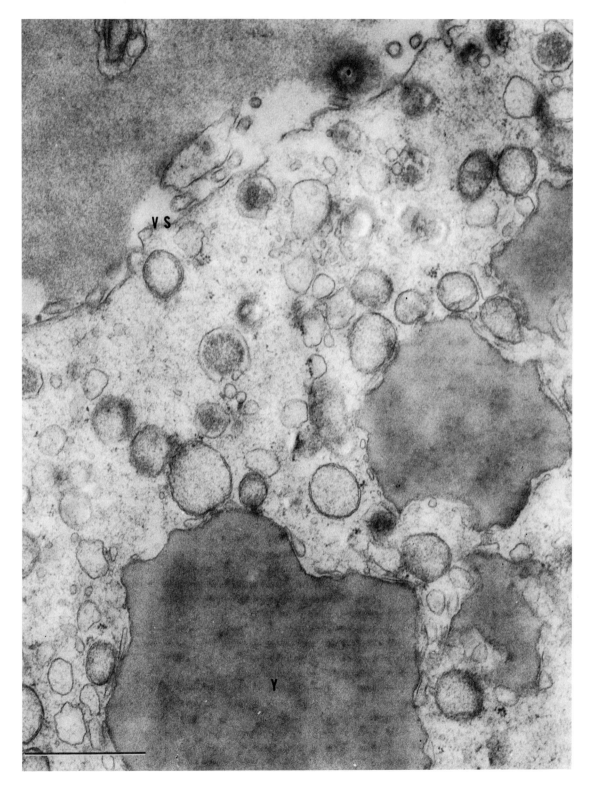

III.74

FIGURE III.75

DISSOCIATING MAMMALIAN YOLK BODIES

CYTOPLASM OF THE PENETRATED RABBIT EGG

One of the structures whose function defied definition were the cytoplasmic membranes (arrow) that were encountered with some regularity in eggs which have been penetrated by the spermatozoon. They always appeared irregular in shape and location. There were two characteristics associated with them: (1) a scroll-like twist on their free end, and (2) occasional remnants of lipid droplets. One solution would be the assumption that they are the remnants of the smooth-walled lipid bodies. Following the disappearance of the lipid, the enclosing wall probably opens, and the limiting membrane would come to lie free within the cytoplasm of the egg. Or they could be remnants of spindle fibers.

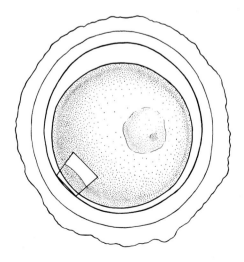

SPECIMEN

III.75. Rabbit zygote 14 hours after ovulation. Veronal acetate-buffered 1% OsO₄; Epon 812; uranyl acetate (× 26,000).
Y, yolk bodies; arrow, free cytoplasmic membrane.

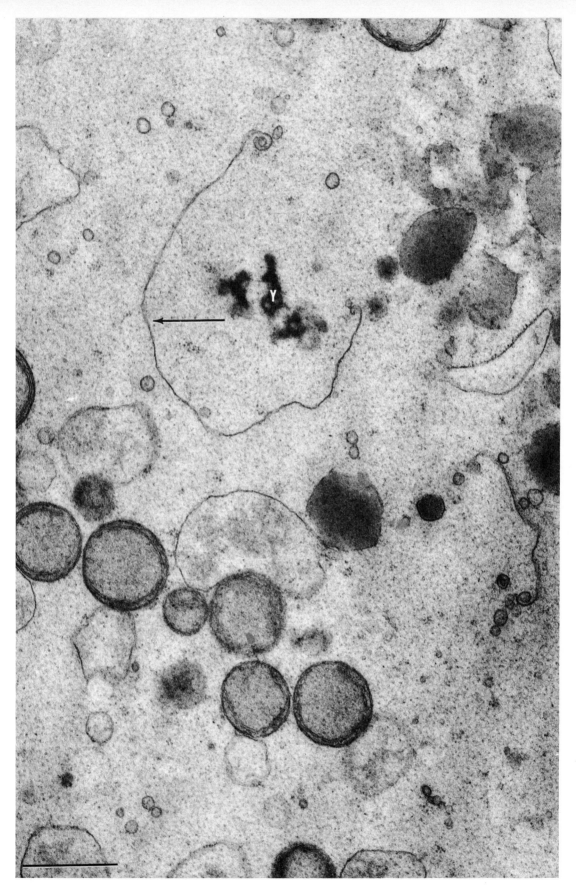

III.75

FIGURE III.76

CYTOPLASMIC STRANDS IN HAMSTER EGG

CYTOPLASM, FRESHLY PENETRATED HAMSTER EGG

Cytoplasmic strands of the hamster oocyte and zygote are apparently composed of fine, granular material (Szollosi, 1965; Hadek, 1966; Weakly, 1967a). They are accumulating into (not particularly well-organized) strands, filling the vitellus of the hamster egg. Between them, as a rule, cytoplasmic organelles are visible. In the egg shown here a remarkably large perivitelline area is present between the zona pellucida and the vitelline membrane. The complete absence of cortical granules is indicative of the fertilization which has taken place.

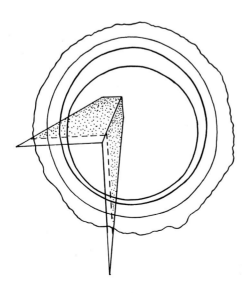

SPECIMEN

III.76. Hamster zygote. Veronal acetate-buffered 1% OsO₄, Epon 815; uranyl acetate (× 8,000).
CS, cytoplasmic strands; PV, perivitelline area; VS, vitelline surface or vitelline membrane; Z, zona pellucida.

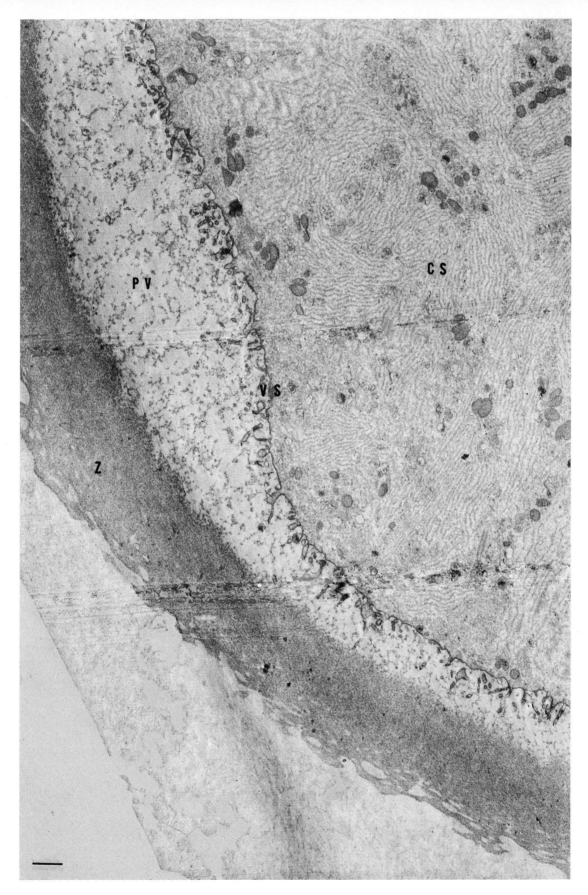

III.76

FIGURES III.77 AND III.78

CYTOPLASMIC STRANDS IN HAMSTER ZYGOTE SHORTLY AFTER FERTILIZATION

Cytoplasmic strands are neither uniform in thickness, nor do they run in identical directions. It is apparent from this picture that cytoplasmic strands may be formed from cytoplasmic microtubules which, in their turn, accumulate granular material. Their dense packing causes the disappearance of their fine, tubular structure, and it leads to the striated appearance of the densely packed, granular matrix. In addition to protein they could also contain RNA.

Between the strands circular, smooth-walled profiles and round, dense mitochondria are also visible.

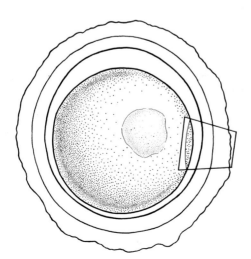

SPECIMENS

III.77. Hamster zygote. Veronal acetate-buffered 1% OsO$_4$; Epon 812; uranyl acetate ($\times$ 22,000).

III.78. Hamster zygote. Veronal acetate-buffered 1% OsO$_4$; Epon 812; uranyl acetate ($\times$ 22,000).

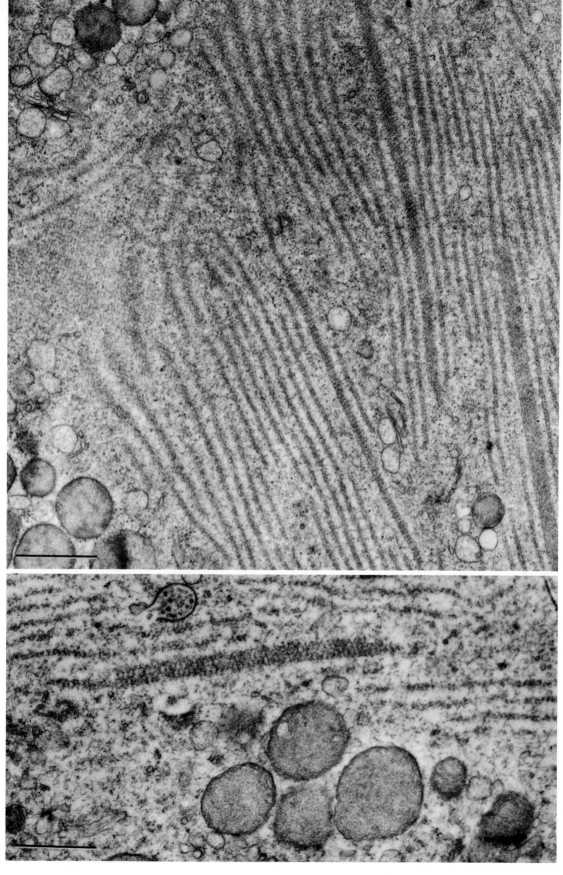

III.77 (↑)   III.78 (↓)

IV

THE FUNCTIONAL
ASPECTS OF
GRANULOSA CELL
ULTRASTRUCTURE

A Short Introduction to Granulosa Cell Functions

It is not the purpose of this study to deal extensively with granulosa cell structure or to dwell on the changing nature of the relationship between granulosa cells and developing egg cell. The granulosa cell and developing egg cell relationship has been amply described, although our basic information did not change since 1960 (Odor, 1960). By now the changing pattern of the cellular border between the egg cell and the granulosa cells in the growing follicle have been described by a number of authors (Weakly, 1966; Bjorkman, 1962; Franchi, 1960; Anderson and Beams, 1960; Baca and Zamboni, 1967). It is known that the two cell membranes go through a smooth, deeply inpocketing and then an interdigital phase in every mammal studied thus far. The contribution of granulosa cell secretion to the liquor folliculi formation has been also shown (Hadek, 1965; Weakly, 1966; and others).

At the time of ovulation the oocyte villi, as a rule, have disappeared, and most of the granulosa cell processes are also absent. Some of them, however, remain within the zona pellucida, most probably breaking off from the granulosa cells. The granulosa cell at that stage is irregularly shaped, measuring 10–15 μ and has a characteristic bilobed nucleus. In the cytoplasm one finds, in addition to the mitochondria, numerous well-developed expanded smooth endoplasmic reticular channels, and far less rough endoplasmic reticulum. Following ovulation the corona radiata cells, those granulosa cells which remain attached to the egg around the zona pellucida, do not show any mitotic division.

One of the remarkable aspects of granulosa or rather corona radiata cell behavior after ovulation are changes in cellular morphology at a phase when it is outside the follicle. The cytological changes which one observes in it indicate that once the gonadotrophic hormones have started to act on the cell, their activity continues even after ovulation. As a result the endoplasmic reticular channel within the cell becomes large; the outline of the cell becomes more irregular; the nucleus and the surface of the cell become far more lobulated than before.

The Functional Aspects of Granulosa Cell Ultrastructure and the Formation of the Zona Pellucida

Since the mammalian egg is not a secretory product, there are essentially three secretions in the mammalian ovary which contribute to the formation of the follicular fluid. One of them is the production of a rather thin flowing serum, the liquor folliculi, the second are Call-Exner bodies, and the third is the follicular fluid which is secreted after ovulation. Observed with the light microscope, the first fill the tissue spaces between the cells, while the second consists of intensively eosinophil round bodies, situated within the cytoplasm of the granulosa cells.

At the inception of follicular secretion, the granulosa cells in the rabbit are cuboidal to polyhedral in shape, measuring about 15 μ–18 μ in size, and show a bilobed, centrally placed nucleus. Although liquor secretion in the vicinity of the egg starts in the unilaminar follicle, the major secretion occurs in the multilaminar stage. The secreting granulosa cells are characterized by the presence of large numbers of mitochondria evenly dispersed within the cytoplasm. The Golgi complex prior to secretion is in the vicinity of the nucleus, but after its start the Golgi elements are gradually approaching the vitelline membrane.

Evidence has been found that follicular fluid originating from the granulosa cells evolves within the Golgi complex. The process starts with the distension of narrow Golgi vesicles into somewhat expanded, smooth-walled vessels, the wider components becoming less electron dense than the surrounding cytoplasm. While the Golgi vesicles continue in the gradually expanding phase, parallel with their expansion, they gradually advance toward the cell border. Once the expanded vessel has reached the ectoplasm, the secretory material and its membranous wall separate from the rest of the vesicular system, and the droplet advances toward the vitelline membrane. After reaching the cell border, the secretory droplet is separated from the cell into the intercellular area within the follicle. Differences can be observed between the various laboratory animals. For example, in the mouse there is a tendency for the secretory droplets to be round, whereas, in the rabbit, as a rule, they are polymorph.

The second type of secretory product, which is observable in the Graafian follicle, is the formation of Call-Exner bodies. With ultrastructure techniques Call-Exner bodies can be perceived within the cytoplasm of the granulosa cells as circular, smooth-walled enclosures, which have, as a rule, strongly electron-dense fillings. Actually the density of the filling can alternate between wide boundaries. On many occasions the Call-Exner bodies have a light center and dense periphery.

The third type of secretion which occurs after ovulation will not be considered in this study.

The first two kinds of secretions are often produced in different granulosa cells. The cells in which the Call-Exner bodies appear, as a rule, have narrow Golgi lacunae and canaliculi, which apparently are not involved in the formation of this secretion. The area within the cell in which the Call-Exner bodies are formed is the ectoplasm, and they are surrounded by a single smooth membrane.

The mammalian zona pellucida, a tough, transparent elastic structure, is actually a secondary membrane which is completely separated from the egg cell and assumedly produced by the secretion of the follicular supporting granulosa cells. Although it does not correspond to any cell membrane, nevertheless, under certain circumstances, it appears to assume a character of its own.

The mammalian zona pellucida in the laboratory animals is laid down comparatively early after the start of follicular secretion. Actually, a secretion around the oocyte is apparent already in the unilaminar follicle. As a matter of fact, it appears parallel with the oocyte microvilli, although it cannot be recognized yet as the zona pellucida.

While the formation of the zona pellucida has been observed very often, due to the lack of adequate morphological and (or) chemical tagging of the materials which contribute to its formation, no definite information exists. Rather, opinions have evolved on the strength of circumstantial evidence. There are three views about the origin and formation of the zona pellucida. However, prior to discussing them, light microscopic and ultrastructure morphology of the forming zona pellucida should be briefly considered. They are:

1. In most mammals the zona pellucida is laid down at a time when liquor folliculi secretion is already progressing.

2. The zona pellucida itself has a smooth inner surface corresponding to the surface of the oocyte and an irregular (rough) outer surface, which apparently is the negative imprint of the granulosa cell surfaces around the egg.

3. At the time of the formation of the zona pellucida, the oocyte villi and granulosa cell processes are already established, thus nothing needs to penetrate, (or grow) through the zona pellucida.

4. The cytological landmarks which accompany zona pellucida formation are enumerated below.

At the time of zona pellucida secretion, the oocyte mitochondria apparently regroup, quite a few of them taking up new locations in the ectoplasm. The Golgi complex and enlarged cytoplasmic channels become located at the cortex of the oocyte under the vitelline membrane and apparently empty their secretion into the area between the oocyte and the granulosa cells. Parallel with this secretory process, the deposition of fine filamentous material can be perceived between the egg and granulosa cells. This is accompanied subsequently with a density increase in the interstitial material between the oocyte and granulosa cells. Histochemical studies reveal two bands within the zona pellucida of the rabbit, a strong acid mucopolysaccharide reaction in the peripheral layer and a neutral mucopolysaccharide reaction in the vicinity of the egg (Hadek, 1965). Since acid mucopolysaccharide reaction can be observed within the secretory droplets of the granulosa cells, the zona pellucida is assumed to be nothing else but jelled follicular fluid; hence the duality of reaction (Hadek, 1965; Hope, 1965). Consequently, the first view is that the zona pellucida is of double origin. However, Chiquoine, (1959, 1960) assumes that jelling of the liquor folliculi occurs in the vicinity of the egg without assuming any secretion on the part of the egg.

The second view is expressed by a number of investigators who assume a purely granulosa cell origin for the zona pellucida; among them are Stegner and Wartenberg (1961), Trujillo-Cenoz and Sotelo (1959), and Merker (1961).

The third purely oocyte origin of the zona pellucida has been proposed by Zamboni and Mastroianni (1966a), Odor (1960), Liss (1964), Baca and Zamboni (1967), and Franchi (1960).

The corona radiata, or those granulosa cells which remain attached to the egg after ovulation has taken place, apparently continue their secretory activity, which is the third type of liquor folliculi. These granulosa cells are characterized by the extreme vesiculation of their cytoplasm. The place of the ground substance is taken by greatly enlarged smooth-walled channels apparently filled with material of moderate density.

Although the zona pellucida has apparently no biological function, nevertheless, it is involved at least as a passive participant in the various stages of egg development. For example, around the unfertilized rabbit egg, the zona pellucida is accumulating a large amount of mucus. Slits or narrow channels through the zona pellucida are produced by the penetrating rabbit spermatozoon. The channel appears to extend for a distance around the sperm head, indicating two possibilities: (1) enzymes released by the sperm head dissolve the zona in a concentric manner; (2) there is a different shrinkage coefficient (possibly due to fixation) in the sperm head than in the zona pellucida. The diameter of channel around the sperm tail is always smaller than around the head. With the advancing cleavage of the fertilized egg, two definite areas can be observed within the zona pellucida, a denser one nearer to the blastomeres, and a lighter one further away from it. Around the blastocyst it forms four evenly spaced burrs and at the time of, or approaching, blastocyst implantation cytoplasmic processes of the blastomeres penetrate the zona pellucida.

In the late blastocysts, there is a gradual disintegration of the zona pellucida. It appears to separate into segments that are delineated from one another by a material of lower density than the zona pellucida proper. Ultimately, the disappearance of the zona pellucida is brought around by breakage in weakened spots which can be recognized by light microscope as thin streaks going through the zona, with the electron microscope, as small, thin vacuoles penetrating through it. Apparently, these are the places where the zona pellucida breaks and thus the embryo becomes free-lying in the uterine cavity.

Another characteristic of the zona pellucida is "zona reaction" (Braden *et al.*, 1954) which prevents the passage of supernumerary sperm through the zona pellucida of most animals. Of course, a number of physiological mechanisms could be responsible for this variety of zonal behavior. One could assume that there is a change in the zona pellucida structure. Or possibly that the fertilized egg produces a secretion which hinders the accumulation of mucus, or alternately that the secretion of the egg has an effect on the zona itself that makes it impervious to mucus accumulation.

FIGURE IV.1

PRIMARY FOLLICLE, HAMSTER OVARY

TRANSVERSE SECTION THROUGH PRIMARY OVARIAN FOLLICLE

Granulosa cells are characterized by the irregularly shaped nucleus. Practically every granulosa cell nucleus shows a deep indentation and considerable irregularity. That this follicle is still at a comparatively early developmental stage is demonstrated by the fact that the cells are very close to one another. There is practically no interstitial material visible between them, and apparently no secretion has started yet.

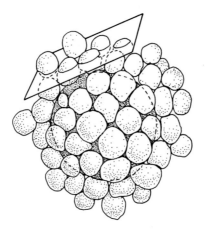

SPECIMEN

IV.1. Two-week-old hamster ovary. Veronal acetate-buffered 1% OsO$_4$; Epon 815; lead citrate ($\times$ 22,000).

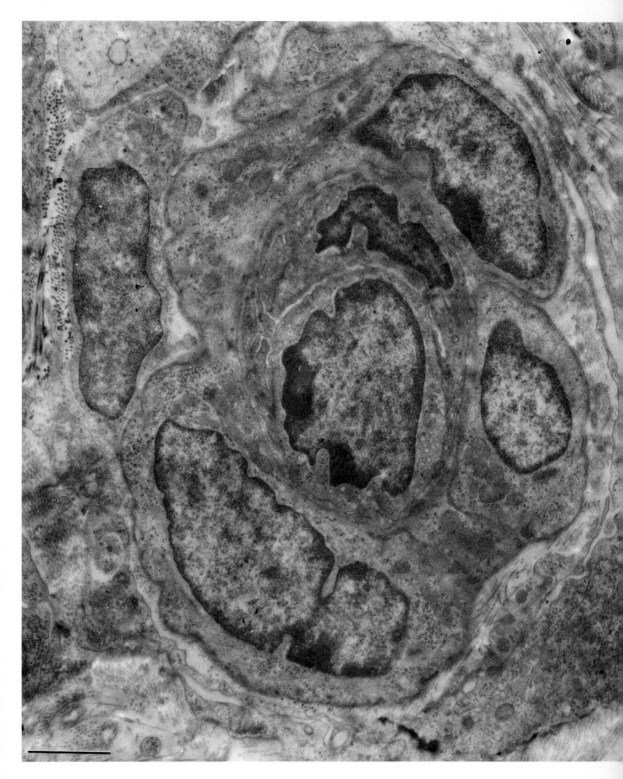

IV.1

FIGURE IV.2

VITELLINE MEMBRANE–GRANULOSA CELL CONNECTIONS IN HAMSTER PRIMORDIAL FOLLICLE

Prior to the start of follicular fluid secretion and establishment of villi on the surface, oocyte cytoplasm forms deep inpocketings into granulosa cell substance. Very few cell organelles are present in each, but there are comparatively large amounts of RNP particles.

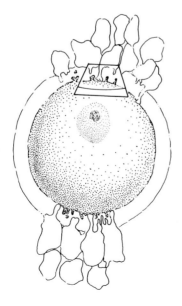

SPECIMEN

IV.2. Two-week-old hamster ovary. Veronal acetate-buffered 1% OsO₄; uranyl acetate (× 18,000).

VS, vitelline surface or vitelline membrane.

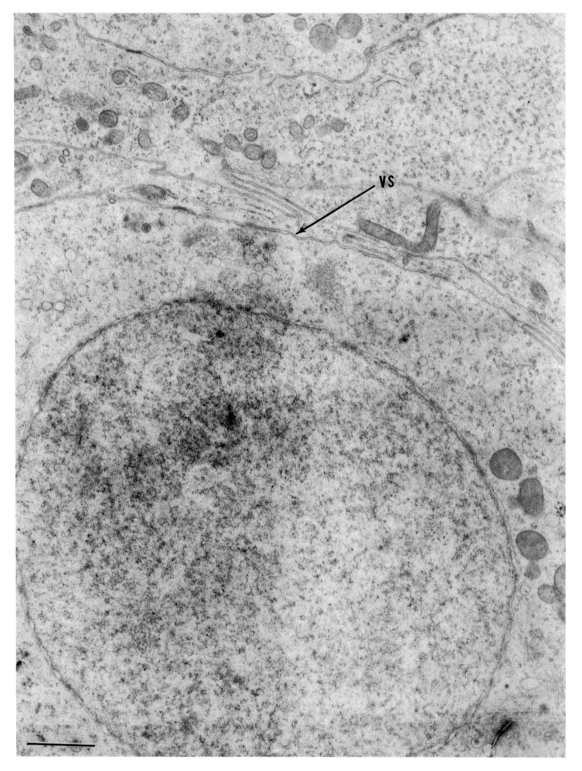

IV.2

FIGURE IV.3

GRANULOSA CELL WITH SMALL CALL-EXNER BODY

MOUSE OVARIAN FOLLICLE

The Golgi area in this particular granulosa cell does not reveal great secretory activity. On the other hand, in its cytoplasm a Call-Exner body is present. It is surrounded by a single membrane and shows a light center and dense periphery. The formation of Call-Exner bodies is apparently a process of storage as opposed to active secretion, as is the case in the elaboration of the follicular fluid and possibly also the zona pellucida.

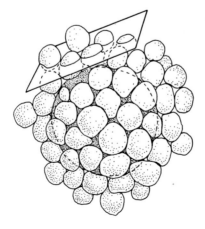

SPECIMEN

IV.3. Two-week-old mouse ovary: Veronal acetate-buffered 1% OsO₄; uranyl acetate (× 18,000).
CX, Call-Exner body; G, Golgi complex.

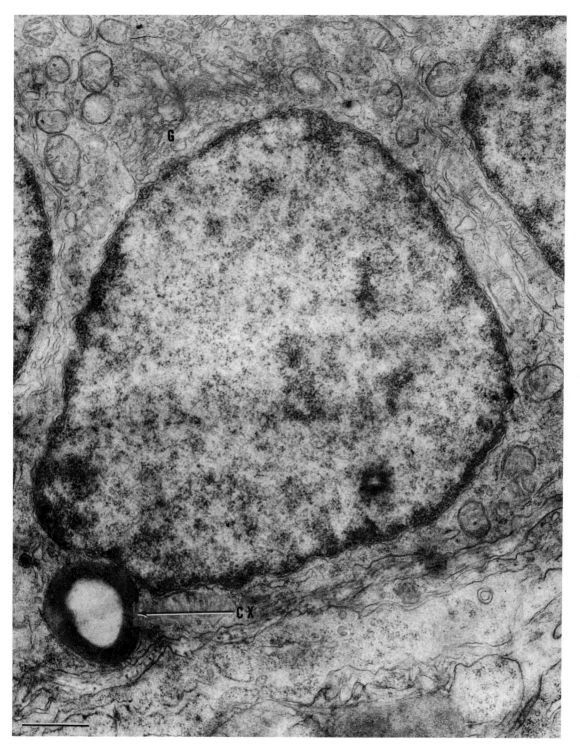

IV.3

FIGURE IV.4

GRANULOSA CELL, PRIMARY FOLLICLE, MOUSE

Elements of Golgi complex (in juxtanuclear position) show localized enlargements due to filling of vesicular lumina with material of low electron density. Some enlarged smooth-walled elements also are visible.

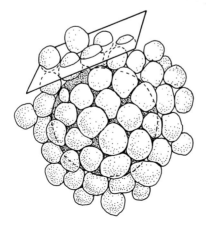

SPECIMEN

IV.4. Two-week-old mouse ovary. Veronal acetate-buffered 1% OsO$_4$; uranyl acetate ($\times$ 18,000).
G, Golgi complex.

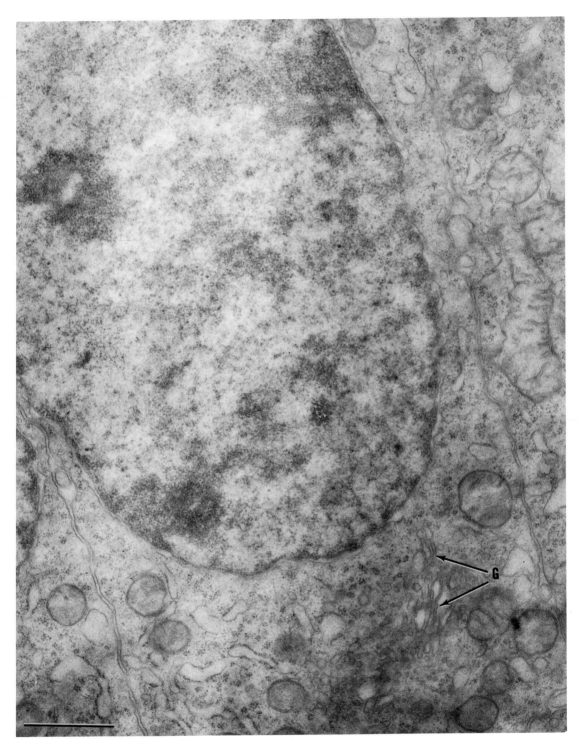

IV.4

FIGURE IV.5

FOLLICULAR FLUID SECRETION IN GRANULOSA CELLS

HAMSTER PRIMARY FOLLICLE

Although some narrow Golgi canaliculi and lacunae are still present, most of the vesicles are greatly enlarged (arrow). Cytoplasm contains extended channels and cisternae filled mostly with material of low electron density. Intense metabolic activity of cells is attested by the large amount of cytoplasmic ribosomes and mitochondria.

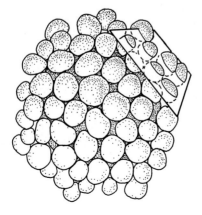

SPECIMEN

IV.5. Two-week-old hamster ovary. Veronal acetate-buffered 1% OsO_4; lead acetate ($\times$ 18,000).

G, Golgi complex; arrow, expanded Golgi canaliculi with secretory material in their lumina.

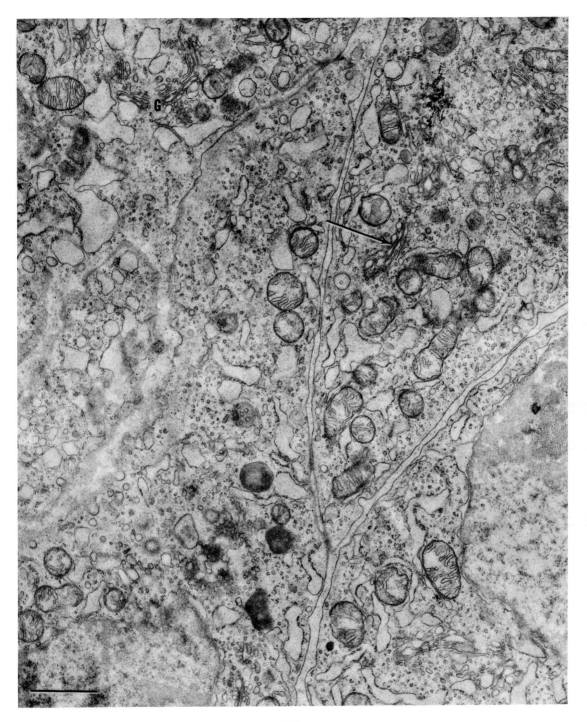

IV.5

FIGURE IV.6

LIQUOR FOLLICULI SECRETION, EXCRETORY PHASE

SECONDARY FOLLICLE, MOUSE

Vesicles filled with secretory material are being detached on cell border. One such droplet is observable in the intercellular area. The amount of cell membrane detached can be assessed from the debris lying between the cells. Large amount of RNP particles, active mitochondria are indicative of cellular involvement in secretion.

In cell on the right one lysosome is visible. In the cell on the left two small Call-Exner bodies, which probably will coalesce to form one large enclosure.

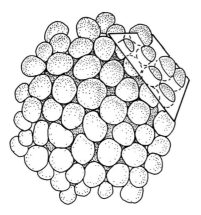

SPECIMEN

IV.6. Secondary follicle, mouse. Veronal acetate-buffered 1% OsO₄; Epon 812; uranyl acetate (× 22,000).
CX, Call-Exner body; L, lysosome. Inset: cellular activity in granulosa cells in which secretion was prevented by administration of AgNO₃.

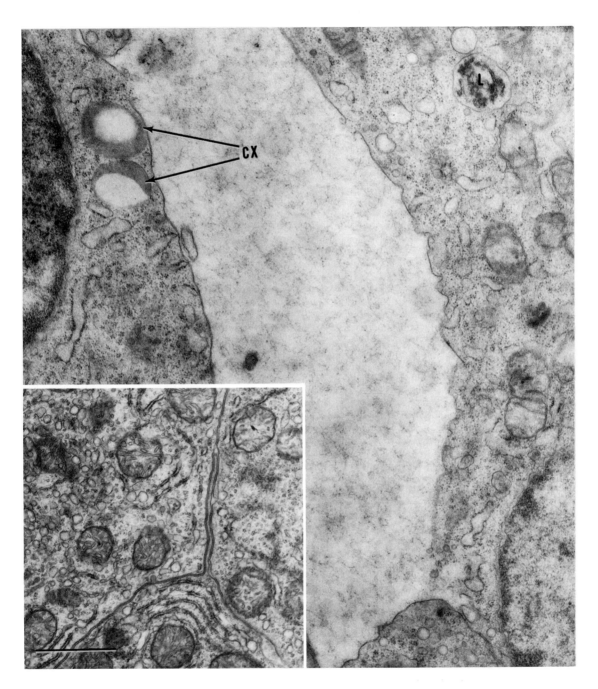

IV.6

FIGURE IV.7

FORMATION OF ZONA PELLUCIDA

MULTILAMINAR OVARIAN FOLLICLE, HAMSTER

The oocyte contains many smooth-walled circular profiles in the vicinity of the vitelline membrane, and also large numbers of mitochondria are located in the cortex. Both are indicative of the secretory activity on the cell border. The borders of opposing granulosa cells in many cases are ill defined and hypertrophied secretory vessels open into the intercellular area. Filamentous material deposited into ground substance between the cells assumedly forms the basis for zona pellucida. This substance shows also increased density when compared to the original secretory product.

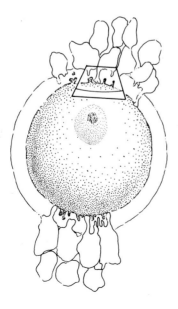

SPECIMEN

IV.7. Ovary, golden hamster. Phosphate-buffered 2% glutaraldehyde; postosmicated; Epon 815; uranyl acetate (× 22,000).
GC, granulosa cell; Z, zona pellucida.

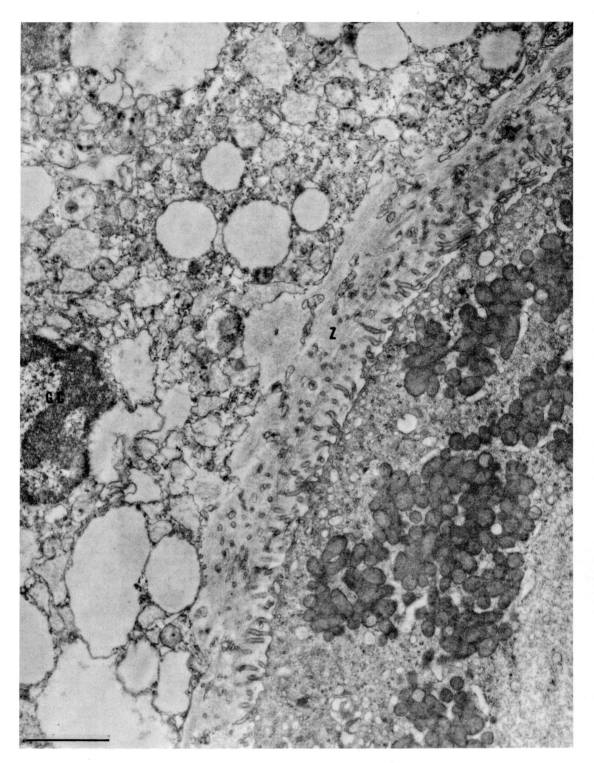

IV.7

FIGURE IV.8

LIQUOR FOLLICULI SECRETION IN MULTILAMINAR OVARIAN FOLLICLE

PERIPHERY OF HAMSTER OVARIAN FOLLICLE

Granulosa cells located in vicinity of follicular boundary (characterized by the presence of basement lamina and irregularly arranged fibrillae). Each cell has a characterized lobulated nucleus. At the start of liquor formation, there is an apparent cytoplasmic accumulation of secretory material which subsequently will break cellular boundaries and release content into the intercellular space. Golgi complex not visible in this picture.

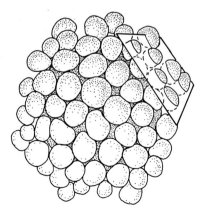

SPECIMEN

IV.8. Hamster ovary. Phosphate-buffered 1% OsO₄; Epon 815; uranyl acetate (× 18,000). BL, basement lamina.

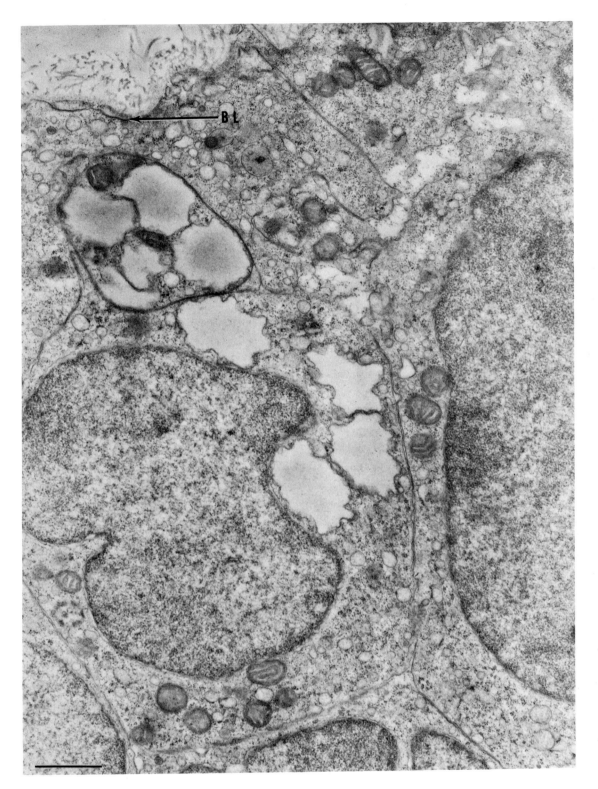

IV.8

FIGURE IV.9

GRANULOSA CELL PROCESSES AROUND FRESHLY OVULATED RABBIT EGG

Around the freshly ovulated rabbit egg, granulosa cell processes are projecting into zona pellucida. These processes contain structureless cytoplasmic matrix in which fine granules are apparent, also greatly extended cytoplasmic channels are visible. On the left of the picture is the rather structureless zona pellucida in which a few granulosa cell processes are evident in transverse section.

Under normal physiological conditions, it is assumed that granulosa cell processes are withdrawn from the zona pellucida of the freshly ovulated egg. Those that break and remain in the vicinity of the egg are segregated by the vitelline membrane projections.

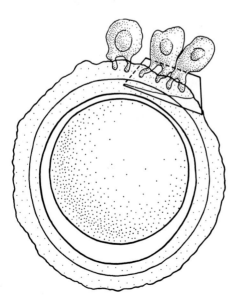

SPECIMEN

IV.9. Rabbit egg. Phosphate-buffered 1% OsO₄; Epon 815; lead citrate (× 18,000). GP, granulosa cell processes; Z, zona pellucida.

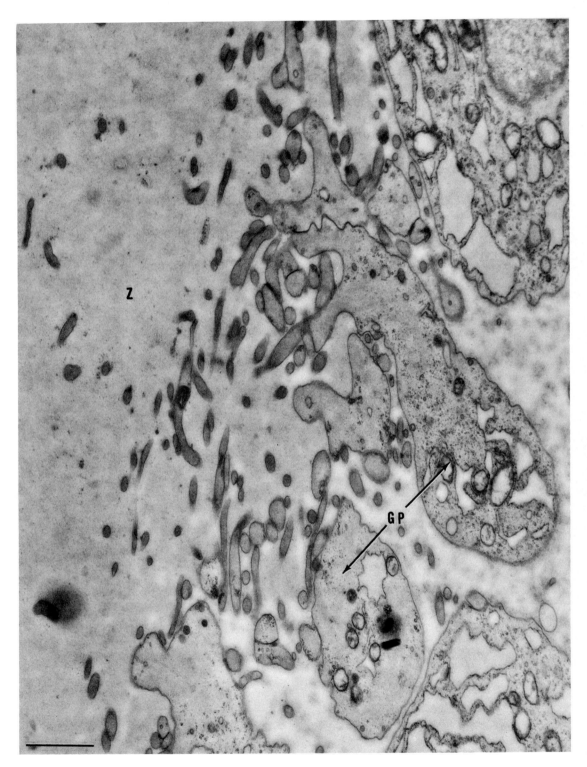

IV.9

FIGURE IV.10

CORONA RADIATA

GRANULOSA CELLS ATTACHED TO NEWLY OVULATED RABBIT OOCYTE

Notwithstanding ovulation, granulosa cell secretion apparently continues. In these typical granulosa cells, each with a cleaved, or lobular nucleus, the cytoplasm is practically extinct because of the greatly increased size of secretory channels and areas. In some of the granulosa cells there are some smooth-walled channels observable. In the rest, the cytoplasm remains only in the shape of little islands. It is remarkable that hardly any mitochondria are left, and that once granulosa cell secretion is under way, the location within the follicle is not a necessity for continued secretory activity.

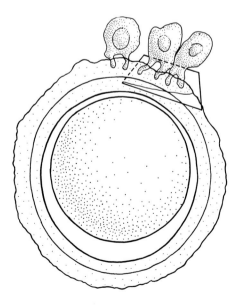

SPECIMEN

IV.10. Rabbit oocyte. Veronal acetate-buffered 1% OsO$_4$; Epon 812; uranyl acetate ($\times$ 12,000).

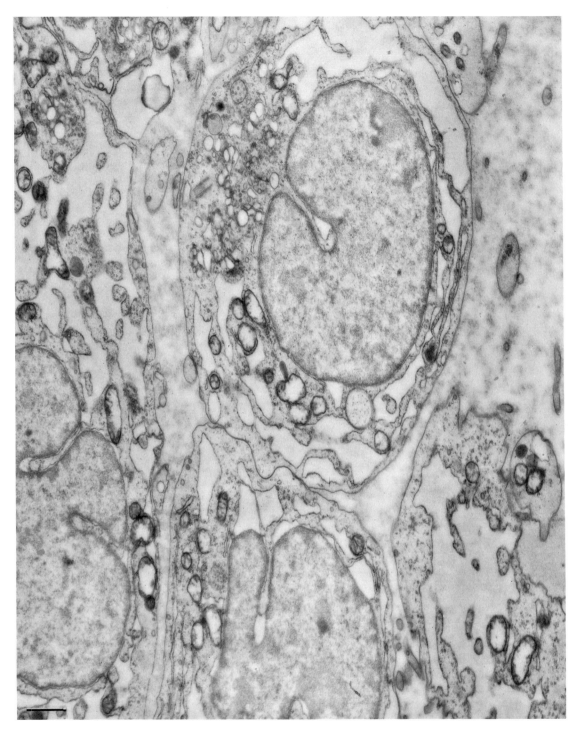

IV.10

FIGURE IV.11

ZONA PELLUCIDA AROUND NEWLY SHED HAMSTER OOCYTE

Studies on the submicroscopic structure of the zona pellucida show it to be composed of amorphous (ground substance) matrix interwoven with extremely fine, thin filaments.

Peripheral irregularity reflects the negative imprint of zona pellucida of neighboring granulosa cells. Pictures like this give the impression that mammalian zona pellucida is only jellied follicular fluid. Although the perivitelline area has very light density fillings, nevertheless it is not empty, only occupied by material of low electron density.

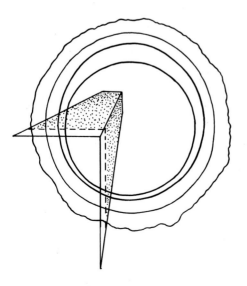

SPECIMEN

IV.11. Hamster oocyte. Veronal acetate-buffered 1% OsO₄; Epon 812; uranyl acetate (× 8,000).

PV, perivitelline area; VS, vitelline surface or vitelline membrane; Z, zona pellucida.

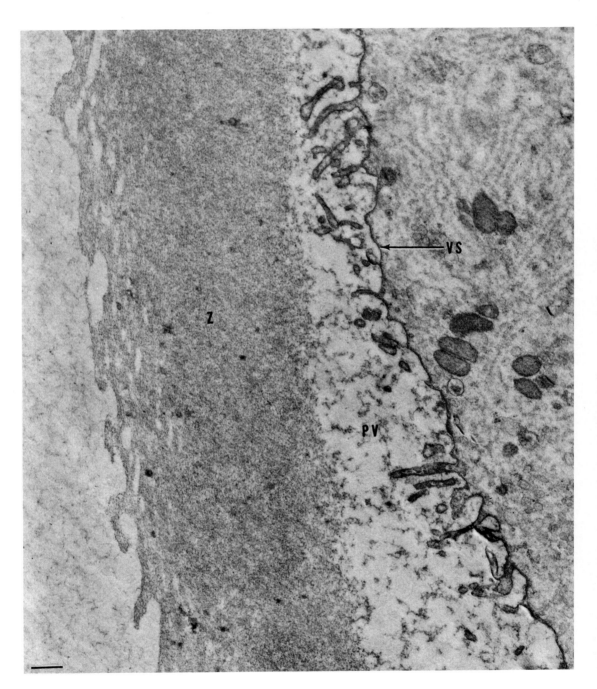

IV.11

FIGURES IV.12–IV.15

DIFFERENT ASPECTS OF ZONA PELLUCIDA STRUCTURE

This quadruple picture shows various aspects of zona pellucida structure and function around postovulatory rabbit egg.

The uppermost picture (IV.12) depicts rabbit zona pellucida around the zygote; it consists of two areas of various densities; apparently it contains filamentous and granular material. The denser area depicts the outer zone of the zona pellucida, whereas the lighter one represents the inner layer closer to the zygote.

The center picture (IV.13) shows the periphery of zona pellucida in the rabbit around the fertilized egg. The slits or channels in the dense area of the zona are assumed to indicate the passage of the spermatozoon (arrow). Around the outer layer of the zona pellucida, the threads that are visible are the gradually accumulating mucous filaments, which gather around the fertilized rabbit egg although in far smaller quantities than around the nonfertilized one.

The lower picture (IV.14) shows the zona pellucida which has surrounded a morula. Three layers can be perceived: one dense outer layer on the right; the middle one, which appears filamentous; and an inner loose layer closest to the cells.

The bottom picture depicts one of the four burrs observable on the inner surface of the zona pellucida (arrow). The alteration in the appearance and the structure of the zona pellucida around the developing egg and early embryo are indicative that it is not quite as passive a layer as it has been assumed, although its presence is not vital for the development of the embryo.

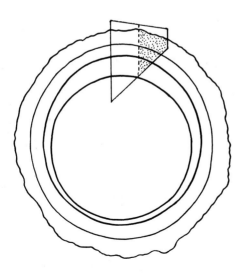

SPECIMENS

IV.12. Rabbit egg. Veronal acetate-buffered 1% OsO$_4$; Epon 812; uranyl acetate (× 30,000).

IV.13. Rabbit egg. Veronal acetate-buffered 1% OsO$_4$; Epon 812, uranyl acetate (× 30,000).
Arrow, slit in zona pellucida.

IV.14. Rabbit morula. Veronal acetate-buffered 1% OsO$_4$; Epon 812; uranyl acetate (× 30,000).

IV.15. Rabbit blastocyst. Veronal acetate-buffered 1% OsO$_4$; Epon 812; uranyl acetate (× 30,000).
Arrow, burrs on inner layer of zona pellucida.

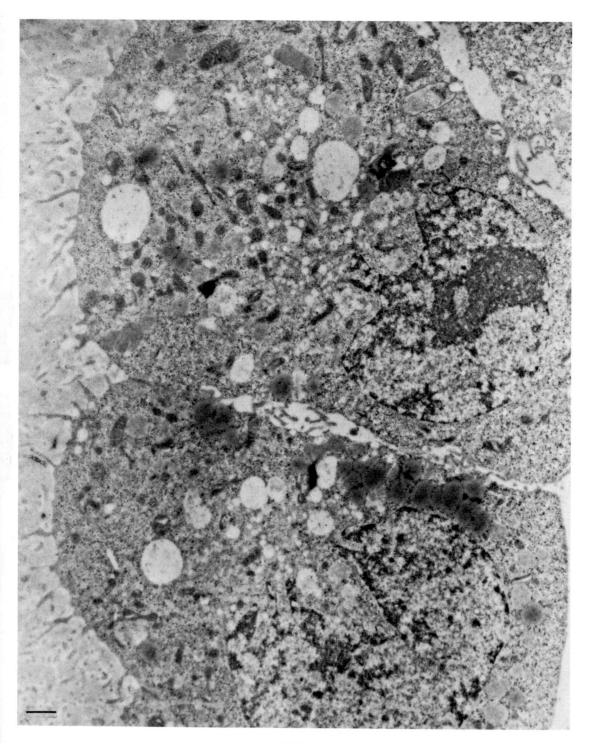

IV.16

FIGURE IV.16

ZONA PELLUCIDA FROM BLASTOCYST

Cytoplasmic processes are penetrating into zona pellucida, and lighter areas around them could be indicative of dissolution of the same (also it may have been caused by different shrinkage coefficients during specimen preparation).

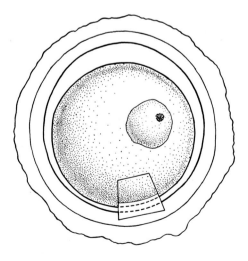

SPECIMEN

IV.16. Rabbit blastocyst. Phosphate-buffered 2% glutaraldehyde postosmicated; Epon 812; lead citrate ($\times$ 8,000).

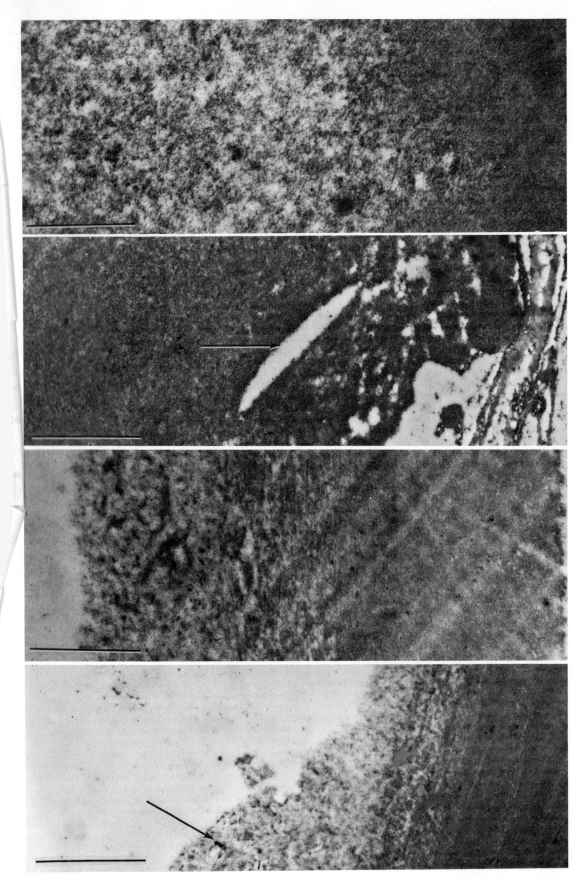

IV.12, IV.13 (↑)   IV.14, IV.15 (↓)

V
EXPERIMENTS

One of the intriguing questions is the feasibility of exchange of material between the oocyte and the perivitelline area. In order to test whether such an exchange is present or not, ferritin was injected into the rabbit egg which was obtained (1) following fertile mating, (2) after sterile mating, and (3) ultimately in multiple cell stage. In each experiment a small amount (0.01–0.03 ml) of suspended ferritin was deposited with a micromanipulator under microscopic control into the perivitelline area of the egg. The uptake of material from the perivitelline area was observed in each egg studied. Ferritin uptake was associated with the surface of villi, or with extremely fine channels within the villi, or with membranes emanating from the surface of the egg.

In those rabbit eggs which have been obtained as a result of fertile matings, it has been observed that ferritin has been progressing into the cytoplasm of the egg along smooth membranes which have shown a connection with the outside. In eggs fixed 5–10 minutes after injection, ferritin was still confined to the cortex of the egg. Within the cortex it has been associated with smooth-walled vessels and channels. In addition, there appeared rather a high concentration of multivesicular bodies in which some of the vesicles contained comparatively large amounts of ferritin.

If the amount of ferritin injected has been increased (0.05–0.1 ml) in addition to its accumulation on cortical smooth membranes, it also appeared in larger amounts in the cytoplasmal matrix, in many cases dispersed without associating with any other structure.

The reaction appeared to be similar in unfertilized egg also, in which smooth membrane projections were observed to bond ferritin and then subsequently carry it into the cytoplasm of the egg.

In multiple-cell stages where a large amount of ferritin (0.05–0.1 ml) was deposited, in addition to a pool in the perivitelline area, one also could observe the uptake of ferritin in villi whose lumens apparently were filled with this material. After the elapse of 15–30 minutes, the perivitelline pool of ferritin became surrounded by membranes, thus forming a typical segrosome in the perivitelline area.

Incorporation of ferritin into the cytoplasm of blastomeres proceeded in the morula the same way as it has been observed in the unfertilized egg. Again, within the cytoplasm of the blastomere, one could observe ferritin associated either with smooth membranes or incorporated into multivesicular bodies or within lysosomes. If excessive amount was injected, then ferritin could be observed lying freely within the cytoplasm of the blastomere, and also stimulating the Golgi complex to such an extent that large amounts of lysosomes were produced. Under exceptional circumstances ferritin also appeared within the mitochondria.

FIGURE V.1

FERRITIN ACCUMULATION IN FRESHLY SHED RABBIT EGG

Ferritin has been injected into rabbit egg 1–5 hours after assumed ovulation and fixed 10 minutes later. As the accompanying electron micrograph shows, ferritin granules are accumulating on cortical villi which are projecting into the perivitelline area and on smooth membranes within the vitellus of the egg. In addition, concentration of multi-vesicular bodies is evident; whether their presence is due to ferritin injection has not been determined. Also some cytoplasmic ferritin pools can be observed, which are still free-lying at this stage.

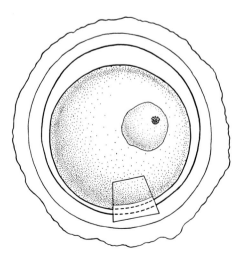

SPECIMEN

V.1. Rabbit egg 1–3 hours after ovulation. Phosphatase-buffered 2% glutaraldehyde; postosmicated; uranyl acetate ($\times$ 22,000). MV, multivesicular body.

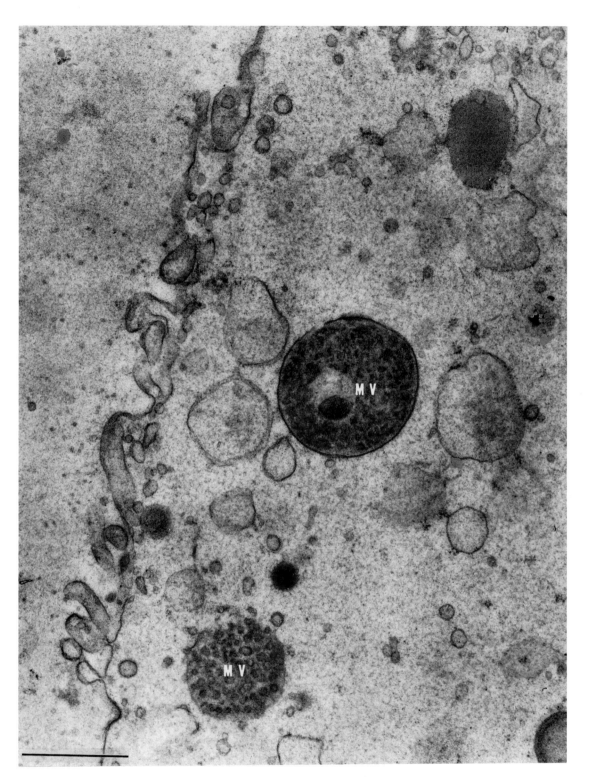

V.1

FIGURES V.2 AND V.3

FERRITIN IN UNFERTILIZED EGG (V.2) AND MORULA (V.3)

The cortical area of unfertilized rabbit egg into which a small amount (0.01 ml) of ferritin was deposited is shown. Ferritin can be observed associated with membranous processes in the perivitelline area and also within the vitellus in association on small membranous profiles (arrows).

If a large amount (0.05 ml) of ferritin is deposited in the perivitelline area as in Fig. V.3, then in addition to forming a pool, ferritin is also taken up by villi pseudopodia (arrow).

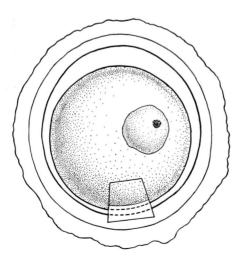

SPECIMEN

V.2, V.3. Rabbit egg. Veronal acetate-buffered 1% OsO_4; Epon 812; uranyl acetate ($\times$ 22,000).

Arrows, ferritin uptake by membranes and villi.

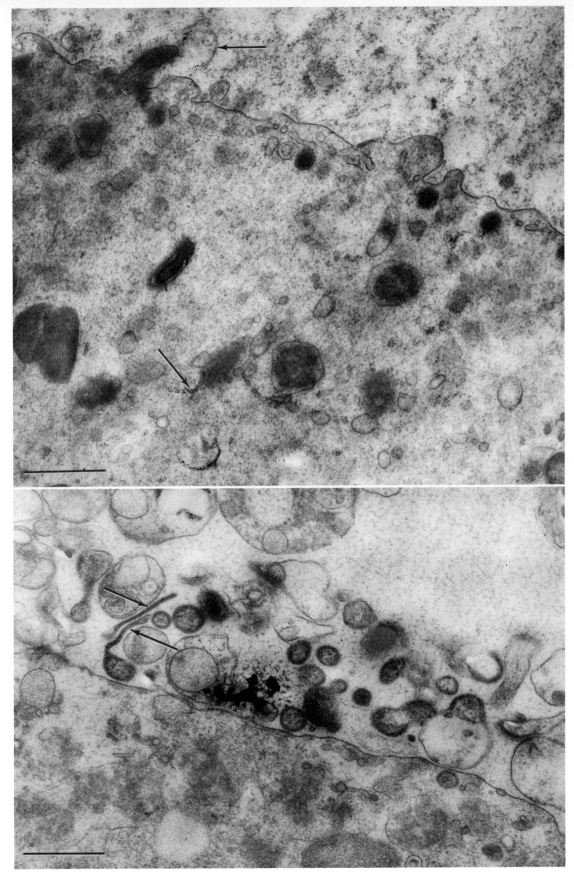

V.2 (↑)   V.3 (↓)

FIGURES V.4 AND V.5

FERRITIN INCORPORATION IN THE PERIVITELLINE AREA OF RABBIT ZYGOTE AND MORULA

These pictures show the effects of a large amount of ferritin injected into the perivitelline area. There is ferritin uptake by the vitelline membrane projections. In addition, there is also a beginning of segrosome formation, as it is evident by the membrane-surrounded body lying free between the cell and zona pellucida.

In the first picture (V.4) surplus ferritin is being separated by segrosome formation. A number of cytoplasmic membranes are surrounding the ferritin pool. Smaller amounts are apparently incorporated by single membranes projecting above the vitelline surface. In the lower picture (V.4) the reaction involves multivesicular body formation in which the dense areas represent the incorporated ferritin granules.

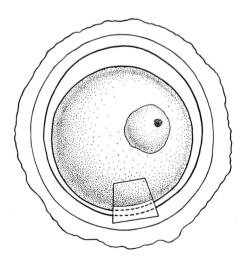

SPECIMENS

V.4. Rabbit zygote; Veronal acetate-buffered 1% OsO_4; Epon 812; uranyl acetate ($\times$ 22,000).

V.5. Rabbit zygote; Veronal acetate-buffered 1% OsO_4; Epon 812; uranyl acetate ($\times$ 22,000).

MV, multivesicular body; SE, segrosome; arrows, smooth membrane uptake of ferritin.

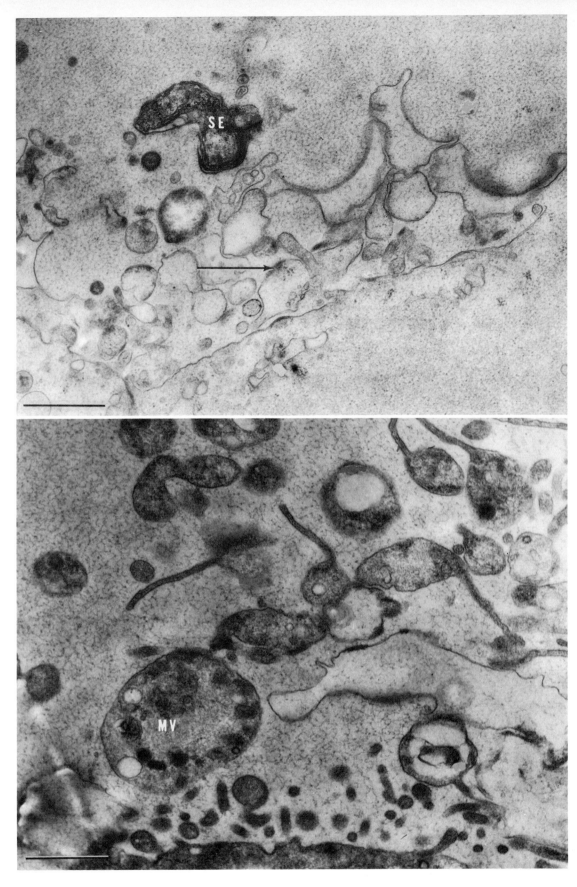

V.4 (↑)   V.5 (↓)

FIGURE V.6

CYTOPLASMIC MECHANISM OF FERRITIN DISPOSAL

In the cytoplasm of an egg injected with a moderate amount (0.02 ml) of ferritin 1 hour after injection, freely lying ferritin accumulations can be observed. In addition, there is ferritin incorporation in multivesicular bodies. In this case the MVB's show irregular (round) outline. Within them ferritin granules are enclosed by smooth membranes. Also, a lysosome is observed apparently in the process of ferritin incorporation. The most remarkable aspects are, however, a number of mitochondria apparently in the process of ferritin incorporation, or transforming into lysosomes.

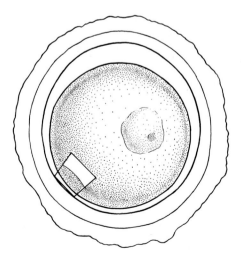

SPECIMEN

V.6. Rabbit egg; Veronal acetate-buffered 1% OsO_4; Epon 812; uranyl acetate ($\times$ 22,000). G, Golgi complex; L, lysosome; M, mitochondria; MV, multivesicular body; arrow, ferritin accumulation.

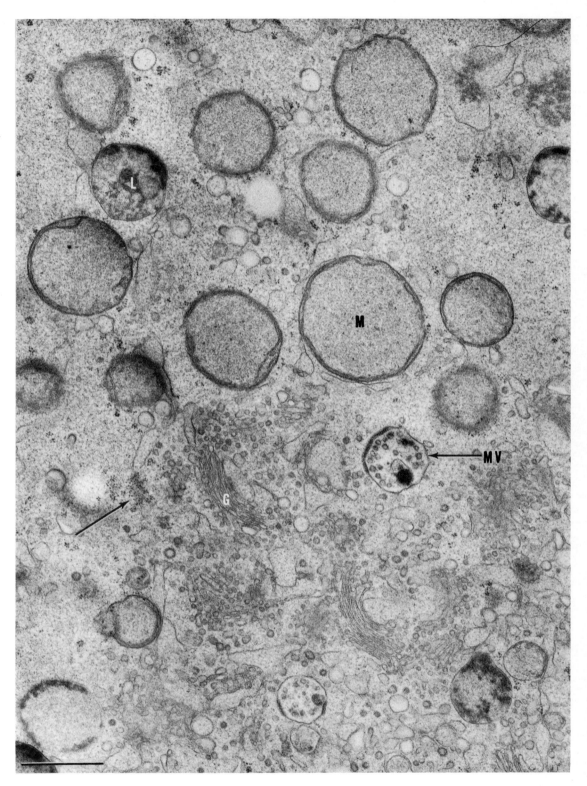

V.6

FIGURES V.7 AND V.8

CYTOPLASMIC MECHANISM FOR FERRITIN DISPOSAL

Cytoplasmic detail of eggs which received large amounts of ferritin deposit in perivitelline area. Ferritin pools are evident, also granules lying freely in cytoplasm. Cellular response is the formation of smooth-walled small caliber vesicles as observable in the hypertrophied Golgi complex. A further reaction is the formation of lysosomes, some partly forming, others fully developed. Also, ferritin accumulation into mitochondria is evident.

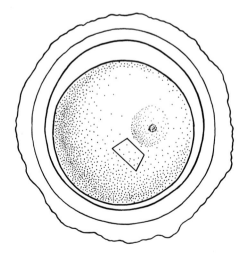

SPECIMENS

V.7. Rabbit egg. Veronal acetate-buffered 1% OsO_4; Epon 812; uranyl acetate ($\times$ 22,000).
V.8. Rabbit egg. Veronal acetate-buffered 1% OsO_4; Epon 812; uranyl acetate ($\times$ 22,000).
G, Golgi complex; L, lysosome; arrow, ferritin pools.

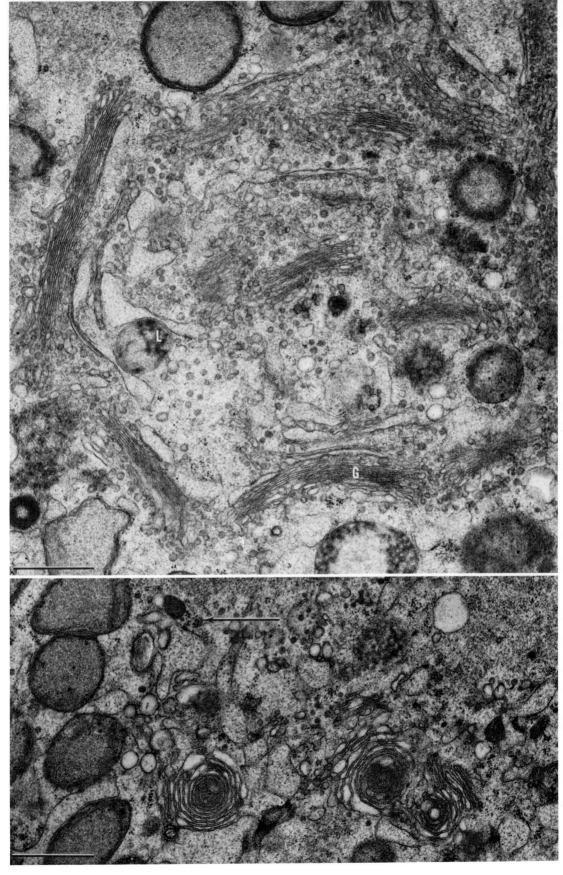

V.7 (↑)   V.8 (↓)

VI

DISCUSSION

Earlier students of cytology who observed mammalian and bird spermatozoa assumed that at the apex of the sperm is a "perforatorium." This structure was expected to facilitate sperm penetration of the zona pellucida and vitelline membrane by piercing or stabbing.

The name "perforatorium" originates from Waldeyer (1906) who first applied this term to a structure in the mouse sperm that stained with basic dyes. The term went into disuse. Recently, however, various structures in the mammalian sperm head have been tagged "perforatorium." For example, in the rat, an apparent thickening of the ventral portion of the head cap could be observed with the light microscope, and investigators assumed this to be the perforatorium (Austin and Sapsford, 1952; Clermont and Leblond, 1955). Austin and Bishop (1958) have assumed the perforatorium, "albeit usually in a less obvious form," in all mammalian spermatozoa to originate from the nuclear membrane; and ultrastructure studies on the toad sperm apparently have revealed some structures which were assumed to be the perforatorium (Burgos and Fawcett, 1956).

The original assumption that the role of the perforatorium is essentially a mechanical activity, fitted the newly described organelle rather well. However, with the development of the idea that sperm penetration is essentially a chemical, and not a mechanical activity, it became apparent that one may have to look for an enzyme pod instead of a spicule.

As a consequence, our present understanding of the relationship between "perforatorium" and acrosomal cap could be summarized as follows:

1. The term "perforatorium," as such, originated at a period when it was assumed that sperm penetration of the egg is a mechanical process.

2. It is now evident that there are no strong fibers in the head to facilitate sperm penetration. Consequently, it is inaccurate to label parts of the head as perforatorium since sperm penetration is a chemical and not a mechanical process. Further, neither the acrosomal cap nor the subacrosomal layer are composed of fibers, but assumedly of enzyme pods which become depleted during sperm penetration.

3. It is now evident that the function ascribed to the "perforatorium," if the word denotes "the structure that facilitates penetration of the zona pellucida," apparently is performed by the acrosomal cap; on the other hand, if the meaning of the word is the "organ which facilitates entry to the egg," then the acrosomal cap cannot be considered to participate in this function since it is depleted by the time the sperm has reached the vitelline membrane. But the one layer which still remains attached to the nucleus and which may participate in the sperm penetration is the subacrosomal, or cytoplasmic layer.

4. As a consequence, it is assumed that the subacrosomal layer, or possibly the "apical body," may fulfill the same function with regard to the vitelline membrane as the "perforatorium" was assumed to perform. Since the term is a misnomer, giving the wrong impression with regard to a structure and function, it is suggested that it be dropped from usage.

Admittedly, there still is controversy between investigators about the very existence of a subacrosomal layer. One of the first who suggested that the acrosome is embedded within a cytoplasmic layer is Horstmann (1961).

While it is evident that the subacrosomal, or cytoplasmic layer which has been described in this study is not comparable to the acrosomal cap, nevertheless, it is constantly present. Further, in its apical part it contains a rough, cone-shaped structure, named the "apical body," which is separated from it by a single membrane (Moricard, 1960; Hadek, 1963c; Bedford, 1964; Wimsatt *et al.*, 1966).

With our present technical methods, this layer becomes more evident in the ejaculated spermatozoon, while it can hardly be observed in the epididymal sperm.

A continuing structural differentiation for guinea pig acrosome after it leaves the testis already had been suggested by Fawcett and Hollenberg (1963); there is no reason why it could not also occur in the subacrosomal layer. Further, it is also true that acrosome does not enclose the caudal aspect of the nucleus, although it forms a sleeve about its posterior aspect. This layer also has been observed by a variety of histochemical techniques [argentophil stain (Williams, 1950); carbolfuchsin and PAS (van Duijn, 1952, 1954)], but it is noted that Clermont and Leblond (1955) could not stain it. Nevertheless, the fact remains that Bishop and Walton (1960) and Saacke and Almquist (1964) have described a double-layered structure, or alternately a porous sheet (Rahlmann, 1961), in the same location in the bovine sperm; while only a single continuous layer was observed in the boar (Nicander and Bane, 1962a) and in the bovine (Saacke and Almquist, 1964). There is no doubt that such a layer is present in the spermatozoon of the rabbit; further, that the filling material in it has an unusual structure.

Clinching the arguments in favor of a cytoplasmic layer which is separate from the acrosomal cap, the cell membrane, and the nuclear membrane, are the observations on the penetrating spermatozoon. Namely, those rabbit spermatozoa which are observed in the process of penetrating the zona pellucida after having lost their acrosomal cap are covered only by this subacrosomal layer.

Thus, one may safely state that a subacrosomal cytoplasmic layer is present in the sperm head. Further, that cranially it is between the acrosome and the nucleus, while caudally it is between the sperm nucleus and the cell membrane. This layer, however, does not cover the posterior aspect of the nucleus; therefore, it cannot be compared to the acrosomal cap and it would be fallacious to call it "postnuclear" cap.

The term "apical body" as used by Blom and Birch-Anderson (1965) designates a hereditary morphology defect in the acrosome of the bull spermatozoon. A similar phenomenon has been described in some rabbit spermatozoa (Bedford, 1964). As it is applied in this study the term has a different meaning.

For the purpose of this study, two types of sperm incorporation patterns were put into juxtaposition with one another: (1) the rabbit, an animal in which multiple spermatozoa penetrate the zona pellucida, and (2) the golden hamster in which the zona acts as a barrier preventing the access of more than one sperm into the perivitelline area. In both species, under physiological conditions, only one sperm penetrates the vitelline membrane (Austin and Braden, 1953). However, when comparing the morphology of the penetrating, or fertilizing sperm, there is a similarity of changes in both species.

In the rabbit, the first change in sperm morphology occurs upon exposing the sperm to oviduct lavage after which separation of the acrosome and subacrosomal layer occurs. The next phase of sperm change in the rabbit occurs during penetration of the zona pellucida. In areas where the zonal material is missing, the acrosome appears in the process of dissolution. In most instances, by the time the spermatozoon has reached the perivitelline area, only the equatorial region of the acrosome cap is present. The rest of the sperm head is covered only by the subacrosomal layer.

It is apparent, therefore, that sperms penetrate the zona pellucida with the help of a lytic enzyme which is released from the acrosomal cap. On the other hand, in some mammals the acrosomal cap may dissolve prior to sperm penetration (Barros *et al.*, 1967; Saacke and Almquist, 1964).

It is evident that in both types of fertilization pattern—(1) the rabbit, in which numerous sperm pass through the zona pellucida, and (2) the hamster, in which only one spermatozoon penetrates—the spermatozoon changes encountered prior to uniting with the egg are similar. In the rabbit, these changes occur while the sperm penetrates the zona pellucida; in the hamster, they occur in the uterus and oviduct during "maturation." None of these changes occur in the vaginal plug.

Conclusions could thus be summarized as follows:

1. No capacitation, or other similar change affecting or preparing the spermatozoon for fertilization, occurs in the vagina or in the vaginal plug.

2. Morphological changes, apparently preparatory to fertilization, occur in the uterus or oviduct of the hamster.

3. Morphological alterations similar to those in the hamster begin to take place in the oviduct of the rabbit, but sperm preparation is completed only after sperm penetration of the zona pellucida.

4. Preparation for fertilization in both animals, the rabbit and the hamster, apparently involves the shedding of the covering layers of the sperm head.

5. If capacitation entails morphological changes, then these sperm changes may amount to capacitation.

6. The presence of the subacrosomal, or "cytoplasmic" layer becomes evident only in those sperm that are observed in the vicinity of the vitelline membrane.

BIBLIOGRAPHY

Adams, E. C. (1958). Egg development in the rabbit; the influence of post-coital ligation of the uterine tube and of ovariectomy. *J. Endocrinol.* **16**, 283–293.

Adams, E. C., and Hertig, A. T. (1964). Studies on guinea pig oocytes. I. Electron microscopic observations on the development of cytoplasmic organelles in oocytes of primordial and primary follicles. *J. Cell Biol.* **21**, 397–427.

Adams, E. C., and Hertig, A. T. (1965). Annulate lamellae in human oocytes in primordial and primary follicles. *J. Cell Biol.* **27**, 119A.

Afzelius, B. A. (1956). The ultrastructure of the cortical granules and their products in the sea urchin egg as studied with the electron microscope. *Exptl. Cell Res.* **10**, 257–285.

Alfert, M. (1950). A cytochemical study of oogenesis and cleavage in the mouse. *J. Cellular Comp. Physiol.* **36**, 381–409.

Anberg, A. (1957). The ultrastructure of the human spermatozoon. *Acta Obstet. Gynecol. Scand.* **36**, Suppl. 2, 1–133.

Anderson, E., and Beams, H. W. (1960). Cytological observations on the fine structure of the guinea pig ovary with special reference to the oogonium, primary oocyte and associated follicle cells. *J. Ultrastruct. Res.* **3**, 432–446.

Andre, J. (1961a). L'evolution ultrastructurale du chondriome au cours de la spermatogenese chez le rat. *Proc. 2nd Reg. Conf. (Eur.) Electron Microscopy, Delft, 1960*, Vol. II, pp. 947–950. Almqvist & Wiksell, Uppsala.

Andre, J. (1961b). Sur quelques details nouvellement connus l'ultrastructure des organites vibratiles. *J. Ultrastruct. Res.* **5**, 86–108.

Austin, C. R. (1951). Observation on the penetration of the sperm into the mammalian egg. *Australian J. Sci. Res.* **B4**, 581–596.

Austin, C. R. (1952). The "capacitation" of the mammalian sperm. *Nature* **170**, 326.

Austin, C. R. (1956). Cortical granules in hamster egg. *Exptl. Cell Res.* **10**, 533–540.

Austin, C. R. (1961). "The Mammalian Egg." Blackwell, Oxford.

Austin, C. R., and Bishop, M. W. H. (1958). Some features of the acrosome and perforatorium in mammalian spermatozoa. *Proc. Roy. Soc.* **B149**, 234–240.

Austin, C. R., and Braden, A. W. H. (1953). An investigation of polyspermy in the rat and rabbit. *Australian J. Biol. Sci.* **6**, 674–692.

Austin, C. R., and Sapsford, C. S. (1952). The development of the rat spermatid. *J. Roy. Microscop. Soc.* [3] **71**, 397–405.

Baca, M., and Zamboni, L. (1967). The fine structure of human follicular oocytes. *J. Ultrastruct. Res.* **19**, 354–381.

Bacsich, P., and Hamilton, W. J. (1954). Some observations on vitally stained rabbit ova with special reference to their albuminous coat. *J. Embryol. Exptl. Morphol.* **2**, 81–86.

Balbiani, E. G. (1864). Sur les movements qui se manifestent dans la tache germinative chez quelques animaux; par M. Balbiani (Luala Societe de biologie dans une de ses seances du mois de fevrier, 1864). *Compt. Rend. Soc. Biol.* **16**, 64–68.

Balbiani, E. G. (1893). Centrosome et "Dotterkern." *J. Anat. Physiol.* **29**, 145–180.

Barka, T., and Anderson, P. J. (1963). "Histochemistry, Theory, Practice, and Bibliography." Harper (Hoeber), New York.

Barros, C., Bedford, J. M., Franklin, L. E., and Austin, C. R. (1967). Membrane vesiculation as a feature of the mammalian acrosome reaction. *J. Cell Biol.* **34**, C1–5.

Baxandall, J., Perlmann, P., and Afzelius, B. A. (1964a). Immuno-electron microscope analysis of the surface layers of the unfertilized sea urchin egg. I. Effects of the antisera on the cell ultrastructure. *J. Cell Biol.* **23**, 609–628.

Baxandall, J., Perlmann, P., and Afzelius, B. A. (1964b). Immuno-electron microscope analysis of the surface layers of the unfertilized sea urchin egg. II. Localization of surface antigens. *J. Cell Biol.* **23**, 629–650.

Bedford, J. M. (1964). Fine structure of the sperm head in ejaculate and uterine spermatozoa of the rabbit. *J. Reprod. Fertility* **7**, 221–228.

Bedford, J. M. (1965). Changes in fine structure of the rabbit sperm head during passage through the epididymis. *J. Anat. (London)* **99**, 891–906.

Bishop, M. W. H., and Walton, A. (1960). Spermatogenesis and the structure of mammalian spermatozoa. *In* "Marshall's Physiology of Reproduction," (A. S. Parkes, ed.), 3rd ed., Vol. I, Part 2, pp. 1–129. Longmans, Green, New York.

Bjorkman, N. (1962). A study of the ultrastructure of the granulosa cells of the rat ovary. *Acta Anat.* **51**, 125–147.

Blanchette, E. J. (1961). A study of the fine structure of the rabbit primary oocyte. *J. Ultrastruct. Res.* **5**, 349–363.

Blandau, R. J. (1945). Is the copulation plug essential for the en masse transport of spermatozoa into the uterine cornua of the albino rat? *Anat. Record* **91**, 266 (abstr.).

Blom, E., and Birch-Andersen, A. (1960). The ultrastructure of the bull sperm. I. The middle piece. *Nord. Veterinarmed.* **12**, 261–279.

Blom, E., and Birch-Andersen, A. (1965). The ultrastructure of the bull sperm. II. The sperm head. *Nord. Veterinarmed.* **17**, 193–212.

Bloom, G., and Nicander, L. (1961). On the ultrastructure and development of the protoplasmic droplet of spermatozoa. *Z. Zellforsch. Mikroskop. Anat.* **55**, 833–844.

Boyd, J. D., and Hamilton, W. J. (1952). Cleavage early development and implantation of the egg. *In* "Marshall's Physiology of Reproduction" (A. S. Parkes, ed.), 3rd. ed., Vol. II, pp. 1–126. Longmans, Green, New York.

Braden, A. W. H., Austin, C. R., and David, H. A. (1954). The reaction of zona pellucida to sperm penetration. *Australian J. Biol. Sci.* **7**, 391–409.

Burgos, M. H., and Fawcett, D. W. (1956). An electron microscope study of spermatid differentiation in the toad, *Bufo arenarum* Hensel. *J. Biophys. Biochem. Cytol.* **2**, 223–240.

Camus, L., and Gley, E. (1896). Action coagulante du liquide prostatique sur le contenu des vesicules seminales. *Compt. Rend. Soc. Biol.* **48**, 787–788.

Camus, L., and Gley, E. (1899). Action coagulante de liquide de la prostate externe du Herisson sur le contenu des vesicules seminales. *Compt. Rend.* **128**, 1417–1419.

Chang, M. C. (1950). The effect of seminal plasma on fertilized rabbit ova. *Proc. Natl. Acad. Sci. U.S.* **36**, 188–191.

Chiquoine, A. D. (1959). Electron microscopic observations on the developmental cytology of the mammalian ovum. *Anat. Record* **133**, 258–259 (abstr.).

Chiquoine, A. D. (1960). The development of the zona pellucida of the mammalian ovum. *Am. J. Anat.* **106**, 149–170.

Clermont, Y., and Leblond, C. P. (1955). Spermiogenesis of man, monkey, ram and other mammals as shown by the "periodic acid-Schiff" technique. *Am. J. Anat.* **96**, 229–253.

Colwin, A. L., and Colwin, L. H. (1961). Changes in the spermatozoon during fertilization in Hydroides hexagonus (Annelida). II. Incorporation with the egg. *J. Biophys. Biochem. Cytol.* **10**, 255–274.

Colwin, A. L., and Colwin, L. H. (1963). Role of the gamete membranes in fertilization in Saccoglossus Kowalevskii (Enteropneusta). I. The acrosomal region and its changes in early stages of fertilization. *J. Cell Biol.* **19**, 477–500.

Courrier, R. (1924). Le cycle sexuel chez la femelle des mammifères. Etude de la phase folliculaire. *Arch. Biol., Paris* **34**, 369–477.

Courrier, R. (1927). Etude sur le determinisme des caractères sexuels secondaires chez quelques mammifères à activité testiculaire periodique. *Arch. Biol., Paris* **37**, 173–334.

Eckstein, P., and Zuckerman, S. (1956). The oestrous cycle in the mammalia. *In* "Marshall's Physiology of Reproduction" (A. S. Parkes, ed.), 3rd. ed., Vol. I, Part 1, pp. 226–396. Longmans, Green, New York.

Endo, Y. (1961a). Changes in the cortical layer of sea urchin eggs at fertilization as studied with the electron microscope. I. Clypeaster Japonicus. *Exptl. Cell Res.* **25**, 383–397.

Endo, Y. (1961b). The role of the cortical granules in the formation of the fertilization membrane in the eggs of sea urchins. II. *Exptl. Cell Res.* **25**, 518–528.

Fawcett, D. W. (1958). The structure of the mammalian spermatozoon. *Intern. Rev. Cytol.* **7**, 195–234.

Fawcett, D. W. (1959). Changes in the fine structure of the cytoplasmic organelles during differentiation. *In* "Developmental Cytology" (D. Rudnick, ed.), pp. 161–189. Ronald Press, New York

Fawcett, D. W. (1965). The anatomy of the mammalian spermatozoon with particular reference to the guinea pig. *Z. Zellforsch. Mikroskop. Anat.* **67**, 279–296.

Fawcett, D. W. (1966). "An Atlas of Fine Structure. The Cell, its Organelles and Inclusion." Saunders, Philadelphia, Pennsylvania.

Fawcett, D. W., and Hollenberg, R. D. (1963). Changes in the acrosome of guinea pig spermatozoa during passage through the epididymis. *Z. Zellforsch. Mikroskop. Anat.* **60**, 276–292.

Fawcett, D. W., and Ito, S. (1965). The fine structure of bat spermatozoa. *Am. J. Anat.* **116**, 567–582.

Franchi, L. L. (1960). Electron microscopy of oocyte-follicle cell relationships in the rat ovary. *J. Biophys. Biochem. Cytol.* **7**, No. 2, 397–398.

Franchi, L. L., and Mandl, A. M. (1962). The ultrastructure of oogonia and oocytes in the foetal and neonatal rat. *Proc. Roy. Soc.* **B157**, 99–114.

Freeman, J. A., and Spurlock, B. O. (1962). A new epoxy embedment for electron microscopy. *J. Cell Biol.* **13**, 437–443.

Gibbons, I. R. (1961). Observations on the structure of cilia and flagella. *Proc. 2nd Reg. Conf. (Eur) Electron Microscopy, Delft, 1960,* Vol. II, pp. 929–933. Almqvist & Wiksell, Uppsala.

Gibbons, I. R., and Grimstone, A. V. (1960). On flagellar structure in certain flagellates. *J. Biophys. Biochem. Cytol.* **7**, 697–716.

Glauert, A. M. (1965). Section staining, cytology, autoradiography and immunochemistry for biological specimens. *In* "Techniques for Electron Microscopy" (D. S. Kay, ed.), 2nd ed., pp. 166–212. F. A. Davis, Philadelphia, Pennsylvania.

Grosser, O. (1903). Die physiologische bindegewebige Atresie des Genitalkanales von Vesperugo noctula nach erfolgter Kohabitation. *Anat. Anz. Ergzngshft.* **23**, 129–132.

Hadek, R. (1958). Intraperitoneal insemination of rabbit doe. *Proc. Soc. Exptl. Biol. Med.* **99**, 39–40.

Hadek, R. (1959). Study of the sperm capacitation factor in the genital tract of the female rabbit. *Am. J. Vet. Res.* **20**, 753–755.

Hadek, R. (1963a). Submicroscopic changes in the penetrating spermatozoon of the rabbit. *J. Ultrastruct. Res.* **8**, 161–169.

Hadek R. (1963b). Submicroscopic study on the sperm-induced cortical reaction in the rabbit ovum. *J.Ultrastruct. Res.* **9**, 99–109.

Hadek, R. (1963c). Study on the fine structure of rabbit sperm head. *J. Ultrastruct. Res.* **9**, 110–122.

Hadek, R. (1964). Some morphological aspects of mammalian fertilization. *Proc. 5th Intern. Congr. Animal Reprod., Trento, 1964,* Vol. II, pp. 138–139.

Hadek, R. (1965). The structure of the mammalian egg. *Intern. Rev. Cytol.* **18**, 29–71.

Hadek, R. (1966). Cytoplasmic whorls in the golden hamster oocyte. *J. Cell Sci.* **1**, 281–282.

Hadek, R., and Swift, H. (1961a). Electron microscopic study on the oocyte and blastocyst in the rabbit. *Anat. Record* **139**, 234.

Hadek, R., and Swift, H. (1961b). A crystalloid inclusion in the rabbit blastocyst. *J. Biophys. Biochem. Cytol.* **8**, 836–841.

Hamilton, W. J., and Laing, J. A. (1946). Development of the egg of the cow up to the stage of blastocyst formation. *J. Anat. (London)* **80**, 194–204.

Hammond, J. (1925). "Reproduction in the Rabbit." Oliver & Boyd, Edinburgh and London.

Hammond, J. (1934). The fertilization of rabbit ova in relation to time. A method of controlling the litter size, the duration of pregnancy and weight of young at birth. *J. Exptl. Biol.* **11**, 140–161.

Hammond, J., and Walton, A. (1934). Notes on ovulation and fertilization in the ferret. *J. Exptl. Biol.* **11**, 307–319.

Hartman, C. G. (1924). Observations on the motility of the opossum genital tract and the vaginal plug. *Anat. Record* **27**, 293–303.

Hartman, C. G. (1933). On the survival of spermatozoa in the female genital tract of the bat. *Quart. Rev. Biol.* **8**, 185.

Hope, J. (1965). The fine structure of the developing follicle of the Rhesus ovary. *J. Ultrastruct. Res.* **12**, 592–610.

Horstmann, E. (1961). Elektronenmikroskopische Untersuchungen zur Spermiohistogenese beim Menschen. *Z. Zellforsch. Mikroskop. Anat.* **54**, 68–89.

Leuckart, R. (1847). "Zur Morphologie und Anatomie der Geschlechtsorgane." Gottingen. Quoted by Stockard and Papanicolaou (1919).

Lewis, W. H., and Wright, E. S. (1935). On the early development of the mouse egg. *Contrib. Embryol. Carnegie Inst.* **25**, 113–143.

Liss, R. H. (1964). A study of the fine structure of a mammalian ovary (Felis domestica). *Anat. Record* **148**, No. 2, 385.

Long, J. A., and Evans, H. M. (1922). The oestrous cycle in the rat and its associated phenomena. *Mem. Univ. Calif.* **6**, 1–111.

Luft, J. H. (1956). Permanganate—a new fixative for electron microscopy. *J. Biophys. Biochem. Cytol,* **2**, 799–809.

Luft, J. H. (1961). Improvements in epoxy resin embedding methods. *J. Biophys. Biochem. Cytol.* **9**, 409–414.

McDonald, L. E., and Sampson, J. (1957). Intraperitoneal insemination of the heifer. *Proc. Soc. Exptl. Biol. Med.* **95**, 815–816.

Mann, T., and Lutwak-Mann, C. (1951). Secretory function of male accessory organs of reproduction in mammals. *Physiol. Rev.* **31**, 27–55.

Matthews, L. H. (1937). (1) The form of the penis in the British rhinolophid bats, compared with that in some vespertilinoid bats; and (2) the female sexual cycle in the British horseshoe bats, Rhilophus ferrum-equinum insulaneus Barrett-Hamilton and R. hipposiderós minutus Montagu. *Trans. Zool. Soc. London* **23**, 213.

Merker, H. J. (1961). Elektronenmikroskopische Untersuchungen über die bildung der zona pellucida in den follikeln des kaninchenovars. *Z. Zellforsch. Mikroskop. Anat.* **54**, 677–688.

Merton, H. (1939). Studies on reproduction in the albino mouse. III. The duration of life of spermatozoa in the female reproductive tract. *Proc. Roy. Soc. Edinburgh* **B59**, 207–218.

Miller, F., and Palade, G. E. (1964). Lytic activities in renal protein absorption droplets. An electron microscopical and cytochemical study. *J. Cell Biol.* **23**, 519.

Millonig, G. (1961). Advantages of a phosphate buffer for OsO_4 solutions in fixation. (Abstr.) *J. Appl. Phys.* **32**, 1637.

Millonig, G. (1962). Further observations on a phosphate buffer for osmium solutions in fixation. *Proc. Fifth Intern. Conf. on Electron Microscopy, Philadelphia 1962.* Vol. II, p. 8.

Moricard, R. (1960). Observations de microscopie électronique sur des modifications acrosomiques lors de la pénétration spermatique dans l'œuf du mammifères. *Compt. Rend. Soc. Biol.* **154**, 2187–2189.

Moser, F. (1939). Studies on cortical layer response to stimulating agents in Arabacia eggs.—Response to illumination. *J. Exp. Zool.* **80**, 423–466.

Moses, M. J. (1956). Chromosomal structures in crayfish spermatocytes. *J. Biophys. Biochem. Cytol.* **2**, 215–218.

Munson, J. P. (1912). A comparative study of the structure and origin of the yolk nucleus. *Arch. Zellforsch.* **8**, 663–716.

Nakano, O. (1928). Ueber die Verteilung des Glykogens bei den Zyklischen Veränderungen in den Geschlechtsorganen der Fledermaus, und über die Nahrungsaufnahme der Spermien in dem weiblichen Geschlechtswege. *Folia Anat. Japon.* **6**, 777–828.

Nicander, L., and Bane, A. (1962a). Fine structure of boar spermatozoa. *Z. Zellforsch. Mikroskop. Anat.* **57**, 390–405.

Nicander, L., and Bane, A. (1962b). New observations on the fine structure of spermatozoa. *3rd Meeting Fertility Club, Northern Countries, Stockholm.*

Odor, D. L. (1960). Electron microscopic studies on ovarian oocytes and unfertilized tubal ova in the rat. *J. Biophys. Biochem. Cytol.* **7**, 567–574.

Odor, D. L. (1965). The ultrastructure of unilaminar follicles of the hamster ovary. *Am. J. Anat.* **116**, 493–522.

Orsini, M. W. (1961). The external vaginal phenomena characterizing the stages of the estrous cycle, pregnancy, pseudopregnancy, lactation, and the anestrous hamster, mesocricetus auratus Waterhouse. *Proc. Animal Care Panel, 1961,* pp. 193–206.

Palade, G. E. (1952). A study of fixation for electron microscopy. *J. Exp. Med.* **95**, 285–298.

Parkes, A. S. (1943). Induction of superovulation and superfecundation in rabbits. *J. Endocrinol.* **3**, 268–279.

Pearson, O. P. (1949). Reproduction of a South American rodent, the mountain viscacha. *Am. J. Anat.* **84**, 143–173.

Piko, L., and Tyler, A. (1964). Fine structural studies of sperm penetration in the rat. *Proc. 5th Intern. Congr. Animal Reprod., Trento, 1964,* Vol. II, pp. 372–377.

Pincus, G. (1936). "The Eggs of Mammals," Exptl. Biol. Monographs. Macmillan, New York.

Price, D., and Williams-Ashman, H. G. (1961). The accessory reproductive glands of mammals. *In* "Sex and Internal Secretion" (W. C. Young, ed.), 3rd ed., Vol. I, pp. 366–448. Williams & Wilkins, Baltimore, Maryland.

Rahlmann, D. F. (1961). Electron microscopic study of the mature spermatozoa of the bull. *J. Diary* **24**, *Sci.* **44**, 915–920.

Rendenz, E. (1926). Nebenhoden und Supermienbewegung. *Wurzburg. Abhandl. Ges. Prakt. Med.* **24**, 107–150.

Rollinat, R., and Trouessart, E. (1896). Sur la reproduction des chauve-souris. Le vespertilion murin (vespertilio murinus Schreber). *Mem. Soc. Zool. France* **9**, 214–240.

Rollinat, R., and Trouessart, E. (1897). Sur la reproduction des chauve-souris les Rhinolophes. *Mem. Soc. Zool. France* **10**, 114–138.

Saacke, R. G., and Almquist, J. O. (1964). Ultrastructure of bovine spermatozoa. I. The head of normal, ejaculated sperm. *Am. J. Anat.* **115**, 143–162.

Sabatini, D. D., Bensch, K., and Barrnett, R. J. (1963). Cytochemistry and electron microscopy—the preservation of cellular ultrastructure and enzymatic activity by aldehyde fixation. *J. Cell Biol.* **17**, 19.

Samuel, D. M. (1944). The use of an agar gel in the sectioning of mammalian eggs. *J. Anat. (London)* **78**, 173–175.

Sotelo, J. R., and Porter, K. R. (1959). An electron microscope study of the rat ovum. *J. Biophys. Biochem. Cytol.* **5**, 327–342.

Stäubli, W. (1963). A new embedding technique for electron microscopy, combining a water-soluble epoxy resin (Durcupan) with water-insoluble Araldite. *J. Cell Biol.* **16**, 197–201.

Stegner, H. E., and Wartenberg, H. (1961). Electron microscopic and histotopochemical studies on the structure and formation of the zona pellucida of human ova. *Z. Zellforsch. Mikroskop. Anat.* **53**, 702–713.

Stockard, C. R., and Papanicolaou, G. N. (1919). The vaginal closure membrane, copulation, and the vaginal plug in the guinea pig, with further considerations of the oestrous rhythm. *Biol. Bull.* **37**, 222–245.

Swift, H. (1956). The fine structure of annulate lamellae. *J. Biophys. Biochem. Cytol.* Suppl. 2, 415–418.

Swift, H., and Rasch, E. (1958). Studies on electron microscope cytochemistry. *Sci. Instr. (News)* **3**, 1–4.

Szollosi, D. (1965). Extrusion of nucleoli from pronuclei of the rat. *J. Cell Biol.* **25**, 545–562.

Szollosi, D. (1967a). Modifications of endoplasmic reticulum in some mammalian oocytes. *Anat. Record* **158**, 59.

Szollosi, D. (1967b). Development of cortical granules and the cortical reaction in rat and hamster eggs. *Anat. Record* **159**, 431–446.

Szollosi, D., and Ris, H. (1961). Observations on sperm penetration in the rat. *J. Biophys. Biochem. Cytol.* **10**, 275–283.

Szollosi, D., and Ris, H. (1963). Extrusion of nucleoli from pronuclei of the rat. *J. Cell Biol.* **19**, 69A.

Telkka, A., Fawcett, D. W., and Christensen, A. K. (1961). Further observations on the structure of the mammalian sperm tail. *Anat. Record* **141**, 231–245.

Thibault, C., and Dauzier, L. (1961). Analyse des conditions de la fecondation "in vitro" de l'œuf de la lapine. *Ann. Biol. Animale, Biochim., Biophys.* **1**, 277–294.

Tinklepaugh, O. L. (1930). Occurrence of vaginal plug in the chimpanzee. *Anat. Record* **46**, 329–332.

Tormey, J. McD. (1964). Differences in membrane configuration between osmium tetroxide-fixed and glutaraldehyde-fixed ciliary epithelium. *J. Cell Biol.* **23**, 658–664.

Trujillo-Cenoz, O., and Sotelo, J. R. (1959). Relationship of the ovular surface with follicle cells and origin of the zona pellucida in rabbit oocytes. *J. Biophys. Biochem. Cytol.* **5**, 347–350.

van Duijn, C. H. (1952). The structure of human spermatozoa. *J. Roy. Microscop. Soc.* [3] **72**, 189–198.

van Duijn, C. H. (1954). Cytomicrochemistry of human spermatozoa. *J. Roy. Microscop. Soc.* [3] **74**, 69–107.

Waldeyer, W. (1906). Die Geschlectszellen. *In* "Handbuch der vergleichenden und experimentellen Entwicklungslehre der Wirbeltiere," Jena.

Walker, G. (1910a). A special function discovered in a glandular structure hitherto supposed to form part of the prostate glands in rats and guinea pigs. *Bull. Johns Hopkins Hosp.* **21**, 182–185.

Walker, G. (1910b). The nature of secretion of the vesiculae seminales and of an adjacent glandular structure in the rat and guinea pig, with special reference to the occurrence of histone in the former. *Bull. Johns Hopkins Hosp.* **21**, 185–192.

Ward, M. C. (1946). A study of the estrous cycle and the breeding of the golden hamster, *Cricetus Auratus. Anat. Record* **94**, 139–161.

Wartenberg, H., and Stegner, H. E. (1960). Uber die elektronenmikroskopische Feinstruktur des menschlichen ovarialeies. *Z. Zellforsch. Mikroskop. Anat.* **52**, 450–474.

Weakley, B. S. (1966). Electron microscopy of the oocyte and granulosa cells in the developing ovarian follicles of the golden hamster (Mesocricetus Auratus). *J. Anat.* (*London*) **100**, 503–534.

Weakley, B. S. (1967a). Investigations into the structure and fixation properties of cytoplasmic lamellae in the hamster oocyte. *Z. Zellforsch. Mikroskop. Anat.* **81**, 91–99.

Weakley, B. S. (1967b). "Balbiani's Body" in the oocyte of the golden hamster. *Z. Zellforsch. Mikroskop. Anat.* **83**, 582–588.

Weinman, D. E., and Williams, W. L. (1964). Mechanism of capacitation of rabbit spermatozoa. *Nature* **203**, 423–424.

Williams, W. W. (1950). Cytology of the human spermatozoon. *Fertility Sterility* **1**, 199–215.

Wimsatt, W. A. (1942). Survival of spermatozoa in the female reproductive tract of the bat. *Anat. Record* **83**, 299.

Wimsatt, W. A. (1944). Further studies on the survival of spermatozoa in the female reproductive tract of the bat. *Anat. Record* **88**, 193.

Wimsatt, W. A., Krutzsch, P. H., and Napolitano, L. (1966). Studies on sperm survival mechanisms in the female reproductive tract of hibernating bats. I. Cytology and ultra-structure of intra-uterine spermatozoa in Myotis Lucifugus. *Am. J. Anat.* **119**, 25–60.

Wittich, G. H. (1845). Obserationes quae dam de aranearum ex ovo evolutione. Halis, Sax Formis Ploetzianis.

Yamada, E., Muta, T., Motomura, A., and Koga, H. (1957). The fine structure of the oocyte in the mouse ovary studied with electron microscope. *Kurume Med. J.* **4**, 148–171.

Yanagimachi, R., and Chang, M. C. (1963). Fertilization of hamster eggs in vitro. *Nature* **200**, 281–282.

Zamboni, L., and Mastroianni, L. (1966a). Electron microscopic studies on rabbit ova. I. The follicular oocyte. *J. Ultrastruct. Res.* **14**, 95–117.

Zamboni, L., and Mastroianni, L. (1966b). Electron microscopic studies on rabbit ova. II. The penetrated tubal ovum. *J. Ultrastruct. Res.* **14**, 118–132.